Spider-Man
Confidential

From Comic Icon to Hollywood Hero

Spider-Man
Confidential

EDWARD GROSS

HYPERION

NEW YORK

Library of Congress Cataloging-in-Publication Data

Gross, Edward (Edward A.)
Spider-Man confidential : from comic icon to Hollywood hero /
Edward Gross.
p.   cm.
ISBN 0-7868-8722-2
1. Spider-Man (Comic strip) I. Title.
PN6728.S6   G767   2002
741.5'973—dc21   2001051672

Hyperion books are available for special promotions and premiums.
For details, contact Hyperion Special Markets, 77 W. 66th Street,
11th floor, New York, New York 10023-6298, or call 212-456-0100.

Book design by Lynne Amft

FIRST EDITION

10 9 8 7 6 5 4 3 2 1

To James "Kells" Kelly
September 11, 2001 changed us, as did having you in our lives

Contents

Acknowledgments

ADMITTEDLY IT'S A CLICHÉ, but *Spider-Man Confidential* quite simply wouldn't exist if it hadn't been for the help of a number of individuals. First and foremost, I'd like to begin with the folks at Hyperion, particularly my editor, Jennifer Lang, whose patience during one crisis after another was pretty amazing. I came damn close to blowing the whole thing, but Jennifer's enthusiasm never wavered, and it's something that's truly appreciated.

For invaluable assistance in research and insight, I'd like to thank Peter Sanderson and his encyclopedic knowledge of comic book history; James Van Hise and his research regarding the Steve Ditko–era adventures of Spidey; Allen Lane, who probably remembers more about *Spider-Man and His Amazing Friends* than he'd care to admit; Eric Gilette, whose website devoted to the comic-book exploits of the web-crawler (www.samruby.com) is the most comprehensive resource of information you could hope to find on the subject; Kevin McCorry and his in-depth look at Spidey's first animated series of the 1960s (www.members.tripod. com/KevinMcCorrytv/spidey.html); the good folks at the Unofficial Spider-Man and His Amazing Friends homepage (www.geocities.com/Area51/Labyrinth/2324/AmazingFriends/ Homepage.htm) for info on that show, as well as a guide to *Spider-Man Unlimited;* and Toei's Spider-Man homepage (www.redrival.com/gorma/Spider-Man.htm), which is devoted to the Japanese live-action series of the 1970s.

For taking the time to be interviewed, I need to thank Gerry Conway, who took over the writing of Spider-Man when Stan Lee moved up to the position of publisher of Marvel Comics; animator supreme Ralph Bakshi, who reflected on the 1960s cartoon version of Spider-Man; Gregory Dinallo and Alvin Boertz, both veterans of the CBS live-action Spidey series; *Spider-Man and His Amazing Friends* writer Christy Marx; Larry Brody, who somehow managed to survive *Spider-Man Unlimited;* Dan Poole, whose fan-made live action film, *The Green Goblin's Last Stand* (which can be viewed at www.alphadogproductions. com), completely hooked my kids on the Spider-Man character; and a number of people involved with the making of the *Spider-Man* movie between 1985 and the start of production of Sam Raimi's film: John Brancato, Barney Cohen, Joe Zito, Ethan Wiley, and Neil Ruttenberg.

Special thanks to two people whose contribution to this book has been immeasurable, and who I feel sincere friendship toward: first, John Semper, the creative guiding force behind *Spider-Man: The Animated Series*, whose reflections of working on that show brought the two of us to the point of hysteria, especially when we were "on the roof." And then there's Ted Newsom, who not only served as the perfect tour guide to the winding path of what has become the Spider-Man feature, but also is someone I have been able to call just to shoot the breeze with for the past fifteen years or so. To both, I offer my sincere thanks.

On a more personal level, I need to thank my agent, Laurie Fox, for never losing faith in me and sharing my passion for each book that I write. With Laurie, particularly at the beginning of a new project, it's a genuinely collaborative relationship and something that I cherish.

On the home front, I must both thank and apologize to my sons, Teddy, Dennis, and Kevin, for not always being available to them when they needed me, and for repeatedly filling their ears with the word "Deadline!" I'm sure it's a word that they could happily live the rest of their lives without hearing again. Most of all, I need to express my profound thanks to and love for my bride, Eileen, whose support through the writing of this book was unwavering. Eileen sacrificed a lot and gave me the space I needed to finish this book, and I don't think I'll ever be able to thank her enough. Whoever said that behind every successful man there's a woman, must have had her in mind.

An Introduction

THE UNITED STATES that existed when the first words of this book were written is vastly different from the one that exists now. And unlike the warm recollections of the elderly, who will reflect on how the world they lived in had gradually evolved from one decade to the next, this was, relatively speaking, a change in existence that happened in the blink of an eye.

On September 11, 2001, the supervillains broke free of the confines of the comic-book page. The machinations of such master criminals as Doc Ock, the Joker, the Green Goblin, or Lex Luthor couldn't compare to their real-life counterparts—villains who didn't need sophisticated high-tech weaponry or tools of mass destruction to fill the populace with fear. None of that was necessary to instantly erode the sense of security that has been a perceived entitlement since the end of World War II. Indeed, all it took were three planes filled with jet fuel, our own apathy, and a trio of well-placed targets to change things forever.

What did come out of the smoldering remains of New York's Twin Towers and Washington, D.C.'s Pentagon was a renewed resolve, a uniting of Americans, and the first war of the twenty-first century. All of which is pretty heavy stuff for a book devoted to Spider-Man, yet somehow appropriate.

When Spider-Man debuted in 1962, and throughout the ensuing decade, America was a country in the midst of redefining itself. The Kennedy assassination, the Beatles invasion, Vietnam, the Flower Power movement—one revolution segued into another. Yet through it all, one comic-book character, Spider-Man, seemed to reflect the times and the youth of the country better than any other.

Peter Parker was a teenager forever transformed by outside forces. Out of nowhere he found himself endowed with the proportional abilities of a spider, which, as he would eventually come to realize, ultimately represented a great power that needed an equal amount of responsibility. What is particularly cool about Parker is that even though he may have become Spider-Man, he was still driven by many of the same fears, anxieties, and insecurities that govern most of us at one time or another in our lives. Unlike the majority of superheroes who stood apart from the masses—Superman, Green Lantern, even Batman—Spidey has always remained one of us, and that has played a large role in his enduring appeal.

But where does he stand now? Oh, sure, there's Sam Raimi's blockbuster movie starring Tobey Maguire, which spent some fifteen years in development and legal hell before it was given a green light; a new animated series; and comics that are selling better than they have in a long time. But what is Spider-Man's relevance in today's altered world? In the immediate aftermath of the attacks on America, there was talk of Hollywood going for pure escapism. Maybe it would mean the return of Rambo or Superman, heroes who would easily triumph over incredible odds. You know, mindless entertainment where the good guys come out of battle with barely a scratch and the perfect one-liner. Good old-fashioned frothy entertainment.

But is America crying out for frothy entertainment? Well, for the first month following the eleventh, all we saw on television were firefighters and police officers valiantly struggling to recover *anyone* from the wreckage; or we learned about another mother or father who never returned home. How much of an appetite for escapism could there be? How could readers relate to comic books in general and Spider-Man in particular when real life has become so unbearable?

In truth, Spider-Man might possibly be just what we're looking for. Director Sam Raimi's intention was to capture the essence of the early comic book—the hero and his struggle with the daily frustrations that haunt us; the feeling of being overwhelmed by it all, coupled with the ability to begin each day anew with the determination to rise to the occasion and do what is right . . . and necessary. In that sense, Spidey remains our perfect reflection. He, like you and I, must struggle on no matter what the odds, armed with little more than faith that everything will work out in the end.

The purpose of *Spider-Man Confidential* is to provide a complete history of Spider-Man, beginning with his origin and moving through his various comic-book incarnations, as well as the numerous television shows and, now, motion picture that have brought his adventures to life. As such, this book serves as a loving tribute to the one comic-book hero who has always seemed like he could be the guy next door or the person staring back at us from the mirror.

Edward Gross
October 2001

Spider-Man
Confidential

PART ONE

Spider-Man in the Comics

Over the past several years, Sony Pictures' all-powerful hype machine has had one objective in mind: to get patrons into movie theaters for the premiere of *Spider-Man*. That being said, it's necessary to take a collective breath and remember that Spidey as a comic-book character is celebrating his fortieth anniversary at the same time he's swinging onto the big screen. Whether or not the film breaks box office records or lives up to fan expectations, your friendly neighborhood Spider-Man will undoubtedly continue to live on in four-color panels for decades to come.

To understand the revolutionary significance of Spider-Man as a character, one must first examine what superhero comics were like before his debut in 1962.

Although the superhero had various forebears (notably the comic-strip character the Phantom), the first true superhero was, of course, Superman, who initially appeared in 1938, in *Action Comics* #1, published by the company now known as DC Comics.

Created by teenage friends Jerry Siegel and Joe Shuster, Superman struck a chord in an America mired in the Great Depression and on the verge of a new world war. He provided a highly appealing wish-fulfillment fantasy: the seeming nonentity (Clark Kent) who secretly possessed the will and strength to battle and triumph over the forces that threatened to crush the common man.

Superman's popularity was both immediate and extraordinary, and within a few years he had spread from comic books to newspaper comic strips, radio, animation, and live-action film. During this same period, a deluge of new superhero charac-

Stan Lee and Spider-Man

ters flooded the comics. Batman and Captain Marvel first appeared in 1939, only a year after Superman, and almost immediately began to rival him in popularity.

That same year a comics company called Timely published *Marvel Comics* #1, showcasing a new assortment of superheroes. Right from the beginning, these "Marvel" heroes were different from the standard mold as exemplified by DC's Superman. One of them, the Human Torch, was actually an android—a robot in human form—who initially was feared by the humans he would ultimately end up protecting. The other major character debuting in that comic was Namor, the Sub-Mariner, the half-human prince of an underwater civilization that would later be identified as Atlantis. With America on the brink of war, Namor's creator, Bill Everett, dared to create a series with one of America's enemies as the protagonist. Enraged by American incursions into his kingdom, the inhumanly strong Namor turned terrorist, launching a one-man war against the United States. (When World War II did begin, Namor shifted his attention to combatting the Nazis.)

By 1941, the top creators at Timely were the team of Joe Simon and Jack Kirby, and one of their employees was a teenager named Stanley Leiber, who soon began writing comics under the pen name of Stan Lee. Simon and Kirby soon left Timely for DC, and Stan Lee rose to become editor, a position he would hold for well over two decades.

During those years the fortunes of the comics industry went into severe decline. In particular, the superhero comics began to lose their appeal following World War II. Perhaps the initial fervor for superheroes had been nothing more than a passing trend, or, more likely, America was once again enjoying peace and prosperity, and people may have no longer had such a strong need for these heroic figures. Another possible reason was that the primary readers of comics—many of whom had been GIs—simply had outgrown the medium and were settling down and raising families. By 1951, with only a few exceptions such as Superman and Batman, superheroes had vanished from the comics.

The comics industry continued, shifting its attention to other genres, such as Westerns, romance, and, most famously, horror. Stan Lee continued to guide Timely through these shifts in audience taste and the company's repeated name changes, but there were hard times, during which Lee had to let nearly his entire staff go.

By the early 1960s, Lee was capitalizing on the readership's new enthusiasm for science-fiction stories, notably with comics featuring a series of gigantic monsters, like the immense dragon Fin Fang Foom. Two

of his main artists were his former boss, Jack Kirby, who had ended his partnership with Joe Simon; and Steve Ditko, whose unusual, quirky style was particularly suited to tales that placed flawed, all-too-human protagonists in weirdly paranormal circumstances.

In 1956, DC started to test the waters for a revival of superhero comics through its successful relaunch of one of its most popular 1940s series, *The Flash*. Then DC scored a hit with its new superhero-team book, *Justice League of America*, at the start of the 1960s.

Despite these successes, it quickly became apparent that comic-book superheroes were in a creative rut. Readers pretty much knew that in each issue a villain would attack one metropolis or another, the hero would arrive, triumph over not-so-incredible odds to save the day, and return everything to the status quo until the following month.

Not that anyone believed things would or could be any different. Let's face it: this was an undeniably successful formula, established as far back as the late 1930s, with the creation of Superman, Batman, and other heroes, who defined the genre for the next twenty years or so. While they—and their countless imitators—offered exciting adventures to the reader, there was no denying that this was a fantasy world where good would invariably triumph over evil and no one would be any worse for the wear.

Stan Lee was as aware of the formula as anyone, and he was desperate to break away

Stan Lee with Batman creator Bob Kane

from it. Unfortunately, he had a stumbling block in the way of Marvel publisher Martin Goodman, whose basic attitude was, Why fix it if it wasn't broken? Nonetheless, Lee got a chance to prove his point when Goodman became determined to beat DC's *Justice League of America* after DC's publisher began bragging about sales figures.

"I really wanted to do something new," said Lee, who was in his early forties at the time. "I wanted to quit. I was really so bored and too old to be doing these stupid comic books. I was also frustrated because I wanted to do comic books that were—even though this seems like a contradiction in terms—a more realistic fantasy. Martin wouldn't let me and had wanted the stories done the way they had always been done, with very young children in mind. My wife, Joan, said to me, 'You know, Stan, if they asked you to do a new book about a new group of superheroes, why don't you do 'em the way that you feel you'd like to do a book? If you want to quit anyway, the worst that could happen is that he'll fire you, and so what? You want to quit.' I figured, 'Hey, maybe she's right.' I wanted to create a new group and do them the way I had always wanted to do a comic book, and that's what happened."

Inspired by his wife's suggestion, Lee

collaborated with Jack Kirby in creating the Fantastic Four, whose first issue premiered in 1961 (from Timely's new moniker, Marvel Comics) and effectively changed comic-book storytelling forever.

The Fantastic Four comprised a quartet of irradiated characters who suddenly found themselves endowed with superpowers, yet driven by the same foibles that drive many of us. Supervillains *still* threatened a metropolis (in this case, New York City) and the good guys would *still* triumph over amazingly impossible odds, but in their case they were as likely to get into a fistfight with each other as they were with the bad guy. As such, the group radically altered the superhero genre. Lee's guiding principle with this and the other comics that would follow was to ask himself: What would happen if beings with superhuman powers were actually people with genuine personalities who lived in the real world? This team was not necessarily welcomed by the society they sought to protect: by the second issue, the FF were framed as criminals and hunted down by the army.

Most astonishing, having superhuman powers was no longer presented purely as a wish-fulfillment fantasy. One of the team's members, the Thing, was a human being who had been transformed by radiation into a grotesque, superhumanly strong monster. Moving back and forth between explosive rage and morose depression, the Thing felt alienated from the rest of the

human race. (Appropriately, another member of the FF was a new version of the Human Torch, and by issue number four the team was doing battle against the Sub-Mariner.) From there, Lee and Kirby combined the underlying themes of the Thing and Sub-Mariner in creating *The Incredible Hulk*, in 1962. In this case, the Clark Kent–like protagonist, Bruce Banner, was unwillingly transformed into a super-strong monster that waged war against a human race that sought to destroy him.

The Fantastic Four and the Hulk have proved over the succeeding decades to be classic characters in their own right. At the same time, one can see Stan Lee's work on their initial stories as a necessary stepping-stone toward the creation of the character who most completely embodies the Marvel style of superhero, the hero who for four decades has remained Marvel's flagship character: Spider-Man.

1962: A New Kind of Hero

The popularity of the Fantastic Four and the Incredible Hulk did not necessarily mean that Lee's life in comics got any easier. Despite this success, he once again came up against Goodman when he broached his latest idea, a character named Spider-Man. In the pages of *Origin of Marvel Comics*, Lee explained: "For quite a while I'd been toying with the idea of doing a strip that would violate all the conventions and break all the rules. A strip that would actually feature a teenager as the star, instead of making him an adult hero's sidekick. A strip in which the main character would lose out as often as he'd win—in fact, *more* often. A strip in which nothing would progress according to formula—the situations, the cast of characters and their relationship to each other would all be unusual and unexpected. Yep, I knew what I wanted all right, but where would I ever get a chance to try it? Where except in a magazine that we were planning to kill anyway?"

In 1962, *Amazing Fantasy* was limping along on its last legs, headed for cancellation. Having failed to match the sales success of such mystery/suspense/horror anthology titles as *Tales of Suspense, Tales to Astonish, Journey into Mystery*, and *Strange Tales*, Martin Goodman was ready to trash the title. In a last-ditch effort to boost sales, the company changed the comic's title from *Amazing Adventure* to *Amazing Adult Fantasy* and finally to *Amazing Fantasy*.

As issue #15 was supposed to be the end of the line for the title, the powers at Marvel decided to give a shot to a character deemed "too scary" for young readers and one which Goodman had previously refused to print: Spider-Man.

Lee named Spider-Man after the Spider, the mysterious hero of pulp magazine stories in the 1930s. He felt that the "Spider" concept gave his new character a spooky

feel. Indeed, this has remained an aspect of Spider-Man over the years: stories regularly show him crawling down a wall, insectlike, cornering a terrified criminal in a dark alley. But Lee and Ditko were not seeking merely to come up with a new variation on the Shadow, the Green Hornet, and other pulp vigilantes.

"Martin told me three things that I will never forget," Lee reflected. "He said people hate spiders, so you can't call a hero 'Spider-Man.' Then, when I told him I wanted the hero to be a teenager, as he was in the beginning, Martin said that a teenager can't be a hero, but only a sidekick. Then, when I said I wanted him not to be too popular with the girls and not great-looking or a strong, macho-looking guy, but just a thin, pimply high school student, Martin said, 'Don't you understand what a hero is?' At the same time, I also said that I wanted him to have a lot of problems, like that he doesn't have enough money and he'd get an allergy attack while he was fighting. Martin just wouldn't let me do the book. Normally, I'd have forgotten about it, but when we were doing the last issue of *Amazing Fantasy*, I put it in there. So I must have felt that he was important somehow, or I wouldn't have bothered."

Originally, Jack Kirby, who together with Lee had created the Fantastic Four and the Hulk, was to be Spider-Man's artist, and indeed it was Kirby who drew Spider-Man on the cover of *Amazing Fantasy* #15.

But Kirby drew muscular, dynamically powerful heroic figures, and Lee intended to cast Spider-Man in a different mold altogether. "Jack did a couple of pages," Lee told *Comic Book Marketplace*, "and I said, 'Jack, I don't want Spider-Man to look like Captain America. I don't want him to be a handsome, muscular guy, I want him to look like an ordinary kid—a little bit puny if anything.' But everything Jack drew was so heroic and wonderful and I think maybe he hadn't really been listening to me, so he drew the first experimental pages of Spider-Man like a real hero. You know, big and strong-looking."

As a result, Steve Ditko, the master of drawing angst-ridden everymen and gritty urban environments, was brought in to illustrate this new, experimental series. In the end it would be Ditko who would define the look and feel of Spider-Man that in many ways prevails even to this day.

Readers who turned to the first page of *Amazing Fantasy* #15 (the August 1962 issue) saw handsome young teenage boys and attractive teenage girls talking animatedly. None of them, it turned out, were the heroes of this story. Instead, the protagonist was the slender, bespectacled fifteen-year-old boy standing in the background, his head lowered in an expression of utter misery. This was Peter Parker, the brightest scholar at Midtown High School in Forest Hills, Queens, and for that very reason a social outcast. His fellow students in the

foreground were the school's cool crowd, smugly self-satisfied, shallow, and thoughtlessly cruel toward those they chose to exclude from their clique.

Though later writers have tended to join in their condescension toward this early version of Peter Parker, calling him an introverted bookworm, Lee and Ditko's original stories actually presented him as the archetypal Good Son, hardworking in his studies and devoted to the people who raised him. Those people were *not* his parents. Like many heroic figures in literature, Peter Parker was an orphan, being raised by his Uncle Ben and Aunt May, benign surrogate parents who seemed old enough to be his grandparents. It was clear that they were the only people who genuinely appreciated and cared for Peter; their home in Queens—and his studies in the world of science—provided his sole refuge from the casual contempt of his peers.

It was while in pursuit of his studies that Peter went on a school field trip to an atomic laboratory. There, an ordinary spider inadvertently passed through a beam of radiation. Dying, the spider landed on Peter's hand and bit the unwary teenager. His body's reaction to this radioactive bite was almost immediate, as he quickly discovered that he had been endowed with superhuman abilities. He had the proportional strength of a spider, being able to carry many times his own weight; his feet and hands could adhere to surfaces, enabling him to walk up walls as a spider can. Then, of course, he had the "spider sense," the ability of real-life insects to scurry away to safety just as they're about to be squashed.

In an effort to test his new strength, Peter decided to enter a match against a wrestler named "Crusher" Hogan, who welcomed challenges from all comers, professional or not. But despite his delight in his new physical prowess, Peter was still the deeply shy boy of the story's beginning. He could only bring himself to show off in public if he wore a crude mask. This was enough, as the anonymous masked marvel easily defeated the massive Hogan. Impressed by this display, a theatrical agent in the audience gave the masked boy his business card, triggering an innovative thought in Peter's head.

Up until that point, whenever any hero first received his powers in the comics, he immediately decided to turn crime fighter, working not for money but for sheer altruistic satisfaction. With Peter Parker, Stan Lee and Steve Ditko asked, What would a person in *real life* do if he got superpowers? Naturally, he would use them to get rich and famous and there would be no better way to do so than to enter show business.

To curtail his extreme shyness, Peter created an alternate identity for himself: the Amazing Spider-Man. He quickly designed the now-familiar costume and, in a burst of creative brilliance, concocted a fluid that he could shoot to create artificial webbing.

Using the webbing, he could swing from tall buildings or entrap opponents.

The mysterious, masked Spider-Man, with his incredible powers, immediately caught the imagination of the public, and the web-slinger became not a superhero but a superstar, appearing in theaters and on television. Meanwhile, Peter kept his double identity secret, even from his uncle and aunt. He took joy in having a spectacular secret life that no one knew about but himself.

But with the accolades of the public, the introverted boy quickly shifted to the other extreme, turning as arrogant as the bullies who had mocked him. On one occasion, upon finishing a television appearance, Spider-Man sees a guard pursuing a thief through a studio corridor. Unconcerned, Spider-Man allows the crook to escape; when the guard demands to know why, Spider-Man replies that it is none of his business.

In reality, it is. Soon afterward, Peter returns home to discover that his uncle has been shot dead by a burglar. Changing into his Spider-Man costume, the horrified, furious boy monitors the police scanner broadcast and races to the burglar's hideout, where the police have him surrounded. Breaking in, the enraged Spider-Man quickly overpowers the burglar, only to recognize him as the same man he had refused to stop at the television studio. From that moment on, he is haunted by the memory of what his uncle Ben had taught him long ago: "With great power there must come great responsibility."

All in all, this was pretty tough to beat in terms of character angst, and it was this part of Spider-Man's origin that separated him from most other superheroes. Whereas Bruce Wayne became Batman as a result of his parents being murdered right in front of him, and Superman's powers were born out of circumstance, Peter Parker had selfishly shirked the responsibility that accompanied great power and had paid the ultimate price for it. It was at that moment of realization—that he was indirectly responsible for Ben's death—that Parker went from super-powered geek to superhero.

No matter that the creation of Spider-Man had been tremendously fulfilling for Lee and Ditko; *Amazing Fantasy* hit news-stands and—as promised—was quickly cancelled. "The book was dropped," said Lee, "and we all forgot about it. I'd gotten the Spider-Man character out of my system and could now go back to our other superstars. Then the sales figures came out a couple of months later. I'll never forget Martin walking into my office and saying, 'Remember that character of yours, that crazy idea that we both liked, Spider-Man? Why don't you do a series of it?'"

Amazing Fantasy #15 was a top seller, and as best could be determined, Spider-Man was the reason. Shortly thereafter, the web-crawler was given his own comic book, which kicked off with a retelling of Spider-Man's origin.

From the moment he arrived on news-stands, Spider-Man struck a chord with the reading public. Offered William Schoell in his book *Comic Book Heroes on the Screen*: "[This] first story is an interesting mini-drama that shows that we cannot ignore our responsibility to others, that our loved ones are 'somebody else' to other people. It also functions as a neat study of loneliness and its effect on young outsiders, in this case the development of a self-promotional and callow flamboyancy on the part of Parker, whose real, more subdued persona is hidden behind a mask . . . Parker may have become a superhero, but he was still a high school boy at heart, a troubled human being, and the stories never forgot that."

It wasn't long before Spider-Man established himself as the quintessential hero for the 1960s. In a sense, Spider-Man/Peter Parker, with his turbulent life and his constant introspection and self-doubt, captured what America itself would be going through during that decade. The fact that the approach to his character predated the youthful turbulence of those years merely meant that the young readers of the comic found someone who reflected their own anxieties. In a sense, Peter Parker put into words what many of his readers could not articulate: the turbulence of growing up and attempting to grapple with often cruel realities. Interestingly, this is the same approach

Stan Lee with his creation, Spider-Man

that television producer Joss Whedon has taken with his *Buffy the Vampire Slayer* series, which owes more than a passing nod to the Marvel style of storytelling.

While the concept of the hero/villain was by no means new, Spider-Man proved himself to be a different breed. Whereas characters like the Spider and the Green Hornet are sought by the police while they battle crime, those characters never agonize over the cruelties of that dichotomy the way Spider-Man does. They never try to turn the public's opinion of them around to no avail, as Spider-Man does. They go about their business, while Spider-Man curses a cruel and seemingly inescapable fate.

Right from the beginning, Lee and Ditko made Spider-Man someone who stands apart. The character tries his best, but is inevitably beaten down by the world. *Daily Bugle* editor J. Jonah Jameson immediately brands Spider-Man a menace, ruining his potential income as an entity in the entertainment world. When Spidey saves the editor's astronaut son, he is branded a criminal who staged an incident to take the credit from a "true" American hero. When he fights the Chameleon, who has committed a crime disguised as Spider-Man, he finds himself having to escape the police, who believe him to be the Chameleon as well. At the conclusion of that particular story, we see a young man who has failed and is at the bottom of the heap, even though he has powers and abilities that are

beyond anyone's imagination (well, anyone except Superman, the Fantastic Four, the Justice League, etc.). He even spends that whole first issue of *Amazing Spider-Man* trying to earn money to help his aunt pay their rent, and fails to do so.

One had to wonder what kind of hero Spider-Man was going to be if he is hounded by police, branded a criminal by Jameson, and driven by desperation. There is even an unprecedented moment when Parker considers what he could accomplish if he applied his powers for evil purposes—obviously this was not your father's superhero.

When *The Amazing Spider-Man* debuted in March 1963, Ben's death is still resonating in Peter's psyche. Tragedy has thrust responsibility upon the mourning teenager, and with Ben Parker's death, Peter's Aunt May suddenly faces severe financial difficulties. It is up to Peter to somehow support her, a personal vow made more difficult to fulfill by the fact that he is no longer driven by greed for fame and fortune, having sworn that he would let no other innocent person come to harm if he could help it. In a nutshell, those are the parameters that guide the character through his early adventures.

Steve Ditko's philosophy about drawing Spider-Man was that he did not want the character to seem larger than life. In fact, those issues often seemed uncomfortably close to reality. New York was never gloomier or grittier than when drawn by Ditko. No one could deny that these characters lived in the real world. Each panel failed to glitter with some slick new look such as Jack Kirby had given his books, and it was an approach that made perfect sense. After all, the Fantastic Four were wealthy, while Peter Parker lived with his aunt. Stan Lee's stories, coupled with Ditko's art (as well as his plotting and a lot of uncredited writing), drew us into the world of Peter Parker. Its earthy, straightforward approach, along with the stories, made it a strip much easier to identify with than any other work being done. Other comics may have been flashier and prettier, but Spider-Man had reality on his side.

While today there have been hundreds of Spider-Man stories that have continuously explored all of the possible plots for the character, at the time there were no limits. Each issue had an atmosphere of exploration and discovery. Would Spider-Man be pushed over the edge? Wouldn't we, under the same circumstances? While readers may have imagined themselves as the Human Torch or the Flash, Peter Parker's life was uncomfortably close to home; his worries similar to our own.

Whereas the superhero stories of the 1930s were usually little more than simplistic confrontations between good and evil, *Spider-Man* had much more complex psychological and—believe it or not—social concerns. The origin story presents a protagonist with a complex psyche: divided between deep insecurity and arrogant egotism, learning to be self-reliant while desperate for acceptance from friends and society at large; accepting his mission in life from an inextricable mixture of genuine idealism and a self-loathing sense of guilt. Superman was idolized by the masses, but Spider-Man is rejected by the society around him, both in his costumed identity and as Peter Parker. He is the hero as misfit, a symbol of any individual who struggles to abide by his sense of morality and yet is unappreciated, misunderstood, and unrewarded by his fellow man. He is a nonconformist who seeks acceptance by an establishment that rejects him. The power fantasies implicit in the superhero genre are balanced by the evocations of modern urban neuroses and angst.

And yet *Spider-Man* does not sink into adolescent self-pity; its hero continually confronts his demons and struggles onward. Peter Parker may live in an ironic world, but he has developed an ironic worldview that enables him to cope. Reflecting the new urban American style of humor emerging in the 1960s in comedy writing, Spider-Man combats his adversaries with jokes as much as with his fists (*Buffy* again, anyone?). He is the stand-up comedian as superhero, puncturing his enemies' pomposities with his witty rejoinders to their tirades, exorcising the evils around him through ridiculing them.

Through Spider-Man and the other heroes they created in the 1960s, Stan Lee and his collaborators signaled that the superhero genre was far more than pleasant juvenile entertainment. It could deal perceptively and affectingly with moral, psychological, and social issues. However fantastic they might be on the surface, its characters could be identifiably human and psychologically complex. Others who followed would take Lee's innovations much further in decades to come, plumbing the metaphorical depth and literary potential of these archetypal heroes and their quests. Without pioneers like Stan Lee and Steve Ditko, none of this might ever have happened.

The 1960s: The Ditko Years

As previously noted, during the first four years of *The Amazing Spider-Man* Lee and Ditko set the tone and style of all of the hundreds of Spider-Man stories to come and created the majority of the primary supporting characters who have populated the series for four decades.

Perhaps foremost among these supporting players is *Daily Bugle* publisher J. Jonah Jameson. He is Spider-Man's most persistent nemesis, rarely letting up in his public campaign to discredit the wall-crawler, and even sometimes commissioning attempts to capture and unmask him (though Jameson draws the line at killing him). Simultaneously, Jameson is a priceless figure of com-

edy, with his constant blustering, knee-jerk anti–Spider-Man fanaticism and cheapness with money. He also can be a serious, even moving figure; a staunch advocate of personal liberties and crusader against organized crime. Peter Parker ends up paying his bills by becoming a freelance photographer for the *Bugle*, secretly using his automatic camera to snap pictures of himself as Spider-Man. Though Jameson continually harangues Parker, it is at times clear that Jameson, beneath his hair-trigger temper, cares for him as a second son.

Jameson's young secretary, Betty Brant, was the series' first leading lady. Peter dates Betty for a while, but their relationship never grows as deep as some of his later romances. Promoted to reporter, Betty remains Peter's friend and a prominent character in the series to this day.

The heads of the high school clique that torment Peter are football star Flash Thompson and heiress Liz Allan. Ironically, Flash proves to be Spider-Man's biggest fan, believing in him when all of New York seems to turn against him. As time passes and the characters mature, Liz and even Flash slowly turn from their disdain for Peter and become his staunch friends.

Whereas in other comics time stands still, in the Marvel universe time passes and the characters age, albeit extremely slowly. Peter eventually graduates from high school and enters Empire State University (inspired by New York University). Here we meet two more long-running characters who initially treat him with contempt but later change their minds: Harry Osborn and Gwen Stacy. Harry would become Peter's college roommate, and Gwen turns out to be Peter's first true love.

In its scope and the brilliance of its concepts, Spider-Man's rogues' gallery surpasses that of any other superhero except for Batman himself, which is why it's important to discuss the Lee/Ditko issues in some detail.

Issue #2 introduces the Vulture, who provides one of Ditko's most memorable images: a wizened, elderly man in a winged costume that grants him the power of flight, a nightmarish figure of age and death sent to combat the youthful Spider-Man.

Issue #3 introduces who is undoubtedly Marvel's most popular villain, next to Dr. Doom: Doctor Octopus. Doc Ock (as he's been known for years) started as scientist Dr. Otto Octavius, who found the mechanical arms he used during his experiments fused to his body through a freak accident. While the Vulture is certainly an interesting foe, the dramatic possibilities for him seem rather limited. Dr. Octopus, on the other hand, is not just a crook with a

Stan Lee surrounded by Wolverine, the Hulk, and Spider-Man

gimmick that allows him to pull off daring crimes. He is not an ordinary villain. His mind was unbalanced by his accident and he brings a genuine emotional presence to the page.

The fourth issue brings Flint Marko, a dangerous killer on the FBI's Ten Most Wanted list, who ventures too close to an atomic test that ultimately bonds the molecules of his body to those of the sand on a beach. Thus Marko becomes the Sandman, a shape-shifting menace who can transform all or part of his body into a sandlike substance that can flow like water or become as hard as granite.

In the fifth issue came Fantastic Four villain Doctor Doom, and it was intriguing to see the good doctor go up against Spidey rather than the FF. By 1963, Doctor Doom was already Marvel's premier villain. The fact that he remains one of their top villains says a lot about the level of creativity of yesterday versus today. Stories and characters done in the early sixties continue to have reverberations in the present. Interestingly, Marvel's attention to continuity was already becoming evident in *Spider-Man #5*, which, clearly, picks up where *Fantastic Four #17* leaves off. Unlike other companies, which would have villains just turn up again and again because they escaped or were released from prison, Marvel's villains move through complex webs of plot and subplot, and, at least in the sixties, are seldom used gratuitously. Events tie into events, until years

later they result in a fascinating tapestry worthy of exploration.

While most of Spidey's adventures take place in New York, issue #6 sends Peter Parker on assignment to Florida to investigate a mysterious being known as the Lizard. This epitomizes the type of story that Marvel excelled at in that the villain is not responsible for his actions. Dr. Curt Connors, in trying to grow a new arm, instead becomes a human lizard when his formula (derived from lizard enzymes) backfires on him. This time, instead of a gizmo, Spider-Man whips up a concoction that returns Connors to normal. The Lizard has returned over the years, but is never as poignantly portrayed as he was in the original appearance, when readers saw him slowly losing his humanity and reacting to his family in more sinister ways. The story is somewhat reminiscent of the old horror film *The Alligator People*. The Lizard is, of course, another spinoff of the Jekyll/Hyde story, as his human and reptilian personalities are diametrically opposed. Like the Hulk, his inhuman side is brutal and challenging to all who cross his path. There are some interesting differences, though, such as when the Lizard recognizes his son and flees at the sound of his wife's voice. The Lizard, although inhuman, retains his ties to humanity in that he keeps the clothes he had worn as Dr. Curt Connors, including the long lab coat. Interestingly, the Lizard is not a foe that Spider-Man finds himself able to fight in the same way he can the Sandman or Doc Ock, since this menace is also a victim. Inside the inhuman form of the Lizard is Connors, desperately struggling to reemerge, and Spider-Man feels obliged to help him, even though the Lizard personality is preparing to attack the world. In a nice bit of continuity, Dr. Connors returns the favor in issue #32, when Aunt May is near death and needs an antidote of her own.

The Vulture returns in issue #7, and while there are no major villains to speak of in #8, an artistic shift becomes apparent. Peter Parker has gradually started looking less geeky and more handsome over the months, but on page two of the story, when his glasses are broken, he's clearly not the same guy we saw in the origin story.

In issue #9, a telephone lineman named Max Dillon accidentally becomes the human electrical battery called—unsurprisingly—Electro. This is followed by a pretty forgettable group known as the Enforcers, while issues 11 and 12 feature the return of Doc Ock. Next up is Mysterio, a villain who seems to have genuine magic powers, but, in fact, is a specials effects technician who can use his tricks to turn Spider-Man's sense of reality upside down.

Things get really interesting with issue #14, which introduces readers—and Spider-Man—to the Green Goblin—probably Marvel's answer to DC's the Joker.

The Green Goblin (who happens to be the villain of the Spider-Man movie) is a grotesque, grinning imp who seems to have sprung from medieval times into the present. Riding through the air on a one-man glider shaped like a bat, this living gargoyle shoots deadly energy blasts from his fingers and hurls jack o' lanterns that explode on impact. Though some of the Goblin's gimmicks may seem humorous, his goals are deadly serious. Determined to dominate New York's criminal underworld, the Goblin decides that he would most impress them by slaying their costumed nemesis, Spider-Man. At first, then, the Goblin has no personal animus against the wall-crawler, but as they clash time and again, he becomes obsessed with Spider-Man's destruction. One thing that makes him different from other villains is that we don't know who he really is any more than Spider-Man does. His face is always obscured and, in fact, it takes a number of issues for the character who turns out to be the Green Goblin to even be introduced. The two antagonists are unmasked to each other in issues #39 and #40, which together tell a pivotal story in the Spider-Man canon.

Issue #15 introduces Kraven the Hunter, who has set his big-game sights on Spider-Man. In this story, Kraven reveals to the Chameleon (from issue #1) that he obtained superhuman strength and speed by drinking a secret potion stolen from the witch doctor of a hidden African tribe. He claims that he can stop the charge of a bull elephant with one punch. While the character looks like a bush-league Tarzan, there is a more disturbing side to him, which Spider-Man recognizes from the start, when he observes. "He's the worst kind of enemy—a nut who fights you for the sheer *fun* of it." It should be noted that this issue introduces the character of Mary Jane Watson, the niece of Peter Parker's next-door neighbor and the woman who would, many years later, become Mrs. Peter Parker.

The Ringmaster, villain of issue #16, isn't quite as interesting as Spider-Man's battle with new Marvel hero Daredevil. Just as the Fantastic Four appear in *Amazing Spider-Man* #1 to help launch that fledgling title, now Daredevil appears in *Spider-Man* so that Spidey's fans will check out this new hero.

The Green Goblin returns in issue #17, which presents an interesting moment when, during a battle with the Goblin at the *Daily Bugle*, Spider-Man overhears someone taking a message for Peter Parker that Aunt May has been hospitalized. This story brings Spider-Man to the greatest low in his career since the one where he saves the astronaut son of J. Jonah Jameson and is branded a criminal. Now he's branded a coward because a room full of people (including Jameson) see him flee the battle.

Issue #18 continues the theme of Spidey's seeming cowardice as he avoids a confrontation with the Sandman so he can tend to Aunt May, who is home from the hospital; but he happily takes on the villain in #19 when he realizes that his aunt is going to be okay. Issue #20 introduces the Scorpion, a villain that Jameson pays to have created in the hopes of capturing Spider-Man in his seeming ignorance of the fact that once this mortal turns superhuman, there is no reason why he should take orders.

And on it would go from there, with some villains returning and others being introduced. Throughout it all, Lee and Ditko continued to pursue their theme of how the heroics of a Spider-Man are stymied by the frustrations of everyday life. Spider-Man goes into combat handicapped by a cold; he is hired to star in a movie and then fired on a whim of the producer; he loses his costume and has to get an ill-fitting knockoff from a Halloween costume shop; he even ends up consulting a psychiatrist at one point! No matter what successes Spider-Man scores against crime, he still has to return to his life as Peter Parker, trying to find a way to pay the rent or explain to Betty why he couldn't make their date without admitting he was too busy fighting Doctor Octopus, or whoever. And sometimes Spider-Man seems inadvertently to cause more harm than good, as when Betty's ne'er-do-well brother is killed during one of his adventures.

The 1960s: The Romita Years

By the mid-1960s, Stan Lee was editor and principal writer of over a dozen comic book titles each month. As remarkably prolific as Lee was, he could not have written so many books in the 1960s had he not devised what became known as the Marvel method of doing comics. At DC, for example, writers did full scripts, complete with descriptions of the action in each comic panel and dialogue—all *before* the artist began work.

Stan Lee, on the other hand, started by formulating a plot, usually in a conversation with the artist. Lee would leave it to the artist to break the plot down into individual panels, to pace the story, and to fill in many of the details. Once the artist had penciled the story, then Lee would write the dialogue. This method made Marvel stories more visually dynamic, since it was the artist who decided how to visualize the plot. Moreover, artists like Jack Kirby and Steve Ditko were highly imaginative and talented in their own right in terms of plotting stories and in creating concepts for characters. Hence, Lee increasingly left much of the work of plotting stories to Kirby and Ditko. For example, Kirby is said to have plotted a four-issue story from a three-sentence outline Lee gave him.

In his later issues of *Amazing Spider-Man*, Steve Ditko is credited for the plots of the stories and Lee credited for the dialogue. Heavily influenced by the conservative ideology of the writer Ayn Rand, Ditko's world view greatly underlies the early *Spider-Man* stories. His later work, notably *The Question*, tends to pit a lone, misunderstood individualist with a strict moral code against

a narrow-minded social and political establishment; the conflict between Spider-Man and J. Jonah Jameson fits the pattern. Nonetheless, Stan Lee's contribution to the *Spider-Man* series should not be minimized. Lee's dialogue often may seem bombastic, melodramatic, and corny, but it nonetheless endows his Spider-Man stories with sharp humor, incisive characterizations, and surprisingly affecting drama.

As time went on, Ditko grew increasingly restless and resentful at collaborating with Lee, and he finally quit Marvel to pursue projects at other comics companies. Issue #38, dated July 1966, was Ditko's last: he had drawn the series for just short of four years. Although Ditko would go on to create minor classics like the Creeper and Shade the Changing Man at DC, none of them would ever prove to be as commercially successful or artistically important and influential as Spider-Man or his other collaboration with Stan Lee, *Doctor Strange*. Furthermore, although Ditko has continued to work for Marvel from time to time over the years, he has steadfastly refused to draw either Spider-Man or Doctor Strange, claiming he does not want his current art to be compared to his past work. While his co-creation, Spider-Man, continues to grow in popularity and commercial success, Ditko's style, unfortunately, long ago fell from favor with the majority of the comics audience. Although comics professionals and long-time comics aficionados recognize the greatness of his achievements in the medium, he seldom has new work published anymore.

When Ditko left *Amazing Spider-Man*, Lee made a surprising choice to replace him: John Romita, an artist perhaps best known till then for his work in romance comics. It would probably be safe to say that no one was more surprised about the assignment than Romita himself, as he related to the *Comic Book Marketplace*.

"I didn't think I was on it permanently," he said. "Stan had asked me, 'Would you mind doing Spider-Man for a while?' I took that literally. I thought that Ditko would go away, relax and then come back and want it back again. I never dreamed I'd be on it for six or seven years. So the whole thing was a shock to me, because I never really felt at home on that strip. I always felt like it was Ditko's book."

It probably would have been impossible at that time to find a comics artist who could work in Ditko's unusual style. But perhaps Lee saw in Romita a way of taking *Spider-Man* to a new level of popularity. Ditko's idiosyncratic art style could really only win a cult following, but Romita's style, with large, open panels and conventionally attractive human faces and figures, had much more mainstream appeal. Peter Parker had already been growing more handsome and less scrawny under Ditko, but Romita transformed the character into a teenage leading man appropriate for one of Marvel's then-current love comics. Although Peter still

was not one of Kirby's musclemen, Romita had filled out his build, and he was no longer the kind of guy that girls would ignore as they did in the early Ditko stories.

Moreover, Romita had a spectacular skill at something Ditko could not do at all: drawing beautiful women. Ditko's version of Gwen Stacy was undistinguished; Romita transformed her into the perfect 1960s comics leading lady, combining a softly vulnerable and innocent face with a genuinely sexy build. But Lee and Romita put Gwen on a pedestal, so idealizing her as Peter's true love that she came off as sweet but basically bland and lacking in depth.

In the long run, Romita and Lee were more successful in creating a *new* leading lady for *Spider-Man*: Mary Jane Watson. In the Ditko stories, Aunt May keeps trying to set Peter up with Mary Jane, the niece of her next-door neighbor, Anna Watson. Peter continually resists, imagining that whoever his elderly aunt thinks is a good match for him would surely be plain and boring. We are not shown Mary Jane's face, but Ditko and Lee make it clear from the reactions of other characters who do see her that she is a raving beauty. Had Ditko drawn Mary Jane's face, she probably could not have lived up to readers' expectations, but when Romita finally unveiled her at the end of his fourth issue (#42, November 1966), she surpassed them. "Face it, Tiger, you've hit the jackpot!" she tells the astonished Peter, and he had. Romita gave her a highly distinctive charac-

John Romita

ter, simultaneously gorgeous and filled with high spirit. Perhaps because Lee and Romita did not intend for MJ, as she was known, to dislodge Gwen as the series' leading lady, they felt free to differentiate her from the kind of saintly, long-suffering girlfriends common in 1960s Marvel series. A cross between a 1960s go-go girl (a job she actually holds for a while) and a 1930s screwball comedy heroine, Mary Jane is funny, sexy, self-confident, and some-

thing of a rebel. She has a flirtatious relationship with Peter, who nonetheless remains devoted to Gwen. It would remain for later writers to realize that the wisecracking, unconventional party girl MJ actually was a good match for the young man who was secretly the wisecracking, unconventional superhero, Spider-Man.

It was also Lee and Romita who introduced Joe "Robbie" Robertson, the *Bugle's* editor, and one of the first African-American characters in a position of authority in comics.

Romita's most memorable *Spider-Man* cover is surely the one for issue #50, "Spider-Man No More!," showing a ghostly figure of the hero hovering above a disconsolate Peter Parker as he walks away from his discarded costume. Unable to cope with the havoc his Spider-Man career wreaks on his personal life, Peter Parker gives up his costumed identity to start life anew. Eventually, however, events conspire to remind him of his life philosophy, that "with great power must come great responsibility," and Peter dons the costume again, rededicating himself to his purpose. From that point on, subsequent writers would attempt variations on that theme: every few years Peter briefly gives up being Spider-Man in an attempt to renew his sense of idealism.

The story line that began with issue #50 also introduces one of Spider-Man's greatest nemeses, the crime boss known as the Kingpin. Seemingly obese, the Kingpin is actually built like a sumo wrestler, strong enough to stand up even to Spidey in hand-to-hand combat. More important, the Kingpin's massive size and assured demeanor convey a sense of sinister authority that make him the perfect arch-villain for Frank Miller's acclaimed *Daredevil* stories in the 1980s.

Stan Lee again altered the face of comics through *Amazing Spider-Man* when he defied the Comics Code Authority, the comics industry's own self-censorship board, which had been established in response to congressional investigations of comics in the 1950s. Lee was bent on using the comics medium to help persuade young people of the dangers of drug addiction. He and artist Gil Kane produced *Amazing Spider-Man* #96–#98, in which Peter's best friend, Harry Osborn (the son of the Green Goblin), becomes hooked on pills of an unidentified sort. Since the Comics Code forbade any references to drugs whatsoever, Lee and Marvel daringly published those three issues without the Code's seal of approval. Lee's gamble paid off: the Comics Code was soon modified to permit negative portrayals of the effects of addictive drugs, and another step was taken in moving this "children's" medium toward more adult subject matter.

Marvel had proved astonishingly successful, and in the late 1960s the company began expanding its line of titles. One experiment that misfired was the *Spectacular Spider-Man* magazine, an attempt to publish Spider-Man stories in a more expensive format, one that presumably would have more appeal to adults than the usual four-color comic books. Launched in 1968, *Spectacular*, with stories written by Lee and drawn by Romita, lasted only two issues.

The 1970s: Extending the Web

As the 1960s turned into the 1970s, Stan Lee gave up his comic-book assignments one by one. Inspired by the great work at Marvel in the 1960s, talented young fans like Roy Thomas and Gerry Conway had started writing for Marvel, taking over the superhero titles. Lee's greatest collaborator, Jack Kirby, had left to go to DC, and Romita was working on fewer *Spider-Man* issues as time went on. Moreover, as the company grew, Lee's corporate responsibilities grew with them, leaving little time for writing. *Spider-Man*, a personal favorite, was the last that he relinquished. Roy Thomas wrote issues #101 through #104, and then Lee returned briefly before finally turning the series over to Gerry Conway with issue #111 (August 1972).

But this was hardly the end of Stan Lee's involvement with Spider-Man! In the mid-1970s he and John Romita began collaborating on a daily *Spider-Man* newspaper strip, and though Romita left after the first year, to be followed by a succession of various other artists, Lee continues working on the strip to this day. Moreover, although John Romita only occasionally draws new comics stories, his son, John Romita, Jr., is one of today's leading *Spider-Man* artists.

Gerry Conway put his mark on the series through two landmark events. The first changed the tone of superhero comics permanently. Conway was seeking to shake up the status quo of the series when John Romita made a startling suggestion: killing off Gwen Stacy. No one would ever expect that Superman would fail to save Lois Lane from a death trap; one simply does not kill off the hero's leading lady. But Marvel was comics with a difference: the Marvel heroes *could* suffer tragedies. Spider-Man already had, through the death of his uncle and the death of Gwen's father, retired police captain George Stacy, in one of Stan Lee's stories.

And so it was that in *Amazing Spider-Man* #121 (June 1973) the Green Goblin, who years before had discovered Spider-Man's true identity, abducts Gwen and takes her to the top of the Brooklyn Bridge. (Oddly, although artist Gil Kane clearly drew the Brooklyn Bridge, Conway's script refers to it as the George Washington Bridge.) Before Spider-Man can stop him, the Goblin pushes Gwen off. Spider-Man swings to the rescue, but as he catches Gwen with his webbing, there is a snapping noise. Gwen is dead. Spider-Man attributes her demise to the shock of falling, but perceptive fans realized that the truth is far worse. It was the impact when Spider-Man caught the falling Gwen that snapped her neck. Not only had Spider-Man failed to rescue her, he had arguably accidentally helped to kill her.

In the following issue, the vengeful Spider-Man fights the Goblin, who falls on the sharp end of his own one-man glider and is left for dead. (He stayed "dead" for decades, to be succeeded by several other Goblins, before Marvel finally brought him back to life in the late 1990s.)

Although Stan Lee didn't discuss the death of Gwen Stacy very often, in a printed "interview" with Spider-Man he related his feelings about Conway's scenario: "You'll never know how it broke me up when I had to put you in the care of others," he told the web-slinger. "But there was no way out. My life just became too complicated for me to continue as a scriptwriter. . . . As for what happened to Gwen, I think I felt as broken up as you did about her tragic fate—after all, you just fell in love with her, but Jazzy Johnny Romita and I created the lady."

As Conway explains it, the death of Gwen Stacy was an attempt to "up the stakes" and keep *Spider-Man* mythic, dramatic, and dealing with things that had never happened before.

"What I wanted to do," he says, "was to create the same kind of feeling and mythic impact that I had enjoyed in the first thirty or forty issues of *Spider-Man*. Specifically I had in mind the period that introduced the Green Goblin, that had the Master Planner stories with Doctor Octopus, and that had this great sense of continuity and this kind of sense of impending doom every issue. Something was going to happen next month, and something was going to happen at the end of this issue that you've never seen before. That was true, in my experience, only up to issue 30 or 40 of the original book, and after that the book just never seemed to have the same intensity of plotting and adventure.

"So I was looking to do something different, and killing off Spider-Man's girlfriend certainly had never been done before," he continues with a laugh. "It was very serious. While I'll take some credit for co-conceiving the idea, I didn't do it myself."

The shock that readers felt at Gwen's death was aptly captured decades later by writer Kurt Busiek and painter Alex Ross in their limited series *Marvels*. This series, which retells various key events from Marvel history, including Gwen's death, makes it clear that it was a turning point in the evolution of the superhero genre. From that point on, nothing was certain. The heroine could die. The superhero could fail. Order would not necessarily be restored. Evil could triumph. The relative innocence of the Marvel stories of the 1960s was beginning to give way to the "grim and gritty" comics that would dominate the 1980s and early 1990s.

"I've done a lot of thinking about this in the last ten years because the story has been retold now several times by different people," Conway muses. "I think this story line summed up the difference between superheroes prior to 1973 and the superheroes since 1973. In a real sense, that was a turning point for the concept of comics. After that point, anything could happen and did."

Conway used *Amazing Spider-Man* to create one of the signature characters of the grim and gritty era: the Punisher, a vigilante in a black costume with a skull insignia who first appears in *Amazing Spider-Man* #129 (February 1974), drawn by longtime Spider-artist Ross Andru. Inspired by pulp novel characters, the Punisher is a Vietnam veteran whose family has been murdered by criminals. Inhumanly obsessed with vengeance, the Punisher conducts a one-man war on crime. What distinguishes him from the superheroes of that time is the fact that he has crossed a moral divide: the Punisher ruthlessly kills his adversaries. This would seem to put the Punisher and Spider-Man on opposite sides, but the Punisher proves a popular character. The web-slinger often finds himself working alongside this killer, though never adopting his methods.

The Punisher was ahead of his time—and of most of the comics audience. But a decade later, when the grim and gritty trend began to gather strength, the Punisher won his own book, and at the height of this fervor for anti-heroes, the Punisher would star in four monthly comics series simultaneously.

Conway and Andru also created a new villain, the Jackal, who creates not only a clone of the deceased Gwen Stacy with which to torment Spider-Man, but also a clone of Spider-Man himself! The clone is killed in *Amazing Spider-Man* #149 and its body destroyed in the following issue—or so readers, editors, and writers at that time are led to believe. As we shall see, few deaths—except for Gwen's and Uncle Ben's—are permanent in superhero comics,

and long-forgotten characters can resurface decades later in undreamed-of circumstances.

Although the original *Spectacular Spider-Man* failed, Marvel merely misjudged the growth of the Spider-Man readership by a few years. In 1972, Marvel successfully expanded the Spider-Man franchise by launching *Marvel Team-Up*, which paired up Marvel heroes for new adventures. Spider-Man teams up with the Fantastic Four's Human Torch in the first two issues; after that, either Spider-Man or the Torch teams up with another Marvel hero or team. Soon, however, Spider-Man becomes the star of the book, joining forces with a different guest star in each issue.

Marvel Team-Up ran for over 150 issues. Its best creative period came in the late 1970s, when writer Chris Claremont and artist John Byrne, the pair who revolutionized the *X-Men*, collaborated on the series. Claremont also wrote *Marvel Team-Up*'s most unusual issue, in which Spider-Man crosses paths with the original cast of TV's *Saturday Night Live*!

Since it dealt with combinations of heroes, *Marvel Team-Up* was conceptually different from *Amazing Spider-Man*, which remained focused on the web-slinger's solo exploits. Spider-Man, though, had become Marvel's best-selling character, and had displaced *Fantastic Four* as the company's flagship title. Hence, the temptation was there to clone *Amazing* and thus create a third

Spider-title. It finally happened when the prolific writer Gerry Conway returned to Marvel after a stint at DC and wanted to write *Spider-Man* again. Rather than displace *Amazing*'s current writer, Marvel gave Conway a new companion title to write: *Peter Parker, The Spectacular Spider-Man*, which began in December 1976. The name of the series was in part recycled from the failed *Spectacular Spider-Man* magazine. From time to time during *Spectacular*'s history, there were attempts to distinguish it from *Amazing*. *Amazing* would concentrate on Peter's life with the *Daily Bugle* characters, for example, while *Spectacular* would feature the supporting cast from Empire State University. In the end, though, the only real differences among *Amazing, Spectacular*, and other Spider titles to come lay in the contrasting styles of the writers and artists of the books. Indeed, by the 1990s, story lines would frequently run from one Spider-series into another and back again.

It was also in the early 1970s that Marvel entered into a partnership with the Children's Television Workshop, which produced *Sesame Street*. As a result a live-action (but mute) Spider-Man appeared on episodes of *The Electric Company*, the Workshop's 1970s series aimed at teaching children how to read. In turn, Marvel published *Spidey Super Stories*, a comic for very young children, starting in October 1974. Designed as an aid to teach reading, *Spidey Super Stories* utilized a simple, limited

vocabulary to tell stories involving Spider-Man and various other Marvel characters.

Another obvious way to expand the Spider-Man franchise was to create—what else?—a Spider-Woman. In fact, if Marvel had not created a Spider-Woman, inevitably some other comic book company would trademark the name (for example, DC has Wonder Woman, but Marvel has a Wonder Man). Marvel's first Spider-Woman appeared in *Marvel Spotlight* #32 in February 1977, and was presented as an actual spider who, through genetic engineering, had been transformed into a humanoid being! Ultimately, it was decided that this was simply too weird, and it was subsequently explained that Jessica Drew, the Spider-Woman, was indeed a real human being who had been given spiderlike abilities. These differed somewhat from Spider-Man's: she was super-strong, too, but she also could shoot "venom" bolts—bioelectrical energy blasts—from her hands.

Spider-Woman soon won her own series, written by Marv Wolfman and drawn by Carmine Infantino, starting in April 1978. Wolfman distinguished the *Spider-Woman* series from *Spider-Man* by slanting it toward supernatural fantasy: her archenemy, for instance, is the sorceress Morgan le Fey from the legends of King Arthur. Taking a different approach, writer Chris Claremont set Jessica up as a private investigator in San Francisco. The series' last writer, Mark Gruenwald, succeeded in combining the film-noir milieu with paranormal menaces, but the book nevertheless was cancelled with issue #50.

The 1980s: Wedding Bells and Serial Killers

Longtime Marvel editor-in-chief Jim Shooter introduced a concept that quickly became a standard in the comics business: the companywide crossover story. The first of these, *Marvel Super Heroes Secret Wars*, was a limited series that ran for twelve issues, starting in 1984, pitting Marvel's leading superheroes against its most infamous villains on a distant planet. Shooter, who wrote the series, intended that it would make changes in the status quo of the characters, some of them permanent. The most vivid of these was Spider-Man's new costume, all black except for the spider insignia and eyepieces. Since his standard costume was damaged in combat, Spider-Man acquired the black, alien costume, which he wears when he returns to Earth in *Amazing Spider-Man* #252, cover-dated May 1984.

At the time, Shooter declared that Spider-Man's change of costume was permanent, and collectors therefore snapped up copies of its first appearance. The webslinger was indeed still wearing this ninja-like outfit when Marvel launched its fourth monthly Spider-Man comic, *Web of Spider-Man*, in April 1985. It was probably inevitable, though, that the red-and-blue

Spider costume would return: solid black hardly suits the cheerful, bright, wisecracking side of Spider-Man's personality, and with no visible web pattern, it just doesn't look like a spider!

One person who wasn't particularly fond of the black costume was Stan Lee, who did *not* incorporate the change into the comic strip. "I've always been happy with the old costume," he said at the time. "The new costume is fine, even very dramatic, but there's no reason for me to change it in the strip. And, truthfully, I don't worry about continuity between the strip and the comics, because there are so many different things anyway. We don't check with each other as to what stories they're doing in the comics or what stories I'm doing in the strip. That doesn't seem to bother any of the newspaper readers and I don't imagine it bothers any of the comic book readers either."

Writer David Michelinie admitted that he, too, preferred the old costume. "That's a dangerous question," he laughed. "If we're talking about Spider-Man in person, I've seen the guy who makes personal appearances wearing both costumes and the black one really looks terrific. But for the comic book, I'm a fan from way back and I guess I still prefer the red and blue."

Interestingly, there had been talk of developing yet another version of the costume. "It was going to get some red highlights and outlines around the eyes,"

Michelinie noted. "When Jim Salicrup came in as the new editor, he tossed out that idea. Originally the costume was going to change at the end of a two-part battle with the Hobgoblin."

In the end, Michelinie did come up with a cunning story-twist for getting rid of the black costume. He revealed that the costume was actually a living being that was attempting to bond itself to Peter Parker! Aided by the Fantastic Four, Spider-Man frees himself from the costume and imprisons it in a glass tube. But Michelinie had more up his sleeve. He and his new collaborator, artist Todd McFarlane, crafted a story line in which the black costume escapes and bonds with a disgruntled reporter named Eddie Brock, who resents Spider-Man. The living costume also has a grudge against the wall-crawler, feeling rejected by him. Joined together physically and mentally, Brock and the costume become a murderous, nightmarish version of Spider-Man, calling himself Venom.

Debuting in the 25th anniversary issue of *Amazing Spider-Man*, #300 (May 1988), Venom swiftly became the most popular villain in Spider-Man's rogues' gallery since the time that Stan Lee was writing the comic. Dressed like a monstrous version of Spider-Man, Venom seems like the web-slinger's depraved evil twin.

But times had changed a great deal since the 1960s. Readers in the late 1980s and early 1990s were enamored of "grim and gritty" comics, in which the level of violence had sharply escalated from the more innocent stories of earlier decades. Venom, who takes pleasure in threatening not simply to kill Spider-Man, but to devour his brain, is in the forefront of this new, more vicious wave of comics characters. Even more disturbing is the fact that Venom grew so popular that he became an anti-hero, starring in numerous back-to-back comics miniseries in the 1990s. By this point he has called a truce of sorts with Spider-Man and is battling other villains.

Since Venom had become a nominal good guy, albeit a particularly ruthless one, Michelinie came up with Carnage, a serial killer bonded to another alien costume, as a new villain for both Venom and Spider-Man to battle.

Venom and Carnage seemed ubiquitous in the 1990s, but as the decade wore on, tastes shifted again: Carnage has pretty much disappeared from the Spider-titles, and Venom is only an infrequent visitor nowadays.

In issue #7 (October 1984), *Marvel Super Heroes Secret Wars* introduced the second Spider-Woman, who would turn out to be single mother Julia Carpenter. Her powers, too, differ somewhat from Spider-Man's: she creates her "webbing" from sheer mental energy. Spider-Woman II joined *Avengers West Coast* (a spinoff from Marvel's classic *Avengers* series), starred in her own limited series, written by Roy

Thomas, and ended up in the short-lived team book *Force Works*. But when *Force Works* came to an end, so did Julia's superhero career. Two Spider-Women down; one more to come!

One of the hallmarks of Spider-Man is that his life does change over time: he starts out in high school and then goes on to college. Time may pass more slowly in the Marvel Universe than it does in real life, but pass it does. Mind you, Stan Lee probably never dreamed that the series would last for four decades. If he had, then perhaps he wouldn't have moved Peter Parker into college as early as the mid-1960s!

Still, it should be no surprise that it was Stan Lee himself, who, in the mid-1980s, decided that it was finally time for Peter Parker to get married. The obvious candidate for bride of Spider-Man was Mary Jane Watson. She was the longtime leading lady of Stan Lee's Spider-Man comic strip, and in the comic books, Tom DeFalco had unintentionally laid the groundwork for an eventual wedding by having Mary Jane reveal to Peter that she has long known his secret identity. (Indeed, a later graphic novel, *Parallel Lives*, written by Gerry Conway, establishes that Mary Jane, visiting her aunt's house, had seen Peter leave the Parker house as Spider-Man on the night of Uncle Ben's death, and put two and two together!)

As to the development of the idea of marriage, Lee reflected: "One day I just said, 'Gee, he's been dating this girl long enough,

it might be fun to see what the life of a superhero would be like if he had a wife.' Except for Reed Richards of the Fantastic Four, I can't recall any individual married superheroes."

The wedding was announced by Lee and Jim Shooter while they were on a convention panel, and they noted that the story would take place in that year's annual. "In the three issues building up to the annual," said Michelinie, "Peter Parker reassesses his entire life, not only as Spider-Man but as Peter Parker; Mary Jane reassesses her life as well. He reevaluates his early goal to be a scientist. Being Spider-Man was an excuse to make a living by going out and taking pictures of himself and selling them. He comes to the conclusion that he has been Spider-Man at the expense of his other goals in life."

The wedding of Peter Parker and Mary Jane Watson in 1987 became something of a multimedia event. It took place simultaneously in the newspaper comic strip and in *Amazing Spider-Man Annual* #21. "To my knowledge," said Michelinie, "one has never followed the course of the events in the other. But to alter the character radically by having him get married made it necessary to match up the story lines. Otherwise it would be too different. It's not like having Peter Parker break his arm or something that could be healed in a few weeks."

Interestingly, there was even a "real life" wedding ceremony involving actors (one in

Stan Lee gives a thumbs-up to a recent Spider-Man comic book

Spider costume) held in New York City's Shea Stadium! When Clark Kent finally married Lois Lane years later, Marvel published an ad congratulating the DC hero and, not incidentally, gently observing that he was following in his competitor's footsteps.

The 1990s: Sending in the Clones

Venom's co-creator, Todd McFarlane, is surely the most influential Spider-Man artist since Steve Ditko and John Romita, Sr. In fact, McFarlane's style in certain aspects seems like an updated version of Ditko's. Rather than aim at total realism, McFarlane consciously draws "cartoony" faces and figures, but conveys a dynamic power through their poses and his panel layouts, while at the same time creating a dark and forbidding urban environment. McFarlane also found ways to emphasize the sheer strangeness of Spider-Man, greatly enlarging the eyepieces of his mask and making him move as if he were indeed a spider scuttling along walls. A new generation of comics readers responded with tremendous enthusiasm, making Todd McFarlane the biggest name in comics in the early 1990s.

McFarlane's rise in fame came simultaneously with the great speculator boom in comics, when sales throughout the industry rose to unprecedented heights. McFarlane longed to write as well as draw his stories, and

he got his chance when Marvel launched its fourth series about the wall-crawler, called simply *Spider-Man*, starting in August 1990. The initial issue sold millions of copies to speculators who somehow persuaded themselves that a book that was printed in such vast quantities would be worth something someday. The speculator bubble in comics was fated to explode, and the industry has yet to recover. But the boom was a blessing for the careers of McFarlane and several of his artist friends. Their popularity was so great at the time that they soon were able to break away from Marvel and form their own company, Image, for which McFarlane created his best-selling comic, *Spawn*.

In the early 1990s, Marvel launched its *2099* line of titles, depicting one of many possible futures for the Marvel Universe. These books were heavily influenced by "cyberpunk" science fiction, of which the film *The Matrix* is a prominent recent example. Such works extrapolate fantastic futuristic uses of computer technology while depicting a world dominated by powerful corporations. The most prominent of the titles was *Spider-Man 2099*, created by writer Peter David and artist Rick Leonardi (the first issue dated November 1992). The central character is Miguel O'Hara, a genetic engineer who has made a study of the original Spider-Man. O'Hara was unwillingly injected with genetic material from a spider, causing him to mutate in grotesque fashion. This Spider-Man does not need web-shooters: he can actually produce organic webbing from his body. As often occurs with Marvel's attempts to create fictional realities other than its present-day universe, the *2099* line was a commercial failure, and *Spider-Man 2099* was cancelled.

In the mid-1990s, Spider-Man editor Danny Fingeroth and his writers decided that the character had strayed too far from his roots. The main problem was Peter Parker's marriage to Mary Jane. For one thing, it was felt that this made Peter seem too old in comparison to the teenage readers Marvel was trying to target. Moreover, the Spider-Man writers and editors postulated that Peter Parker was supposed to be something of a loser in his personal life, continually beset by bad luck. How badly off could he be, they thought, when he was married to a gorgeous and successful supermodel?

But the editors and writers thought it would make Peter Parker look bad if he and Mary Jane were divorced, and they didn't want to kill her off. So how could the dilemma be resolved?

There was another problem in the minds of the editors and writers. As the decades go by, there is a growing feeling among many comics professionals that the characters' long histories become a burden, making the stories inaccessible to new readers. Whether or not this really bothers readers is a matter of debate; it may simply be that many of the professionals don't want to bother keeping up with the characters' continuity.

Nonetheless, discarding and revamping past continuity had become popular in the comics since the mid-1980s and in DC Comics' *Crisis on Infinite Earths*. This series started a wave of "reboots" at DC, in which the histories of almost all the company's major characters were heavily revised or started over from scratch. The most prominent relaunch was that of Superman himself, in John Byrne's *The Man of Steel* limited series. In that one six-issue series, Byrne started the Superman legend anew, coming up with his own version of Krypton and doing away with Superman's years as a teenage superhero, among many other radical changes.

In contrast, Marvel stood firm in maintaining its own continuity from 1961 intact, probably mainly because the editors and writers believed that the 1960s stories, by comics giants like Stan Lee and Jack Kirby, were still viable by contemporary standards. So how could Spider-Man's history be changed without ignoring over thirty years of stories?

Fingeroth and company devised a surprising solution to these problems they saw in the books. They decided that the Spider-Man clone from *Amazing Spider-Man #149* was not dead, after all. Peter Parker's exact look-alike, who had been leading a nomadic existence all these years, turned up under the name Ben Reilly. Ben even took on his own costumed identity as the Scarlet Spider, and for two months the Spider-Man titles were renamed after him: hence there was *The Amazing Scarlet Spider* comic, from November through December of 1995, instead of *The Amazing Spider-Man*.

But there was more: the writers declared that the "real" Spider-Man whose life the books chronicled was actually the clone! Fingeroth and company intended for Ben Reilly to be the real, original Peter Parker.

Ultimately, the man we had known as Peter Parker since late 1975 gave up being Spider-Man. He and Mary Jane, who was now pregnant, moved to Portland, Oregon—in other words, a continent away from the Spider-Man cast—to start their lives anew. Hence, Peter and Mary Jane virtually disappeared from the Spider-books. Ben Reilly took over the role of Spider-Man in all the comics, and Marvel even launched a new series, *The Sensational Spider-Man*, spotlighting this "new/old" Spider-Man, starting in January 1996 (this series replaced *Web of Spider-Man*, which was cancelled with the September 1995 issue).

In the course of these events, another tragedy struck the life of Peter Parker. In a moving story written by J. Marc DeMatteis for *Amazing Spider-Man* #400 (April 1995), Peter's beloved, frequently ailing Aunt May passes away. May's death is another factor that frees Peter and Mary Jane to move off to Portland.

Fingeroth eventually left Marvel to become editor of Byron Preiss Publications' online comics (which proved short-lived), and was succeeded as Spider-editor by Bob Budiansky. Both Fingeroth and Budiansky felt they had "fixed" Spider-Man. He was no longer married, happy, or prosperous. Now, as Ben Reilly, he had a menial job in a coffee shop and lived in a tiny apartment in a rundown building. Those readers who liked Mary Jane could take satisfaction that she was happily married to the "other" Spider-Man off in Portland.

Moreover, the editors and writers had thus reassigned the last nearly twenty years of continuity to the clone. Ben Reilly's history as Spider-Man was limited to the stories that appeared between 1962 and 1975, most of which had been written by Stan Lee. These were the stories that the writers and editors, who had grown up during that period, considered essential.

It was a complicated but clever solution. And it didn't work.

The majority of the comics audience of the 1980s, which regarded many DC series as dated, welcomed that company's revamps. But Marvel readers were horrified to find that the Spider-Man they had been following for two decades was suddenly declared to be a fake. The editors and writers may have told themselves that Ben Reilly was the same Spider-Man they had read about back in the 1960s, but by the mid-1990s, the majority of Spider-Man's readership had started following the character after 1975. Their Spider-Man was the one married to Mary Jane, not this drifter who had suddenly usurped the title!

And so, the Spider-Man writers and editors were abruptly forced to change direction. Ben Reilly would be revealed to be the clone, after all, and the self-exiled Peter Parker would turn out to be the original Spider-Man.

But how could Marvel explain all of this away? Simple: the editors and writers would claim that all the confusion was caused by a master villain who was trying to get revenge on the real Spider-Man by taking away his own sense of identity. And who would be an imposing-enough mastermind to have come up with such a convoluted scheme? None other than Norman Osborn, the original Green Goblin!

It would now turn out that the serum that turned Osborn into the Green Goblin had also given him superhuman healing abilities, enabling him to recover from the mortal wound he had suffered following the death of Gwen. Osborn had surreptitiously left for Europe, and had been manipulating Spider-Man's destiny from afar.

Osborn reassumes his Green Goblin identity and murders the Ben Reilly Spider-Man. Reilly's body dissolves before Peter Parker's eyes, proving that Reilly was the clone. Peter then becomes Spider-Man once more, once again affirming that with great power must come great responsibility.

There was one more "problem" to be solved: if Marvel feared that Peter Parker would seem too old in readers' eyes if he was married, it would be worse if he became a father! When Mary Jane finally gives birth to a baby girl named "May," she is told the infant was stillborn, and an agent of Osborn carries the baby off. But is the baby dead? For now, the Spider-Man department was content: the baby had, in any event, been written out.

(If you feel confused trying to follow all of these convoluted plot twists, imagine how the fans reading the comics felt! No wonder the clone saga came to be regarded as a disaster.)

Nostalgia for the *Spider-Man* of the 1960s led to the creation of *Untold Tales of Spider-Man*, written by Kurt Busiek (whose career was rising rapidly), and drawn by Pat Olliffe. This series started in September 1995 and ran for two years. Busiek's idea was to tell stories about Spider-Man in his high school days that would fit in between the original Lee-Ditko tales. Busiek was remarkably successful in capturing the spirit of *Amazing*'s early years; Olliffe, in turn, was faithful to the look of those early stories. Whereas contemporary Spider-book writers tend to condemn the early Peter Parker as a nerd or geek, Busiek treated Peter with sympathy and understanding, much as Stan Lee had.

While longtime readers could pick up on the links to old-time continuity, *Untold*

Tales was also designed to be accessible to new readers who might prefer reading about a high-school-age hero. Marvel also decided to do an *Amazing Fantasy* limited series to cover what might have happened between *Amazing Fantasy* #15 and *Amazing Spider-Man* #1; Busiek wrote this series as well. But perhaps the majority of Spider-Man readers regarded *Untold Tales* as peripheral, since it did not take place in the present; it came to an end all too soon.

Though *Spider-Man 2099* didn't last, Marvel tried depicting another future successor to the web-slinger with *Spider-Girl* by Tom DeFalco and Pat Olliffe. Introduced in *What If?* #105, Spider-Girl began her own comic book in October 1998. This was part of DeFalco's *M2* line of books, which depicted a possible Marvel Universe over fifteen years in the future. In this alternate future Peter Parker has retired as Spider-Man due to the loss of one of his legs in combat. His daughter, May, now a high school student, has inherited his superpowers, and has become the crime-fighting Spider-Girl. This comic has outlasted the rest of the *M2* line, but now that the infant May seems to be dead in the modern-day Spider-books, Spider-Girl's possible future seems impossible.

Longtime Marvel editor Ralph Macchio eventually took over the Spider-Man titles. Macchio, writer Howard Mackie, artist John Byrne, and others sought to put the "clone" era behind them and return, as they

saw it, to more traditional kinds of Spider-Man stories. But they too believed that over the decades Spider-Man had strayed too far from his roots. They made two controversial moves to restore what they believed to be the character's proper status quo.

First, Macchio and company deemed it essential that Aunt May be part of the series. She served as a living reminder of Uncle Ben, and hence of the sense of the guilt that motivated Spider-Man's mission to fight crime. Kurt Busiek made the point that it was important too that Spider-Man have a family member to whom he related solely as Peter, not as a superhero.

The writers established that Osborn's agents were holding someone named "May" captive, and readers assumed that it was baby May. So it was even more of a surprise when the prisoner turned out to be Aunt May, still alive; the "May" who had died was an impostor whom Osborn had altered via plastic surgery! Readers who had been moved by J. Marc DeMatteis's depiction of the death of Aunt May felt cheated, but a character deemed essential to the series had been restored. (And the baby's fate has still not been proved one way or the other!) Mary Jane's modeling career revived, and now she, Peter, and Aunt May live together happily in an expensive Manhattan apartment. It seems that Peter has everything he ever wanted. But Macchio, Mackie, and Byrne would soon pull the rug out from under him.

To mark the fact that a chapter was closing in Peter's life, Marvel brought the original *Amazing Spider-Man* comic to an end with issue #441 in November 1998. That same month saw the cancellation of the three other Spider-books: *Spectacular Spider-Man, Sensational Spider-Man*, and just plain *Spider-Man*.

Two months later, Marvel relaunched the line of Spider-titles, led by *Amazing Spider-Man* Volume 2, starting with a new issue #1 for January 1999, written by Howard Mackie and drawn by John Byrne. A new series, *Peter Parker, Spider-Man*, debuted, written by British talent Paul Jenkins. A short-lived third series, *Webspinners: Tales of Spider-Man*, would debut a year later, in January 1999: this would comprise a succession of multi-part stories by different writer-artist teams, set in different periods of Spider-Man's history.

And then the previously mentioned rug was pulled. Mary Jane gets aboard an airplane that explodes in midair in *Amazing Spider-Man* Vol. 2, #13. Peter is suddenly a young widower, and debts wipe out Mary Jane's riches, leaving him penniless. The hard-luck Spider-Man is back with a vengeance.

Again there was some backlash among the readers, many of whom seemed to feel that Mackie and Byrne had made the series too dark and depressing. This had not been their intention. Indeed, once Peter got over his depression over Mary Jane's demise, the books certainly had a more traditional feel than they had in quite some time. They were surely brighter in tone than the Carrion tales or the grim clone saga of the previous decade.

Though Marvel traditionally paid strict adherence to past continuity, editor-in-chief Bob Harras was not averse to making revisions in the classic tales of the 1960s. In the new series *Spider-Man: Chapter One*, he gave carte blanche to writer/artist John Byrne, the man who had revamped *Superman*. The limited series began in December 1998 and ran for a year. Through it, Byrne retold many of the classic Lee/Ditko stories, making alterations where he saw fit. A great admirer of Lee and Ditko's work, Byrne saw no reason to do a complete overhaul as he had with Superman. Most of the changes turned out to be cosmetic, updating the look of the characters and their surroundings. Peter looks the same, but now Flash wears a baseball cap backward, and Liz wears miniskirts. Instead of a microscope, Uncle Ben and Aunt May give Peter a personal computer. There were some substantial changes, though: for instance, Byrne merged the origins of Spider-Man and Doctor Octopus. It turns out that the nuclear accident that gave Octopus his powers also irradiated the spider that bit Peter—a theme possibly picked up from the Ted Newsom and John Braccato draft of the Spider-Man movie from 1985.

Revisions of history do not tend to last

at Marvel, however. In *Chapter One*, for example, Byrne was intent on throwing out Kurt Busiek's *Amazing Fantasy* limited series. At present, since neither Bob Harras nor Byrne works at Marvel any longer, there is some question as to whether any of the story changes made in *Chapter One* will remain canonical.

John Byrne also wrote a new, short-lived *Spider-Woman* series, drawn by Bart Sears, which depicted the third version of Spider-Woman, a young woman named Mattie, who turned out to be J. Jonah Jameson's niece. Launched in July 1999, the new *Spider-Woman* comic came to an abrupt end in December 2000.

Into the New Century

In the year 2000, Bill Jemas became Marvel's president of publishing, and he appointed Joe Quesada as Marvel's latest editor-in-chief. With the Spider-Man movie on the horizon, Jemas and Quesada believed one of their priorities was to revamp the Spider-Man line.

"The Spider-books," offered Quesada, "lost the essence of what Spidey was. First of all, let's give credit where credit is due: Ralph Macchio did the undoable; he made people forget 'The Clone Saga' as best we possibly could. He cleaned up a lot of horrific decisions that were made in the past, but the character was still not where it should have been."

Jemas and Quesada also believed that the current Spider-Man titles were inaccessible to new, young readers. Like many, they seemed to find Spider-Man most appealing when he was high-school age. But they seemed to be dissatisfied with both Kurt Busiek's and John Byrne's recent series about Spider-Man's early years. It was their intention to start the Spider-Man saga over from the beginning and make it, in their view, more relevant to today's teens.

And so, *Ultimate Spider-Man* came about, written by Brian Michael Bendis, a new star from the world of independent comics, and longtime Spider-Man artist Mark Bagley.

"Basically, comics are in a sales slump," offered Bendis in explanation of the title. "There's just no two ways about it. There's not enough people reading mainstay comics to sustain them commercially. People try to pretend that's not the truth because it upsets them, but it's the way it is. A plan was put down to create a line of comics using the most beloved characters. Supposedly Spider-Man is just the hugest license. Anything they put it on does hugely well, *except* for the comics. That means that people love the character, but just aren't grabbing on to the comics.

"So the idea," he continued, "was that Marvel had these characters and felt that they should be brought down to the basic idea—deshackle them from continuity. They did some research, and people felt that if they picked up a copy of *Spider-Man*, they'd need to read a thousand issues to really get a sense of the whole picture."

Ultimate Spider-Man's first issue was cover-dated October 2000. In effect, this series presented an alternate version of Spider-Man for new readers.

"I wanted to go back to the initial concept that Peter Parker is fifteen years old and gets bit by a spider," Bendis explained. "That was the origin of Spider-Man. Now he's in his thirties and on his second wife or something. Whatever it is, it's off the mark from the initial concept. So let's go back to the initial concept, except that it takes place today. Tell the story as logically and emotionally as possible, using this basic concept that it takes place today.

"Comics are a little bit more of a mature medium than they were in the 1960s," he elaborated. "A lot more can and needs to be expressed to tell a more fully layered story. The original *Amazing Fantasy* number fifteen is only, like, fifteen pages long, whereas we're taking the same story and are sort of spreading it out over a six-issue arc. We wanted to get a sense of Peter's home and who he was beforehand. In the original, somebody said, 'Hey, Parker, you loser,' and he goes into the lab and gets bitten by the spider. And we see Uncle Ben for like one panel before he dies. Of course it works, because we're with him and it's sad to imagine somebody in your family dying. Today, that's not something we can really

get away with. Our obligation is to flesh out Peter's relationship with Ben so that when that inevitable bad thing happens, hopefully it will be devastating. So we're telling the same story, but in more of, I guess, a cinematic way and in more mature language, but in an innocent way for people to enjoy it. People are very hung up on this being a marketed-for-kids thing. The idea, really, is to write something as emotionally honest as possible. Kids don't want to be talked down to. If you tell an honest story and put it out there, people will come to it. But if you start trying to pander, man, people hate that. We're not pandering. We're telling a very loving story of Spider-Man and Peter Parker."

As noted, this was a Peter Parker who was in high school in the year 2000. The new versions of Aunt May and Uncle Ben, who ties his hair in a ponytail (!), have clearly grown up in the 1960s (which undoubtedly has made longtime readers feel old). When Peter gets his job at the *Daily Bugle*, it's at the paper's brand-new Internet site. Changes have gone beyond topical updates: now Mary Jane is Peter's high school classmate, and Norman Osborn, as the Green Goblin, is not the thin, cackling adversary Ditko drew, but a lumbering, heavily muscled opponent.

The first six issues of *Ultimate Spider-Man* reworked Spider-Man's origin, following the same basic story that Lee and Ditko had told nearly forty years earlier. This new version of Spider-Man would also appear in the *Ultimate Team-Up* series, which introduces revamped versions of other classic Marvel heroes.

The *Ultimate* books existed side by side with *Amazing Spider-Man* and other traditional Spider-books, meaning that Marvel was now publishing two versions of Spider-Man. Longtime readers could still follow the old continuity in *Amazing* and related titles and ignore *Ultimate* if they wished. New readers could follow the *Ultimate* books and ignore the rest. As it turned out, many longtime Spider-Man readers embraced *Ultimate Spider-Man* as a well-executed variation on Lee and Ditko's classic themes.

"I harken it to a lot of people who saw the X-Men movie who never read the X-Men comics," Bendis said. "They had nothing to compare it to and they enjoyed it immensely. Then you get those guys who compare it to the Byrne X-Men or to the Paul Smith X-Men. I sort of invited people to separate themselves from the marketing of it and just enjoy the book. Most people who have been able to do that have been able to see that we came to the project with a lot of love. I have a lot of affection toward the history of the character and what our responsibilities are. My job is to take the basic idea of the book and go back to it. What we're doing is crafting the story for a general audience to sort of introduce it to people. That's all we've done. It's a great gig and the response has been real pleasant.

"I had read a lot of *Spider-Man* and I'm actually a huge fan of John Romita, Sr.," he added. "That, to me, is the level of achievement in characterizations and ideas worth striving for. In the beginning of *Spider-Man*—and I think Stan Lee will admit to this—they were making up the rules as they went along a little bit. I sort of can see that Stan got into a groove of really understanding the character. The popularity of the character was sort of defining itself and the rules of the character. I'm just a huge fan of that stuff. I haven't read it in a while. That's not to take away from anything those guys were doing, but I think it's probably one of the reasons I was a good choice to write this book. I was coming at it pretty fresh, with a lot of love and overall feeling toward the character, rather than being immersed in it. That's what I can bring to it. I'm in love with the essence of the character rather than the specifics of what's been going on."

The real question, of course, is, Why has this character captured the writer's imagination the way that it has? "When you make generalizations," Bendis mused, "people always stand up and say, 'Hey, not me!' But I do feel I was, just like many of my friends who were into comics, physical underachievers in the group—the geeks and the dorks. Peter Parker is a dork. I saw that Sam Raimi said about the movie that the appeal of Spider-Man is that Clark Kent was always pretending to be a dork, but Peter always *was* a dork. Even after he got his powers he was *still* a dork. *That's* the appeal. Everyone can sort of relate to trying to break out of that shell. Of all the characters ever in comics, I literally thought I was Peter Parker—except for the cool job, powers, and ability to be a brilliant scientist.

"That being said," he continued, "it's very easy for me to tap into the psyche and charm of the guy. Also, in my own writing, outside of the work-for-hire stuff, I've never yet dealt with my personal adolescent neurosis. So it was fun to open that box again and find out how fresh the wounds were. It's been eighteen years and I'm still pissed. See, that's where Stan Lee's genius was. The idea of creating these superheroes with a lot of personal problems is such a brilliant idea and it never gets tired. That's why the X-Men movie was a hit. People can relate to it. People don't see themselves as Superman. They probably think that even if they had superpowers, they'd still have to deal with a lot of crap in their lives. Also, and not to get too cheesy, there's something about the spider powers being a metaphor for adolescence. There's something about the growing pains of him getting the powers when he's a kid. It fascinates me."

Ralph Macchio was given the assignment of editing *Ultimate Spider-Man*, while the "traditional" Spider-titles were reassigned in 2000 to new Marvel editor Axel Alonso, whose previous experience had been as an editor in DC's acclaimed Vertigo line of sophisticated fantasy comics. "We

need fresh blood," offered Quesada in explanation of the change. "We need someone from the outside who has a different perspective. Look at some of the stuff he's created at Vertigo—the guy has a consistent track record, not only of creating exciting commercial properties within an imprint that's traditionally noncommercial. He's also got a great reputation amongst the freelance community. To me, we went out shopping for a home-run hitter and we got one."

Planning to leave *Amazing Spider-Man* anyway, Howard Mackie took the change of editorship as an opportunity to resign as its writer. Before he left, he brought Mary Jane back from apparent death (she hadn't been onboard the plane when it exploded). It was still believed, however, that Peter should be single. This time Marvel bit the bullet, and Mary Jane started divorce proceedings, weary of the constant tension of Peter's life as a superhero.

Alonso's choice for Mackie's successor was astonishing: J. Michael Straczynski, the creator of the cult science-fiction TV series *Babylon 5*, who was also a staunch comics fan.

Joe Quesada is of the belief that Straczynski is an important creative move for Spider-Man. "Number one," he said, "a whole new set of readers. Number two, a style of storytelling that maybe we haven't seen at Marvel. He comes from a completely different world. He has that sort of neophyte exuberance of, 'I've never worked at Marvel before. This is the most exciting thing on the planet.' That kind of stuff is really contagious and I think if you get that kind of excitement on Spider-Man, it'll be contagious across the whole line."

In explaining his take on the character, the writer noted, "What I want to do is bring Peter Parker into the twenty-first century. Right now, if you take nearly any of the current titles and put them next to an issue from the 1980s or 1990s, I'd defy an outsider to tell you the difference. The character really hasn't grown. Things around him have changed, the cast of characters has ebbed and flowed, but the growth we saw as integral to the character in the beginning has fallen by the wayside. The comic has to have an edge to it. It has to feel contemporary, as much a part of this time as Peter was a part of the sixties. It would have to take chances, at times be somewhat experimental. What are the problems facing us right now? What would someone with these abilities want to do with them about those problems? Not all of the bad guys wear costumes and have superpowers, but are in some ways even more deadly. How does he react to skinheads? Bureaucrats? Goths? The lost and the dispossessed? What is his responsibility to them? Let's make the book relevant again, not just have him out fighting aliens and intelligent costumes from space.

"There's also something missing from the equation that's at the very core of Spider-Man," Straczynski continued. "'With great power comes great responsibility.' Okay, fine. But what's the next level? 'With great responsibility comes . . .' What? Guilt? Maturity? Vision? Does it free you or limit you? I'd like to explore that aspect."

In his initial story line, drawn by John Romita, Jr., and published in 2001, Straczynski envisioned another side to Spider-Man's origin, tying it to the manipulations of a cult of mystics. Paul Jenkins remained on *Peter Parker, Spider-Man*, which concentrates on Peter Parker's personal life. Alonso also launched a new series in 2001, *Tangled Web*, which views Spider-Man's life through the perspectives of other characters; each story arc in *Tangled Web* would be authored by a different guest writer.

At present, then, Marvel's flagship character is still going strong, appearing each month in new stories in *Amazing Spider-Man; Peter Parker, Spider-Man; Tangled Web; Ultimate Spider-Man*; and *Ultimate Team-Up*. The original, classic Spider-Man tales by Stan Lee, Steve Ditko, and John Romita live on, reprinted in the *Essential Spider-Man* trade paperbacks and *Marvel Masterpieces* hardcover volumes. Much of the rest of Spider-Man's past history also is available in Marvel's line of trade paperbacks. And, after over twenty-five years, Stan Lee continues to script new adventures for his most famous character in the daily *Spider-Man* newspaper strip, and it's Lee who will adapt the screenplay for the movie into comic form.

Those who first discover who Spider-Man is from the movie will surely be astounded to learn how voluminous his past history in the comics medium has been. And yet, despite all the twists and turns over the decades, Spider-Man has basically remained unchanged. He is still, in his own words, the "Hard-Luck Harry" of the super-hero business; the guy who has abilities and responsibilities he never asked for. He never gets much help or appreciation, and stands as living proof that no good deed goes unpunished.

His job might be fighting super-villains, but in the end he too is just trying to make his way through a hard life the way so many people in the real world do. As Brian Michael Bendis suggested, Superman is what people *wish* they were; Spider-Man represents who we actually are.

Amazing Spider-Man Checklist

Amazing Spider-Man

#1: MARCH 1963

"SPIDER-MAN": 14 pages

"SPIDER-MAN VS. THE CHAMELEON": 10 pages

WRITER: Stan Lee

ARTIST: Steve Ditko

GUEST STARS: The Fantastic Four

VILLAIN: The Chameleon

#2: MAY 1963

"DUEL TO THE DEATH WITH THE VULTURE":
14 pages

"THE UNCANNY THREAT OF THE TERRIBLE
TINKERER": 10 pages

WRITER: Stan Lee

ARTIST: Steve Ditko

VILLAINS: Vulture, Terrible Tinkerer, Quentin
Beck

#3: JULY 1963

"SPIDER-MAN VERSUS DOCTOR OCTOPUS":
21 pages

WRITER: Stan Lee

ARTIST: Steve Ditko

GUEST STAR: The Human Torch

VILLAIN: Doctor Octopus

#4: SEPTEMBER 1963

"NOTHING CAN STOP THE SANDMAN": 21 pages

WRITER: Stan Lee

ARTIST: Steve Ditko

VILLAIN: Sandman

#5: OCTOBER 1963

"MARKED FOR DESTRUCTION BY DOCTOR
DOOM": 21 pages

WRITER: Stan Lee

ARTIST: Steve Ditko

GUEST STARS: The Fantastic Four

VILLAIN: Doctor Doom

#6: NOVEMBER 1963

"FACE TO FACE WITH THE LIZARD": 21 pages

WRITER: Stan Lee

ARTIST: Steve Ditko

VILLAIN: The Lizard

#7: DECEMBER 1963

"THE RETURN OF THE VULTURE": 21 pages

WRITER: Stan Lee

ARTIST: Steve Ditko

VILLAIN: The Vulture

#8: JANUARY 1964

"THE TERRIBLE THREAT OF THE LIVING
BRAIN": 17 pages

"SPIDER-MAN TACKLES THE TORCH": 6 pages

WRITER: Stan Lee

ARTIST: Steve Ditko

GUEST STARS: The Fantastic Four

VILLAIN: The Living Brain

#9: FEBRUARY 1964

"THE MAN CALLED ELECTRO": 22 pages
WRITER: Stan Lee
ARTIST: Steve Ditko
VILLAIN: Electro

#10: MARCH 1964

"THE ENFORCERS": 22 pages
WRITER: Stan Lee
ARTIST: Steve Ditko
VILLAINS: The Enforcers, Bigman

#11: APRIL 1964

"TURNING POINT": 21 pages
WRITER: Stan Lee
ARTIST: Steve Ditko
VILLAINS: Doctor Octopus, Blackie Gaston

#12: MAY 1964

"UNMASKED BY DOCTOR OCTOPUS": 22 pages
WRITER: Stan Lee
ARTIST: Steve Ditko
VILLAIN: Doctor Octopus

#13: JUNE 1964

"THE MENACE OF MYSTERIO": 22 pages
WRITER: Stan Lee
ARTIST: Steve Ditko
VILLAIN: Mysterio

#14: JULY 1964

"THE GROTESQUE ADVENTURE OF THE GREEN GOBLIN"
WRITER: Stan Lee

ARTIST: Steve Ditko
GUEST STAR: The Hulk
VILLAINS: Green Goblin, The Enforcers

#15: AUGUST 1964

"KRAVEN THE HUNTER": 22 pages
WRITER: Stan Lee
ARTIST: Steve Ditko
VILLAINS: Kraven the Hunter, Chameleon

#16: SEPTEMBER 1964

"DUEL WITH DAREDEVIL": 22 pages
WRITER: Stan Lee
ARTIST: Steve Ditko
GUEST STAR: Daredevil
VILLAINS: Ringmaster and his Circus of Crime

#17: OCTOBER 1964

"THE RETURN OF THE GREEN GOBLIN":
    22 pages
WRITER: Stan Lee
ARTIST: Steve Ditko
GUEST STAR: The Human Torch
VILLAIN: Green Goblin

#18: NOVEMBER 1964

"THE END OF SPIDER-MAN": 22 pages
WRITER: Stan Lee
ARTIST: Steve Ditko
GUEST STARS: Fantastic Four, Avengers,
    Daredevil
VILLAINS: Sandman, Green Goblin, Doctor
    Octopus, Kraven, the Vulture

45

#19: DECEMBER 1964

"SPIDEY STRIKES BACK": 22 pages

WRITER: Stan Lee

ARTIST: Steve Ditko

GUEST STAR: The Human Torch

VILLAINS: Sandman, The Enforcers

#20: JANUARY 1965

"THE COMING OF THE SCORPION": 20 pages

WRITER: Stan Lee

ARTIST: Steve Ditko

VILLAINS: The Scorpion, Dr. Farley Stillwell

#21: FEBRUARY 1965

"WHERE FLIES THE BEETLE": 20 pages

WRITER: Stan Lee

ARTIST: Steve Ditko

GUEST STAR: Human Torch

VILLAIN: Beetle

#22: MARCH 1965

"PREEEEEESENTING THE CLOWN AND THE MASTERS OF MENACE": 20 pages

WRITER: Stan Lee

ARTIST: Steve Ditko

VILLAINS: Ringmaster and his Circus of Crime, Princess Python

#23: APRIL 1965

"THE GOBLIN AND THE GANGSTERS": 20 pages

WRITER: Stan Lee

ARTIST: Steve Ditko

VILLAIN: Green Goblin

#24: MAY 1965

"SPIDER-MAN GOES MAD": 20 pages

WRITER: Stan Lee

ARTIST: Steve Ditko

VILLAIN: Dr. Ludwig Rinehart

#25: JUNE 1965

"CAPTURED BY J. JONAH JAMESON": 20 pages

WRITER: Stan Lee

ARTIST: Steve Ditko

VILLAINS: Spencer Smythe, Spider-Slayer

#26: JULY 1965

"THE MYSTERY OF THE CRIME-MASTER'S MASK": 20 pages

WRITER: Stan Lee

ARTIST: Steve Ditko

VILLAINS: Crime Master, Green Goblin

#27: AUGUST 1965

"BRING BACK MY GOBLIN TO ME": 20 pages

WRITER: Stan Lee

ARTIST: Steve Ditko

VILLAINS: Crime Master, Green Goblin

#28: SEPTEMBER 1965

"THE MENACE OF MOLTEN MAN": 20 pages

WRITER: Stan Lee

ARTIST: Steve Ditko

VILLAINS: Molten Man, Spencer Smythe

#29: OCTOBER 1965

"NEVER STEP ON A SCORPION": 20 pages

WRITER: Stan Lee

ARTIST: Steve Ditko

VILLAIN: The Scorpion

#30: NOVEMBER 1965

"THE CLAWS OF THE CAT": 20 pages

WRITER: Stan Lee

ARTIST: Steve Ditko

VILLAIN: Cat Burglar

#31: DECEMBER 1965

"IF THIS BE MY DESTINY": 20 pages

WRITER: Stan Lee

ARTIST: Steve Ditko

VILLAINS: Master Planner's (Doctor Octopus) Henchmen

#32: JANUARY 1966

"MAN ON A RAMPAGE": 20 pages

WRITER: Stan Lee

ARTIST: Steve Ditko

VILLAINS: Doctor Octopus, Master Planner's Henchmen

#33: FEBRUARY 1966

"THE FINAL CHAPTER": 20 pages

WRITER: Stan Lee

ARTIST: Steve Ditko

VILLAINS: Doctor Octopus (Master Planner), Master Planner's Henchmen

#34: MARCH 1966

"THE THRILL OF THE HUNT": 20 pages

WRITER: Stan Lee

ARTIST: Steve Ditko

VILLAIN: Kraven the Hunter

#35: APRIL 1966

"THE MOLTEN MAN REGRETS . . . !": 20 pages

WRITER: Stan Lee

ARTIST: Steve Ditko

VILLAIN: Molten Man

#36: MAY 1966

"WHEN FALLS THE METEOR"

WRITER: Stan Lee

ARTIST: Steve Ditko

VILLAIN: Looter (Meteor Man)

#37: JUNE 1966

"ONCE UPON A TIME THERE WAS A ROBOT . . . !": 20 pages

WRITER: Stan Lee

ARTIST: Steve Ditko

VILLAIN: Mendel Stromm (Robot Master)

#38: JULY 1966

"JUST A GUY NAMED JOE": 20 pages

WRITER: Stan Lee

ARTIST: Steve Ditko

VILLAIN: Guy Named Joe (Smith)

#39: AUGUST 1966

"HOW GREEN WAS MY GOBLIN!": 20 pages

WRITER: Stan Lee

ARTIST: John Romita

VILLAIN: Green Goblin (revealed to be Norman Osborn)

#40: SEPTEMBER 1966

"SPIDEY SAVES THE DAY: THE END OF THE GREEN GOBLIN!": 20 pages

WRITER: Stan Lee

ARTIST: John Romita

VILLAIN: Green Goblin

#41: OCTOBER 1966

"THE HORNS OF THE RHINO": 20 pages

WRITER: Stan Lee

ARTIST: John Romita

VILLAIN: The Rhino

#42: NOVEMBER 1966

"THE BIRTH OF A SUPER-HERO": 20 pages

WRITER: Stan Lee

ARTIST: John Romita

VILLAIN: The Rhino

#43: DECEMBER 1966

"RHINO ON THE RAMPAGE": 20 pages

WRITER: Stan Lee

ARTIST: John Romita

VILLAIN: The Rhino

#44: JANUARY 1967

"WHERE CRAWLS THE LIZARD!": 20 pages

WRITER: Stan Lee

ARTIST: John Romita

VILLAIN: The Lizard

#45: FEBRUARY 1967

"SPIDEY SMASHES OUT!": 20 pages

WRITER: Stan Lee

ARTIST: John Romita

VILLAIN: The Lizard

#46: MARCH 1967

"THE SINISTER SHOCKER"

WRITER: Stan Lee

ARTIST: John Romita

VILLAIN: The Shocker

#47: APRIL 1967

"IN THE HANDS OF THE HUNTER": 20 pages

WRITER: Stan Lee

ARTIST: John Romita

VILLAIN: Kraven the Hunter

#48: MAY 1967

"THE WINGS OF THE VULTURE!": 20 pages

WRITER: Stan Lee

ARTIST: John Romita

VILLAINS: Vulture, Blackie Drago
(Vulture II)

#49: JUNE 1967

"FROM THE DEPTHS OF DEFEAT!": 20 pages

WRITER: Stan Lee

ARTIST: John Romita

VILLAINS: Blackie Drago (Vulture II), Kraven
the Hunter

#50: JULY 1967

"SPIDER-MAN NO MORE!": 20 pages

WRITER: Stan Lee

ARTIST: John Romita

GUEST STARS: Johnny Carson and Ed
McMahon

VILLAIN: The Kingpin

#51: AUGUST 1967

"IN THE CLUTCHES OF . . . THE KINGPIN!":
20 pages
WRITER: Stan Lee
ARTIST: John Romita
VILLAIN: The Kingpin

#52: SEPTEMBER 1967

"TO DIE A HERO": 20 pages
WRITER: Stan Lee
ARTIST: John Romita
VILLAIN: The Kingpin

#53: OCTOBER 1967

"ENTER: DR. OCTOPUS": 20 pages
WRITER: Stan Lee
ARTIST: John Romita
VILLAIN: Doctor Octopus

#54: NOVEMBER 1967

"THE TENTACLES AND THE TRAP!":
20 pages
WRITER: Stan Lee
ARTIST: John Romita
VILLAINS: Doctor Octopus, Doctor Octopus'
henchmen

#55: DECEMBER 1967

"DOC OCK WINS!": 20 pages
WRITER: Stan Lee
ARTIST: John Romita
VILLAINS: Doctor Octopus, Doctor Octopus's
henchmen

#56: JANUARY 1968

"DISASTER!": 20 pages
WRITER: Stan Lee
ARTIST: John Romita
VILLAINS: Doctor Octopus, Doctor Octopus's
henchmen

#57: FEBRUARY 1968

"THE COMING OF KA-ZAR": 20 pages
WRITER: Stan Lee
ARTIST: John Romita
GUEST STARS: Ka-Zar, Zabu

#58: MARCH 1968

"TO KILL A SPIDER-MAN!": 20 pages
WRITER: Stan Lee
ARTIST: John Romita
VILLAINS: Spider-Slayer II, Spencer Smythe

#59: APRIL 1968

"THE BRAND OF THE BRAINWASHER": 20 pages
WRITER: Stan Lee
ARTIST: John Romita
VILLAIN: The Brainwasher (Kingpin)

#60: MAY 1968

"O, BITTER VICTORY!": 20 pages
WRITER: Stan Lee
ARTIST: John Romita
VILLAIN: The Brainwasher (Kingpin)

#61: JUNE 1968

"WHAT A TANGLED WEB WE WEAVE": 20 pages
WRITER: Stan Lee

49

ARTIST: John Romita

VILLAIN: The Kingpin

#62: JULY 1968

"MAKE WAY FOR . . . MEDUSA!": 20 pages

WRITER: Stan Lee

ARTIST: John Romita

GUEST STAR: Medusa

#63: AUGUST 1968

"WINGS IN THE NIGHT!": 20 pages

WRITER: Stan Lee

ARTIST: John Romita

VILLAINS: The Vulture, Blackie Drago
   (Vulture II)

#64: SEPTEMBER 1968

"THE VULTURE'S PREY": 20 pages

WRITER: Stan Lee

ARTIST: John Romita

VILLAIN: The Vulture

#65: OCTOBER 1968

"THE IMPOSSIBLE ESCAPE!": 20 pages

WRITER: Stan Lee

ARTIST: John Romita

VILLAINS: various prison inmates

#66: NOVEMBER 1968

"THE MADNESS OF MYSTERIO": 20 pages

WRITER: Stan Lee

ARTIST: John Romita

VILLAINS: Mysterio, Green Goblin

#67: DECEMBER 1968

"TO SQUASH A SPIDER": 20 pages

WRITER: Stan Lee

ARTIST: John Romita

VILLAIN: Mysterio

#68: JANUARY 1969

"CRISIS ON CAMPUS": 20 pages

WRITER: Stan Lee

ARTIST: John Romita

VILLAIN: The Kingpin

#69: FEBRUARY 1969

"MISSION: CRUSH THE KINGPIN!": 20 pages

WRITER: Stan Lee

ARTIST: John Romita

VILLAIN: The Kingpin

#70: MARCH 1969

"SPIDER-MAN: WANTED!"

WRITER: Stan Lee

ARTIST: John Romita

VILLAIN: The Kingpin

#71: APRIL 1969

"THE SPEEDSTER AND THE SPIDER":
   20 pages

WRITER: Stan Lee

ARTIST: John Romita

VILLAIN: Toad

#72: MAY 1969

"ROCKED BY . . . THE SHOCKER": 20 pages

WRITER: Stan Lee

ARTIST: John Romita

VILLAIN: The Shocker

#73: JUNE 1969

"THE WEB CLOSES!": 20 pages

WRITER: Stan Lee

ARTIST: John Romita

VILLAINS: Man-Mountain Marko, Caesar
Cicero, Silvermane

#74: JULY 1969

"IF THIS BE BEDLAM!": 20 pages

WRITER: Stan Lee

ARTIST: John Romita

VILLAINS: Man-Mountain Marko, Caesar
Cicero, Silvermane

#75: AUGUST 1969

"DEATH WITHOUT WARNING": 20 pages

WRITER: Stan Lee

ARTIST: John Romita

VILLAINS: The Lizard, Man-Mountain Marko,
Caesar Cicero, Silvermane

#76: SEPTEMBER 1969

"THE LIZARD LIVES": 20 pages

WRITER: Stan Lee

ARTIST: John Buscema

SUPPORTING CAST: Harry Osborn, Aunt May,
Gwen Stacy, Captain George Stacy, Joe
Robinson

VILLAIN: The Lizard

#77: OCTOBER 1969

"IN THE BLAZE OF BATTLE": 20 pages

WRITER: Stan Lee

ARTIST: John Buscema

VILLAIN: The Lizard

#78: NOVEMBER 1969

"THE NIGHT OF THE PROWLER": 20 pages

WRITER: Stan Lee

ARTIST: John Buscema

VILLAIN: The Prowler

#79: DECEMBER 1969

"TO PROWL NO MORE": 20 pages

WRITER: Stan Lee

ARTIST: John Buscema

VILLAIN: The Prowler

#80: JANUARY 1970

"ON THE TRAIL OF THE CHAMELEON":
20 pages

WRITER: Stan Lee

ARTIST: John Buscema

VILLAIN: The Chameleon

#81: FEBRUARY 1970

"THE COMING OF THE KANGAROO":
20 pages

WRITER: Stan Lee

ARTIST: John Buscema

SUPPORTING CAST: Aunt May, J. Jonah
Jameson

VILLAIN: The Kangaroo

#82: MARCH 1970

"AND THEN CAME ELECTRO": 20 pages

WRITER: Stan Lee

ARTIST: John Romita

VILLAIN: Electro

#83: APRIL 1970

"THE SCHEMER": 20 pages

WRITER: Stan Lee

ARTIST: John Romita

GUEST STAR: Vanessa Fisk

VILLAIN: The Schemer (Richard Fisk), The Kingpin

#84: MAY 1970

"THE KINGPIN STRIKES BACK": 20 pages

WRITER: Stan Lee

ARTIST: John Romita

VILLAINS: The Schemer (Richard Fisk), The Kingpin

#85: JUNE 1970

"THE SECRET OF THE SCHEMER": 20 pages

WRITER: Stan Lee

ARTIST: John Romita

VILLAINS: The Schemer (Richard Fisk), The Kingpin

#86: JULY 1970

"BEWARE . . . THE BLACK WIDOW": 20 pages

WRITER: Stan Lee

ARTIST: John Romita

GUEST STAR: Black Widow

#87: AUGUST 1970

"UNMASKED AT LAST": 20 pages

WRITER: Stan Lee

ARTIST: John Romita

VILLAIN: Hobie Brown (The Prowler)

#88: SEPTEMBER 1970

"THE ARMS OF DOCTOR OCTOPUS"

WRITER: Stan Lee

ARTIST: John Romita

VILLAIN: Doctor Octopus

#89: OCTOBER 1970

"DOC OCK LIVES": 20 pages

WRITER: Stan Lee

ARTIST: Gil Kane

VILLAIN: Doctor Octopus

#90: NOVEMBER 1970

"AND DEATH SHALL COME": 20 pages

WRITER: Stan Lee

ARTIST: Gil Kane

VILLAIN: Doctor Octopus

#91: DECEMBER 1970

"TO SMASH THE SPIDER": 20 pages

WRITER: Stan Lee

ARTIST: Gil Kane

VILLAIN: Sam Bullit

#92: JANUARY 1971

"WHEN ICEMAN ATTACKS"

WRITER: Stan Lee

ARTIST: Gil Kane

VILLAIN: Sam Bullit

#93: FEBRUARY 1971

"THE LADY AND . . . THE PROWLER": 20 pages

WRITER: Stan Lee

ARTIST: John Romita

SUPPORTING CAST: Gwen Stacy

VILLAIN: The Prowler

#94: MARCH 1971

"ON WINGS OF DEATH": 20 pages

WRITER: Stan Lee

ARTIST: John Romita

VILLAIN: The Beetle

#95: APRIL 1971

"TRAP FOR A TERRORIST": 20 pages

WRITER: Stan Lee

ARTIST: John Romita

VILLAIN: Unnamed Terrorists

#96: MAY 1971

". . . AND NOW, THE GOBLIN": 20 pages

WRITER: Stan Lee

ARTIST: Gil Kane

VILLAIN: Green Goblin

#97: JUNE 1971

"IN THE GRIP OF THE GOBLIN": 20 pages

WRITER: Stan Lee

ARTIST: Gil Kane

VILLAIN: Green Goblin

#98: JULY 1971

"THE GOBLIN'S LAST GASP": 20 pages

WRITER: Stan Lee

ARTIST: Gil Kane

VILLAIN: Green Goblin

#99: AUGUST 1971

"PANIC IN THE PRISON": 20 pages

WRITER: Stan Lee

ARTIST: Gil Kane

VILLAIN: Turpo (prisoner)

#100: SEPTEMBER 1971

"THE SPIDER OR THE MAN?": 20 pages

WRITER: Stan Lee

ARTIST: Gil Kane

VILLAINS: Hallucinations of The Vulture,
    Doctor Octopus, The Lizard, Green
    Goblin, The Kingpin

#101: OCTOBER 1971

"A MONSTER CALLED MORBIUS": 20 pages

WRITER: Roy Thomas

ARTIST: Gil Kane

VILLAINS: Morbius, The Lizard

#102: NOVEMBER 1971

"VAMPIRE AT LARGE" (PART 1): 12 pages

"THE WAY IT BEGAN" (PART 2): 11 pages

"THE CURSE AND THE CURE" (PART 3): 12 pages

WRITER: Roy Thomas

ARTIST: Gil Kane

VILLAINS: Morbius, The Lizard

#103: DECEMBER 1971

"WALK THE SAVAGE LAND" (PART 1): 12 pages

"GOG" (PART 2): 12 pages

WRITER: Roy Thomas

ARTIST: Gil Kane

VILLAIN: Gog, Kraven the Hunter

#104: JANUARY 1972

"THE BEAUTY AND THE BRUTE": 21 pages

WRITER: Roy Thomas

ARTIST: Gil Kane

VILLAINS: Gog, Kraven the Hunter

#105: FEBRUARY 1972

"THE SPIDER SLAYER": 22 pages

WRITER: Roy Thomas

ARTIST: Gil Kane

VILLAINS: Spider-Slayer III, Spencer Smythe

#106: MARCH 1972

"SQUASH! GOES THE SPIDER": 21 pages

WRITER: Stan Lee

ARTIST: John Romita

VILLAINS: Spider-Slayer III, Spencer Smythe

#107: APRIL 1972

"SPIDEY SMASHES THRU": 21 pages

WRITER: Stan Lee

ARTIST: John Romita

VILLAINS: Spider-Slayer III, Spencer Smythe

#108: MAY 1972

"VENGEANCE FROM VIETNAM": 20 pages

WRITER: Stan Lee

ARTIST: John Romita

VILLAIN: The Giant One

#109: JUNE 1972

"ENTER: DR. STRANGE!": 31 pages

WRITER: Stan Lee

ARTIST: John Romita

VILLAIN: The Giant One

#110: JULY 1972

"THE BIRTH OF THE GIBBON": 20 pages

WRITER: Stan Lee

ARTIST: John Romita

VILLAINS: Gibbon, Kraven the Hunter

#111: AUGUST 1972

"TO STALK A SPIDER": 20 pages

WRITER: Gerry Conway

ARTIST: John Romita

VILLAINS: Gibbon, Kraven the Hunter

#112: SEPTEMBER 1972

"SPIDEY COPS OUT": 20 pages

WRITER: Gerry Conway

ARTIST: John Romita

VILLAINS: Gibbon, Doctor Octopus

#113: OCTOBER 1972

"THEY CALL THE DOCTOR . . . OCTOPUS":
    20 pages

WRITER: Gerry Conway

ARTIST: John Romita

#114: NOVEMBER 1972

"GANG WAR, SHMANG WAR! WHAT I WANT TO
KNOW IS . . . WHO THE HECK IS
HAMMERHEAD?": 20 pages
WRITER: Gerry Conway
ARTIST: John Romita
VILLAINS: Doctor Octopus, Hammerhead, Dr.
Jonas Harrow

#115: DECEMBER 1972

"THE LAST BATTLE": 20 pages
WRITER: Gerry Conway
ARTIST: John Romita
VILLAINS: Doctor Octopus, Hammerhead

#116: JANUARY 1973

"SUDDENLY . . . THE SMASHER!": 20 pages
WRITER: Stan Lee & Gerry Conway
ARTIST: John Romita
VILLAINS: Richard Raleigh, Dr. Thaxton, The
Smasher

#117: FEBRUARY 1973

"THE DEADLY DESIGNS OF THE DISRUPTOR":
20 pages
WRITER: Stan Lee & Gerry Conway
ARTIST: John Romita
VILLAINS: Disruptor, Richard Raleigh, Dr.
Thaxton, The Smasher

#118: MARCH 1973

"COUNTDOWN TO CHAOS": 20 pages
WRITER: Stan Lee & Gerry Conway
ARTIST: John Romita

VILLAINS: Disruptor (revealed to be Richard
Raleigh), Dr. Thaxton, The Smasher

#119: APRIL 1973

"THE GENTLEMAN'S NAME IS THE HULK": 21
pages
WRITER: Gerry Conway
ARTIST: John Romita
GUEST STARS: The Hulk, General
"Thunderbolt" Ross

#120: MAY 1973

"THE FIGHT AND THE FURY": 20 pages
WRITER: Gerry Conway
ARTIST: Gil Kane
GUEST STARS: The Hulk, General
"Thunderbolt" Ross

#121: JUNE 1973

"THE NIGHT GWEN STACY DIED":
20 pages
WRITER: Gerry Conway
ARTIST: Gil Kane
VILLAIN: Green Goblin

#122: JULY 1973

"THE GOBLIN'S LAST STAND": 20 pages
WRITER: Gerry Conway
ARTIST: Gil Kane
VILLAIN: Green Goblin

#123: AUGUST 1973

"JUST A MAN CALLED CAGE": 19 pages
WRITER: Gerry Conway
ARTIST: Gil Kane

GUEST STAR: Luke Cage, Hero for Hire (a.k.a. Power-Man)

#124: SEPTEMBER 1973

"THE MARK OF THE MAN-WOLF": 19 pages

WRITER: Gerry Conway

ARTIST: Gil Kane

VILLAIN: Man-Wolf

#125: OCTOBER 1973

"WOLFHUNT": 19 pages

WRITER: Gerry Conway

ARTIST: Ross Andru

VILLAIN: Man-Wolf

#126: NOVEMBER 1973

"THE KANGAROO BOUNCES BACK": 19 pages

WRITER: Gerry Conway

ARTIST: Ross Andru

VILLAINS: The Kangaroo, Dr. Jonas Harrow

#127: DECEMBER 1973

"THE DARK WINGS OF DEATH": 19 pages

WRITER: Gerry Conway

ARTIST: Ross Andru

VILLAIN: The Vulture III (Dr. Clifton Shallot)

#128: JANUARY 1974

"THE VULTURE HANGS HIGH": 19 pages

WRITER: Gerry Conway

ARTIST: Ross Andru

VILLAIN: The Vulture III

#129: FEBRUARY 1974

"THE PUNISHER STRIKES TWICE": 19 pages

WRITER: Gerry Conway

ARTIST: Ross Andru

VILLAIN: The Jackal

#130: MARCH 1974

"BETRAYED": 20 pages

WRITER: Gerry Conway

ARTIST: Ross Andru

VILLAINS: Hammerhead, The Jackal, Doctor Octopus

#131: APRIL 1974

"MY UNCLE, MY ENEMY?": 19 pages

WRITER: Gerry Conway

ARTIST: Ross Andru

VILLAINS: Doctor Octopus, Hammerhead

#132: MAY 1974

"THE MASTER PLAN OF THE MOLTEN MAN": 19 pages

WRITER: Gerry Conway

ARTIST: John Romita and Paul Reinman

VILLAIN: Molten Man

#133: JUNE 1974

"THE MOLTEN MAN BREAKS OUT": 18 pages

WRITER: Gerry Conway

ARTIST: Ross Andru

VILLAIN: Molten Man

#134: JULY 1974

"DANGER IS A MAN NAMED TARANTULA": 18 pages

WRITER: Gerry Conway
ARTIST: Ross Andru
VILLAINS: Tarantula, Hidalgo

#135: AUGUST 1974

"SHOOT-OUT IN CENTRAL PARK": 18 pages
WRITER: Gerry Conway
ARTIST: Ross Andru
VILLAINS: Tarantula, Hidalgo

#136: SEPTEMBER 1974

"THE GREEN GOBLIN LIVES AGAIN": 18 pages
WRITER: Gerry Conway
ARTIST: Ross Andru
VILLAIN: Green Goblin II

#137: OCTOBER 1974

"THE GREEN GOBLIN STRIKES": 17 pages
WRITER: Gerry Conway
ARTIST: Ross Andru
VILLAIN: Green Goblin II

#138: NOVEMBER 1974

"MADNESS MEANS THE MINDWORM": 17 pages
WRITER: Gerry Conway
ARTIST: Ross Andru
VILLAIN: Mindworm

#139: DECEMBER 1974

"DAY OF THE GRIZZLY": 17 pages
WRITER: Gerry Conway
ARTIST: Ross Andru
VILLAIN: Grizzly, The Jackal

#140: JANUARY 1975

"AND ONE WILL FALL": 17 pages
WRITER: Gerry Conway
ARTIST: Ross Andru
VILLAINS: Grizzly, The Jackal

#141: FEBRUARY 1975

"THE MAN'S NAME APPEARS TO BE . . .
    MYSTERIO": 17 pages
WRITER: Gerry Conway
ARTIST: Ross Andru
VILLAIN: Mysterio II

#142: MARCH 1975

"DEAD MAN'S BLUFF": 18 pages
WRITER: Gerry Conway
ARTIST: Ross Andru
VILLAIN: Mysterio II

#143: APRIL 1975

"AND THE WIND CRIES: CYCLONE": 18 pages
WRITER: Gerry Conway
ARTIST: Ross Andru
VILLAIN: Cyclone

#144: MAY 1975

"THE DELUSION CONSPIRACY": 18 pages
WRITER: Gerry Conway
ARTIST: Ross Andru
VILLAIN: Cyclone

#145: JUNE 1975

"GWEN STACY IS ALIVE . . . AND WELL?":
    18 pages

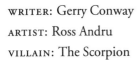

WRITER: Gerry Conway

ARTIST: Ross Andru

VILLAIN: The Scorpion

#146: JULY 1975

"SCORPION . . . WHERE IS THY STING?":
18 pages

WRITER: Gerry Conway

ARTIST: Ross Andru

VILLAINS: The Scorpion, The Jackal

#147: AUGUST 1975

"THE TARANTULA IS A VERY DEADLY BEAST":
18 pages

WRITER: Gerry Conway

ARTIST: Ross Andru

VILLAINS: The Tarantula, The Jackal

#148: SEPTEMBER 1975

"JACKAL, JACKAL, WHO'S GOT THE JACKAL":
18 pages

WRITER: Gerry Conway

ARTIST: Ross Andru

VILLAINS: The Tarantula, The Jackal (revealed
to be Miles Warren)

#149: OCTOBER 1975

"EVEN IF I LIVE, I DIE": 18 pages

WRITER: Gerry Conway

ARTIST: Ross Andru

VILLAINS: The Jackal, The Tarantula

#150: NOVEMBER 1975

WRITER: Archie Goodwin

ARTIST: Gil Kane

VILLAINS: Vulture, Kingpin, Sandman,
Spencer Smythe, and Spider-Slayer

#151: DECEMBER 1975

"SKIRMISH BENEATH THE STREETS":
18 pages

WRITER: Len Wein

ARTIST: Ross Andru

VILLAIN: The Shocker

#152: JANUARY 1976

"SHATTERED BY THE SHOCKER": 18 pages

WRITER: Len Wein

ARTIST: Ross Andru

VILLAIN: The Shocker

#153: FEBRUARY 1976

"THE LONGEST HUNDRED YARDS":
18 pages

WRITER: Len Wein

ARTIST: Ross Andru

#154: MARCH 1976

"THE SANDMAN STRIKES TWICE": 17 pages

WRITER: Len Wein

ARTIST: Sal Buscema

VILLAIN: The Sandman

#155: APRIL 1976

"WHODUNIT": 17 pages

WRITER: Len Wein

ARTIST: Sal Buscema

VILLAIN: Talon

#156: MAY 1976

"ON A CLEAR DAY, YOU CAN SEE THE MIRAGE":
18 pages

WRITER: Len Wein

ARTIST: Ross Andru

VILLAINS: Mirage, Doctor Octopus

#157: JUNE 1976

"THE GHOST THAT HAUNTED OCTOPUS":
17 pages

WRITER: Len Wein

ARTIST: Ross Andru

VILLAINS: Doctor Octopus, Hammerhead

#158: JULY 1976

"HAMMERHEAD IS OUT": 17 pages

WRITER: Len Wein

ARTIST: Ross Andru

VILLAINS: Doctor Octopus, Hammerhead

#159: AUGUST 1976

"ARM-IN-ARM-IN-ARM-IN-ARM-IN-ARM-IN-
ARM WITH DOCTOR OCTOPUS": 17 pages

WRITER: Len Wein

ARTIST: Ross Andru

VILLAINS: Doctor Octopus, Hammerhead,
Terrible Tinkerer, The Toy

#160: SEPTEMBER 1976

"MY KILLER, THE CAR": 17 pages

WRITER: Len Wein

ARTIST: Ross Andru

VILLAINS: Terrible Tinkerer, The Toy

#161: OCTOBER 1976

"AND THE NIGHTCRAWLER CAME PROWLING,
PROWLING": 17 pages

WRITER: Len Wein

ARTIST: Ross Andru

GUEST STARS: Nightcrawler, Wolverine,
Colossus, Punisher

#162: NOVEMBER 1976

"LET THE PUNISHER FIT THE CRIME":
17 pages

WRITER: Len Wein

ARTIST: Ross Andru

GUEST STARS: Nightcrawler, Punisher

VILLAIN: Jigsaw

#163: DECEMBER 1976

"ALL THE KINGPIN'S MEN": 17 pages

WRITER: Len Wein

ARTIST: Ross Andru

VILLAIN: Kingpin

#164: JANUARY 1977

"DEADLINE": 17 pages

WRITER: Len Wein

ARTIST: Ross Andru

VILLAIN: Kingpin

#165: FEBRUARY 1977

WRITER: Len Wein

ARTIST: Ross Andru

VILLAIN: Stegron, The Lizard

#166: MARCH 1977

"WAR OF THE REPTILE-MEN": 18 pages

WRITER: Len Wein

ARTIST: Ross Andru

VILLAINS: Stegron, The Lizard,
Spider-Slayer IV

#167: APRIL 1977

"STALKED BY THE SPIDER-SLAYER": 17 pages

WRITER: Len Wein

ARTIST: Ross Andru

VILLAINS: Spider-Slayer IV, Will-o'-the-Wisp

#168: MAY 1977

"MURDER ON THE WIND": 17 pages

WRITER: Len Wein

ARTIST: Ross Andru

VILLAINS: Spider-Slayer IV, Will-o'-the-Wisp,
Dr. Jonas Harrow

#169: JUNE 1977

"CONFRONTATION": 17 pages

WRITER: Len Wein

ARTIST: Ross Andru

VILLAIN: Doctor Faustus

#170: JULY 1977

"MADNESS IS ALL IN THE MIND": 17 pages

WRITER: Len Wein

ARTIST: Ross Andru

VILLAINS: Doctor Faustus, Burglar

#171: AUGUST 1977

"PHOTON IS ANOTHER NAME FOR?": 17 pages

WRITER: Len Wein

ARTIST: Ross Andru

SUPPORTING CAST: Liz Allen, Harry Osborn

VILLAINS: Photon, AIM

#172: SEPTEMBER 1977

"THE FIEND FROM THE FIRE": 17 pages

WRITER: Len Wein

ARTIST: Ross Andru

VILLAINS: Rocket Racer, Molten Man

#173: OCTOBER 1977

"IF YOU CAN'T STAND THE HEAT . . .":
17 pages

WRITER: Len Wein

ARTIST: Ross Andru

VILLAIN: Molten Man

#174: NOVEMBER 1977

"THE HITMAN'S BACK IN TOWN": 17 pages

WRITER: Len Wein

ARTIST: Ross Andru

VILLAIN: Hitman

#175: DECEMBER 1977

"BIG APPLE BATTLEGROUND": 17 pages

WRITER: Len Wein

ARTIST: Ross Andru

VILLAIN: Hitman

#176: JANUARY 1978

"HE WHO LAUGHS LAST . . .": 17 pages

WRITER: Len Wein

ARTIST: Ross Andru

VILLAIN: Green Goblin III

#177: FEBRUARY 1978

"GOBLIN IN THE MIDDLE": 17 pages

WRITER: Len Wein

ARTIST: Ross Andru

VILLAINS: Green Goblin III, Silvermane

#178: MARCH 1978

"GREEN GROWS THE GOBLIN": 17 pages

WRITER: Len Wein

ARTIST: Ross Andru

VILLAINS: Green Goblin III, Silvermane

#179: APRIL 1978

"THE GOBLIN'S ALWAYS GREENER": 17 pages

WRITER: Len Wein

ARTIST: Ross Andru

VILLAINS: Green Goblin III, Silvermane

#180: MAY 1978

"WHO WAS THAT GOBLIN I SAW YOU WITH?":
18 pages

WRITER: Len Wein

ARTIST: Ross Andru

VILLAINS: Green Goblin III, Green Goblin II,
Silvermane

#181: JUNE 1978

"FLASHBACK": 17 pages

WRITER: Bill Mantlo

ARTIST: Sal Buscema

VILLAINS: The Lizard, Doctor Doom, Doctor
Octopus, Kingpin

#182: JULY 1978

"THE ROCKET RACER'S BACK IN TOWN":
17 pages

WRITER: Marv Wolfman

ARTIST: Ross Andru

VILLAINS: Rocket Racer, Jackson Wheel

#183: AUGUST 1978

"AND WHERE THE BIG WHEEL STOPS, NOBODY
KNOWS": 17 pages

WRITER: Marv Wolfman

ARTIST: Ross Andru

VILLAINS: Big Wheel, Terrible Tinkerer, The
Toy, Rocket Racer

#184: SEPTEMBER 1978

"WHITE DRAGON! RED DEATH!": 17 pages

WRITER: Marv Wolfman

ARTIST: Ross Andru

VILLAIN: White Dragon

#185: OCTOBER 1978

"SPIDER, SPIDER, BURNING BRIGHT": 12 pages

"THE GRADUATION OF PETER PARKER":
6 pages

WRITER: Marv Wolfman

ARTIST: Ross Andru

VILLAIN: White Dragon

#186: NOVEMBER 1978

"CHAOS IS THE CHAMELEON": 18 pages

WRITER: Marv Wolfman

ARTIST: Keith Pollard

VILLAIN: Chameleon

#187: DECEMBER 1978

"THE POWER OF ELECTRO": 18 pages
WRITER: Marv Wolfman
ARTIST: Jim Starlin
VILLAIN: Electro

#188: JANUARY 1979

"THE JIGSAW IS UP": 17 pages
WRITER: Marv Wolfman
ARTIST: Keith Pollard
VILLAIN: Jigsaw

#189: FEBRUARY 1979

"MAYHEM BY MOONLIGHT": 17 pages
WRITER: Marv Wolfman
ARTIST: John Byrne
VILLAINS: Man-Wolf, Spencer Smythe

#190: MARCH 1979

"IN SEARCH OF THE MAN-WOLF": 17 pages
WRITER: Marv Wolfman
ARTIST: John Byrne
VILLAINS: Man-Wolf, Spencer Smythe

#191: APRIL 1979

"WANTED FOR MURDER: SPIDER-MAN":
    17 pages
WRITER: Marv Wolfman
ARTIST: Keith Pollard
VILLAINS: Spencer Smythe, Spider-Slayer V

#192: MAY 1979

"24 HOURS TILL DOOMSDAY": 18 pages
WRITER: Marv Wolfman

ARTIST: Keith Pollard
VILLAINS: Spencer Smythe, Human Fly

#193: JUNE 1979

"THE WINGS OF THE FEARSOME FLY":
    17 pages
WRITER: Marv Wolfman
ARTIST: Keith Pollard
VILLAINS: Human Fly, Burglar, Dr. Ludwig
    Rinehart

#194: JULY 1979

"NEVER LET THE BLACK CAT CROSS YOUR
    PATH": 17 pages
WRITER: Marv Wolfman
ARTIST: Keith Pollard
VILLAINS: Burglar, Dr. Ludwig Rinehart

#195: AUGUST 1979

"NINE LIVES HAS THE BLACK CAT": 18 pages
WRITER: Marv Wolfman
ARTIST: Keith Pollard
VILLAINS: Burglar, Dr. Ludwig Rinehart

#196: SEPTEMBER 1979

"REQUIEM!": 17 pages
WRITER: Marv Wolfman
ARTIST: Al Milgrom
VILLAINS: Dr. Ludwig Rinehart, Kingpin

#197: OCTOBER 1979

"THE KINGPIN'S MIDNIGHT MASSACRE":
    18 pages
WRITER: Marv Wolfman
ARTIST: Keith Pollard

VILLAINS: Burglar, Dr. Ludwig Rinehart, Kingpin

#198: NOVEMBER 1979

"MYSTERIO IS DEADLIER BY THE DOZEN":
17 pages
WRITER: Marv Wolfman
ARTIST: Sal Buscema
VILLAINS: Burglar, Mysterio

#199: DECEMBER 1979

"NOW YOU SEE ME! NOW YOU DIE": 17 pages
WRITER: Marv Wolfman
ARTIST: Sal Buscema
VILLAINS: Burglar, Mysterio

#200: JANUARY 1980

"THE SPIDER AND THE BURGLAR . . . A
SEQUEL": 7 pages
"LESS SPIDER THAN MAN": 5 pages
"LET THE BURGLAR BEWARE": 6 pages
"MURDER MOST FOUL": 5 pages
"THE FINAL CONFRONTATION": 12 pages
"RESOLUTION": 1 page
VILLAIN: Burglar

#201: FEBRUARY 1980

"MAN-HUNT": 17 pages
WRITER: Marv Wolfman
ARTIST: Keith Pollard
GUEST STAR: Punisher

#202: MARCH 1980

"ONE FOR THOSE LONG GONE": 17 pages
WRITER: Marv Wolfman

ARTIST: Keith Pollard
GUEST STAR: Punisher

#203: APRIL 1980

"BEWITCHED, BOTHERED AND BE-DAZZLED":
18 pages
WRITER: Marv Wolfman
ARTIST: Keith Pollard
VILLAIN: Lightmaster

#204: MAY 1980

"THE BLACK CAT ALWAYS LANDS ON HER
FEET": 17 pages
WRITER: Marv Wolfman
ARTIST: Keith Pollard
VILLAIN: Jonas Harrow

#205: JUNE 1980

"IN LOVE AND WAR": 18 pages
WRITER: David Michelinie
ARTIST: Keith Pollard
GUEST STAR: The Black Cat

#206: JULY 1980

"A METHOD IN HIS MADNESS": 17 pages
WRITER: Roger Stern
ARTIST: John Byrne
VILLAIN: Jonas Harrow

#207: AUGUST 1980

"MESMERO'S REVENGE": 17 pages
WRITER: Denny O'Neil
ARTIST: Jim Mooney
VILLAIN: Mesmero

#208: SEPTEMBER 1980

"FUSION": 17 pages
WRITER: Denny O'Neil
ARTIST: John Romita, Jr.
VILLAIN: Fusion

#209: OCTOBER 1980

"TO SALVAGE MY HONOR": 17 pages
WRITER: Denny O'Neil
ARTIST: Alan Weiss
VILLAINS: Calypso, Kraven the Hunter

#210: NOVEMBER 1980

"THE PROPHECY OF MADAME WEB": 22 pages
WRITER: Denny O'Neil
ARTIST: John Romita, Jr.
GUEST STAR: Madame Web

#211: DECEMBER 1980

"THE SPIDER AND THE SEA-SCOURGE":
22 pages
WRITER: Denny O'Neil
ARTIST: John Romita, Jr.
GUEST STAR: Sub-Mariner

#212: JANUARY 1981

"THE COMING OF HYDRO-MAN": 22 pages
WRITER: Denny O'Neil
ARTIST: John Romita, Jr.
VILLAIN: Hydro-Man

#213: FEBRUARY 1981

"ALL THEY WANT TO DO IS KILL YOU, SPIDER-
MAN": 22 pages

WRITER: Denny O'Neil
ARTIST: John Romita, Jr.
VILLAINS: Wizard, Llyra

#214: MARCH 1981

"THEN SHALL WE BOTH BE BETRAYED":
22 pages
WRITER: Denny O'Neil
ARTIST: John Romita, Jr.
VILLAINS: Frightful Four (Wizard, Llyra,
Sandman, Trapster)

#215: APRIL 1981

"BY MY POWERS SHALL I BE VANQUISHED":
22 pages
WRITER: Denny O'Neil
ARTIST: John Romita, Jr.
VILLAINS: Frightful Four

#216: MAY 1981

"MARATHON": 22 pages
WRITER: Denny O'Neil
ARTIST: John Romita, Jr.
GUEST STAR: Madame Web

#217: JUNE 1981

"HERE'S MUD IN YOUR EYE": 22 pages
WRITER: Denny O'Neil
ARTIST: John Romita, Jr.
VILLAINS: Hydro-Man, Sandman

#218: JULY 1981

"EYE OF THE BEHOLDER": 22 pages
WRITER: Denny O'Neil

ARTIST: John Romita, Jr.

VILLAINS: Hydro-Man, Sandman

#219: AUGUST 1981

"PETER PARKER: CRIMINAL": 22 pages

WRITER: Denny O'Neil

ARTIST: Luke McDonnell

VILLAINS: Gray Gargoyle, Jonas Harrow

#220: SEPTEMBER 1981

"A COFFIN FOR SPIDER-MAN": 17 pages

WRITER: Michael Fleisher

ARTIST: Bob McLeod

"THE NURSING HOME CAPER": 5 pages

WRITER: Mike Barr

ARTIST: Win Mortimer

VILLAINS: Mobsters

#221: OCTOBER 1981

"BLUES FOR LONESOME PINKY": 21 pages

WRITER: Denny O'Neil

ARTIST: Alan Kupperberg

VILLAIN: Ramrod

#222: NOVEMBER 1981

"FASTER THAN THE EYE": 21 pages

WRITER: Bill Mantlo

ARTIST: Bob Hall

VILLAIN: Speed Demon

#223: DECEMBER 1981

"NIGHT OF THE APE": 22 pages

WRITER: J. M. DeMatteis

ARTIST: John Romita, Jr.

VILLAINS: Red Ghost and his Super Apes

#224: JANUARY 1982

"LET FLY THESE AGED WINGS": 22 pages

WRITER: Roger Stern

ARTIST: John Romita, Jr.

VILLAIN: The Vulture

#225: FEBRUARY 1982

"FOOLS . . . LIKE US": 21 pages

WRITER: Roger Stern

ARTIST: John Romita, Jr.

VILLAIN: Foolkiller

#226: MARCH 1982

"BUT THE CAT CAME BACK": 22 pages

WRITER: Roger Stern

ARTIST: John Romita, Jr.

GUEST STAR: The Black Cat

#227: APRIL 1982

"GOIN' STRAIGHT": 22 pages

WRITER: Roger Stern

ARTIST: John Romita, Jr.

GUEST STAR: The Black Cat

#228: MAY 1982

"MURDER BY SPIDER": 22 pages

WRITER: Jan Strand

ARTIST: Rick Leonardi

#229: JUNE 1982

"NOTHING CAN STOP THE JUGGERNAUT":
  23 pages

WRITER: Roger Stern

ARTIST: John Romita, Jr.

VILLAINS: Juggernaut, Black Tom Cassidy

65

#230: JULY 1982

"TO FIGHT THE UNBEATABLE FOE": 22 pages

WRITER: Roger Stern

ARTIST: John Romita, Jr.

VILLAINS: Juggernaut, Black Tom Cassidy

#231: AUGUST 1982

"CAUGHT IN THE ACT": 22 pages

WRITER: Roger Stern

ARTIST: John Romita, Jr.

VILLAINS: Cobra, Mister Hyde

#232: SEPTEMBER 1982

"HYDE IN PLAIN SIGHT": 22 pages

WRITER: Roger Stern

ARTIST: John Romita, Jr.

VILLAINS: Cobra, Mister Hyde

#233: OCTOBER 1982

"WHERE THE _____ IS NOSE NORTON?":
22 pages

WRITER: Roger Stern

ARTIST: John Romita, Jr.

VILLAIN: The Tarantula

#234: NOVEMBER 1982

"NOW SHALL WILL-O'-THE-WISP HAVE HIS
REVENGE": 22 pages

WRITER: Roger Stern

ARTIST: John Romita, Jr.

VILLAINS: The Tarantula, Will-o'-the-Wisp

#235: DECEMBER 1982

"LOOK OUT THERE'S A MONSTER COMING":
22 pages

WRITER: Roger Stern

ARTIST: John Romita, Jr.

VILLAINS: The Tarantula, Will-o'-the-Wisp

#236: JANUARY 1983

"DEATH KNELL": 22 pages

WRITER: Roger Stern

ARTIST: John Romita, Jr.

VILLAINS: The Tarantula, Will-o'-the-Wisp

#237: FEBRUARY 1983

"HIGH & MIGHTY": 22 pages

WRITER: Roger Stern

ARTIST: Bob Hall

VILLAIN: Stilt-Man

#238: MARCH 1983

"SHADOW OF EVILS PAST": 22 pages

WRITER: Roger Stern

ARTIST: John Romita, Jr.

VILLAIN: Hobgoblin

#239: APRIL 1983

"HOW STRIKES THE HOBGOBLIN": 22 pages

WRITER: Roger Stern

ARTIST: John Romita, Jr.

VILLAIN: Hobgoblin

#240: MAY 1983

"WINGS OF VENGEANCE": 22 pages

WRITER: Roger Stern

ARTIST: John Romita, Jr.

VILLAIN: The Vulture

66

#241: JUNE 1983

"IN THE BEGINNING": 22 pages
WRITER: Roger Stern
ARTIST: John Romita, Jr.
VILLAIN: The Vulture

#242: JULY 1983

"CONFRONTATION": 22 pages
WRITER: Roger Stern
ARTIST: John Romita, Jr.
VILLAINS: Mad Thinker, Awesome Android

#243: AUGUST 1983

"OPTIONS": 22 pages
WRITER: Roger Stern
ARTIST: John Romita, Jr.
GUEST STAR: The Black Cat

#244: SEPTEMBER 1983

"ORDEALS": 22 pages
WRITER: Roger Stern
ARTIST: John Romita, Jr.
VILLAIN: Hobgoblin

#245: OCTOBER 1983

"SACRIFICE PLAY": 22 pages
WRITER: Roger Stern
ARTIST: John Romita, Jr.
VILLAIN: Hobgoblin

#246: NOVEMBER 1983

"THE DAYDREAMERS": 22 pages
WRITER: Roger Stern

ARTIST: John Romita, Jr.
GUEST STARS: The Black Cat, Watcher

#247: DECEMBER 1983

"INTERRUPTIONS": 22 pages
WRITER: Roger Stern
ARTIST: John Romita, Jr.
VILLAIN: Thunderball

#248: JANUARY 1984

"AND HE STRIKES LIKE A THUNDERBALL":
    11 pages
"THE KID WHO COLLECTED SPIDER-MAN":
    11 pages
WRITER: Roger Stern
ARTISTS: John Romita, Jr., Ron Frenz
VILLAIN: Thunderball

#249: FEBRUARY 1984

"SECRETS": 22 pages
WRITER: Roger Stern
ARTIST: John Romita, Jr.
VILLAINS: Kingpin, Hobgoblin

#250: MARCH 1984

"CONFESSIONS": 22 pages
WRITER: Roger Stern
ARTIST: John Romita, Jr.
VILLAIN: Hobgoblin

#251: APRIL 1984

"ENDINGS": 21 pages
WRITER: Tom DeFalco
PLOTTER: Roger Stern

ARTIST: Ron Frenz

VILLAIN: Hobgoblin

#252: MAY 1984

"HOMECOMING": 22 pages

WRITER: Tom DeFalco

PLOTTER: Roger Stern

ARTIST: Ron Frenz

GUEST STARS: The Avengers, The Black Cat

#253: JUNE 1984

"BY MYSELF BETRAYED": 22 pages

WRITER: Tom DeFalco

ARTIST: Rick Leonardi

VILLAIN: Rose

#254: JULY 1984

"WITH GREAT POWER": 22 pages

WRITER: Tom DeFalco

ARTIST: Rick Leonardi

VILLAIN: Jack O'Lantern

#255: AUGUST 1984

"EVEN A GHOST CAN FEAR THE NIGHT": 22 pages

WRITER: Tom DeFalco

ARTIST: Ron Frenz

VILLAINS: Red Ghost and his Super Apes

#256: SEPTEMBER 1984

"INTRODUCING . . . PUMA": 22 pages

WRITER: Tom DeFalco

ARTIST: Ron Frenz

VILLAINS: Puma, Rose

#257: OCTOBER 1984

"BEWARE THE CLAWS OF PUMA": 22 pages

WRITER: Tom DeFalco

ARTIST: Ron Frenz

VILLAINS: Puma, Rose, Kingpin, Arranger, Hobgoblin

#258: NOVEMBER 1984

"THE SINISTER SECRET OF SPIDER-MAN'S NEW COSTUME": 22 pages

WRITER: Tom DeFalco

ARTIST: Ron Frenz

VILLAINS: Puma, Rose, Hobgoblin

#259: DECEMBER 1984

"ALL MY PASTS REMEMBERED": 22 pages

WRITER: Tom DeFalco

ARTIST: Ron Frenz

VILLAINS: Rose, Hobgoblin

#260: JANUARY 1985

"THE CHALLENGE OF THE HOBGOBLIN": 22 pages

WRITER: Tom DeFalco

ARTIST: Ron Frenz

VILLAINS: Rose, Hobgoblin

#261: FEBRUARY 1985

"THE SINS OF MY FATHER": 22 pages

WRITER: Tom DeFalco

ARTIST: Ron Frenz

VILLAINS: Rose, Hobgoblin

#262: MARCH 1985

"TRADE SECRET": 21 pages
WRITER/ARTIST: Bob Layton

#263: APRIL 1985

"THE SPECTACULAR SPIDER-KID": 22 pages
WRITER: Tom DeFalco
ARTIST: Ron Frenz
GUEST STARS: Spectacular Spider-Kid, The
    Black Cat

#264: MAY 1985

"RED 9 AND RED TAPE": 22 pages
WRITER: Craig Anderson
ARTIST: Paty
GUEST STAR: Red 9

#265: JUNE 1985

"AFTER THE FOX": 22 pages
WRITER: Tom DeFalco
ARTIST: Ron Frenz
VILLAIN: Black Fox

#266: JULY 1985

"JUMP FOR MY LOVE, OR SPRING IS IN
    THE AIR": 23 pages
WRITER: Peter David
ARTIST: Sal Buscema
GUEST STARS: Misfits, The Black Cat

#267: AUGUST 1985

"THE COMMUTER COMETH": 22 pages
WRITER: Peter David

ARTIST: Bob McLeod
GUEST STAR: Human Torch

#268: SEPTEMBER 1985

"THIS GOLD IS MINE": 23 pages
WRITER: Tom DeFalco
ARTIST: Ron Frenz
VILLAINS: Kingpin, Arranger

#269: OCTOBER 1985

"BURN, SPIDER, BURN": 22 pages
WRITER: Tom DeFalco
ARTIST: Ron Frenz
VILLAIN: Firelord

#270: NOVEMBER 1985

"THE HERO AND THE HOLOCAUST": 22 pages
WRITER: Tom DeFalco
ARTIST: Ron Frenz
VILLAIN: Firelord

#271: DECEMBER 1985

"WHATEVER HAPPENED TO CRUSHER
    HOGAN?": 22 pages
WRITER: Tom DeFalco
ARTIST: Ron Frenz
VILLAIN: Manslaughter

#272: JANUARY 1986

"MAKE WAY FOR SLYDE": 22 pages
WRITER: Tom DeFalco
ARTIST: Sal Buscema
VILLAINS: Slyde, Puma

#273: FEBRUARY 1986

"TO CHALLENGE THE BEYONDER": 22 pages

WRITER: Tom DeFalco

ARTIST: Ron Frenz

VILLAIN: Puma

#274: MARCH 1986

"LO, THERE SHALL COME A CHAMPION":
28 pages

WRITER: Tom DeFalco

ARTIST: Ron Frenz, Tom Morgan, James Fry

VILLAINS: Puma, Mephisto, Kingpin

#275: APRIL 1986

"THE CHOICE AND THE CHALLENGE":
26 pages

WRITER: Tom DeFalco

ARTIST: Ron Frenz

VILLAINS: Hobgoblin, Rose, Kingpin,
Arranger

#276: MAY 1986

"UNMASKED": 22 pages

WRITER: Tom DeFalco

ARTIST: Ron Frenz

VILLAINS: Hobgoblin, Rose, The Fly,
Scourge

#277: JUNE 1986

"THE RULE OF THE GAME": 12 pages

WRITER: Tom DeFalco

ARTIST: Ron Frenz

"CRY OF THE WENDIGO": 12 pages

WRITER/ARTIST: Charles Vess

#278: JULY 1986

"IF THIS BE JUSTICE": 22 pages

PLOTTERS: Tom DeFalco & Peter David

WRITER: Jo Duffy

ARTIST: Mike Harris

VILLAINS: Hobgoblin, Death Wraith, Scourge,
Rose

#279: AUGUST 1986

"SAVAGE IS THE SABLE": 22 pages

WRITER: Tom DeFalco

ARTIST: Rick Leonardi

VILLAIN: Jack O'Lantern

#280: SEPTEMBER 1986

"INTRODUCING THE SINISTER SYNDICATE":
22 pages

WRITER: Tom DeFalco

ARTIST: Ron Frenz

VILLAINS: Sinister Syndicate, Kingpin, Rose,
Jack O'Lantern, Hobgoblin

#281: OCTOBER 1986

"WHEN WARRIORS CLASH": 22 pages

WRITER: Tom DeFalco

ARTIST: Ron Frenz

VILLAINS: Sinister Syndicate, Rose, Jack
O'Lantern, Hobgoblin

#282: NOVEMBER 1986

"THE FURY OF X-FACTOR": 22 pages

WRITER: Tom DeFalco

ARTIST: Rick Leonardi

GUEST STARS: The X-Factor

#283: DECEMBER 1986

"WITH FOES LIKE THESE . . .": 23 pages

WRITER: Tom DeFalco

ARTIST: Ron Frenz

VILLAINS: Absorbing Man, Titania,
Hobgoblin

#284: JANUARY 1987

"AND WHO SHALL STAND AGAINST THEM?":
22 pages

WRITER: Tom DeFalco

ARTIST: Ron Frenz

VILLAINS: Hobgoblin, Hammerhead, Rose,
Jack O'Lantern, Silvermane, Arranger

#285: FEBRUARY 1987

"THE ARRANGER MUST DIE": 22 pages

PLOTTER: Tom DeFalco

WRITER: Jim Owsley

ARTIST: Alan Kupperberg

VILLAINS: Hobgoblin, Hammerhead, Rose,
Jack O'Lantern, Arranger

#286: MARCH 1987

"THY FATHER'S SOUL": 22 pages

WRITER: Jim Owsley

ARTIST: Alan Kupperberg

VILLAINS: Hobgoblin, Rose, Jack O'Lantern

#287: APRIL 1987

"AND THERE SHALL COME A RECKONING":
22 pages

WRITER: Jim Owsley

ARTIST: Erik Larsen

VILLAINS: Hobgoblin, Rose, Kingpin, Arranger

#288: MAY 1987

"GANG WAR RAGES ON": 22 pages

WRITER: Jim Owsley

ARTIST: Alan Kupperberg

VILLAINS: Hobgoblin, Rose, Kingpin, Jack
O'Lantern, Hammerhead

#289: JUNE 1987

"THE HOBGOBLIN REVEALED": 40 pages

WRITER: Peter David

ARTISTS: Alan Kupperberg and Tom Morgan

VILLAINS: Hobgoblin II, Rose, Kingpin

#290: JULY 1987

"THE BIG QUESTION": 22 pages

WRITER: David Michelinie

ARTIST: John Romita, Jr.

#291: AUGUST 1987

"DARK JOURNEY": 24 pages

WRITER: David Michelinie

ARTIST: John Romita, Jr.

VILLAINS: Alistaire Smythe, Spider-Slayer

#292: SEPTEMBER 1987

"GROWING PAINS": 23 pages

WRITER: David Michelinie

ARTIST: Alex Saviuk

VILLAINS: Alistair Smythe, Spider-Slayer

#293: OCTOBER 1987

"CRAWLING": 22 pages

WRITER: J. M. DeMatteis

ARTIST: Mike Zeck

VILLAINS: Kraven the Hunter, Vermin

#294: NOVEMBER 1987

"THUNDER": 23 pages

WRITER: J. M. DeMatteis

ARTIST: Mike Zeck

VILLAINS: Kraven the Hunter, Vermin

#295: DECEMBER 1987

"MAD DOGS": 22 pages

WRITER: Ann Nocenti

ARTIST: Cindy Martin

VILLAIN: Brainstorm

#296: JANUARY 1988

"FORCE OF ARMS": 23 pages

WRITER: David Michelinie

ARTIST: Alex Saviuk

VILLAIN: Doctor Octopus

#297: FEBRUARY 1988

"I'LL TAKE MANHATTAN": 23 pages

WRITER: David Michelinie

ARTIST: Alex Saviuk

VILLAIN: Doctor Octopus

#298: MARCH 1988

"CHANCE ENCOUNTER": 22 pages

WRITER: David Michelinie

ARTIST: Todd McFarlane

VILLAIN: Venom

#299: APRIL 1988

"SURVIVAL OF THE HITTIST": 22 pages

WRITER: David Michelinie

ARTIST: Todd McFarlane

VILLAIN: Venom

#300: MAY 1988

"VENOM": 40 pages

WRITER: David Michelinie

ARTIST: Todd McFarlane

VILLAIN: Venom

#301: JUNE 1988

"THE SABLE GAUNTLET": 22 pages

WRITER: David Michelinie

ARTIST: Todd McFarlane

GUEST STAR: Silver Sable

#302: JULY 1988

"(MILD) AMERICAN GOTHIC": 22 pages

WRITER: David Michelinie

ARTIST: Todd McFarlane

VILLAIN: Dr. Royce Nero

#303: AUGUST 1988

"DOCK SAVAGE": 23 pages

WRITER: David Michelinie

ARTIST: Todd McFarlane

VILLAIN: Sandman

#304/#305: SEPTEMBER 1988

"CALIFORNIA SCHEMIN'": 22 pages

"WESTWARD WOE": 22 pages

WRITER: David Michelinie

ARTIST: Todd McFarlane

VILLAIN: Black Fox

#306/#307: OCTOBER 1988

"HUMBUGGED": 22 pages

"THE THIEF WHO STOLE HIMSELF": 22 pages

WRITER: David Michelinie

ARTIST: Todd McFarlane

VILLAIN: Chameleon

#308/#309: NOVEMBER 1988

"DREAD": 22 pages

"STYX AND STONE": 22 page

WRITER: David Michelinie

ARTIST: Todd McFarlane

VILLAINS: Taskmaster, Styx and Stone, Manslaughter

#310: DECEMBER 1988

"SHRIKE FORCE": 22 pages

WRITER: David Michelinie

ARTIST: Todd McFarlane

VILLAIN: Killer Shrike

#311: JANUARY 1989

"MYSTERIES OF THE DEAD": 23 pages

WRITER: David Michelinie

ARTIST: Todd McFarlane

VILLAINS: Mysterio, Green Goblin II, Hobgoblin

#312: FEBRUARY 1989

"THE GOBLIN WAR": 22 pages

WRITER: David Michelinie

ARTIST: Todd McFarlane

VILLAINS: Green Goblin II, Hobgoblin, Lizard

#313: MARCH 1989

"SLITHEREENS": 22 pages

WRITER: David Michelinie

ARTIST: Todd McFarlane

VILLAIN: Lizard

#314: APRIL 1989

"DOWN AND OUT IN FOREST HILLS": 22 pages

WRITER: David Michelinie

ARTIST: Todd McFarlane

#315: MAY 1989

"A MATTER OF LIFE AND DEBT": 22 pages

WRITER: David Michelinie

ARTIST: Todd McFarlane

VILLAINS: Venom, Hydro-Man

#316: JUNE 1989

"DEAD MEAT": 22 pages

WRITER: David Michelinie

ARTIST: Todd McFarlane

VILLAIN: Venom

#317: JULY 1989

"THE SAND AND THE FURY": 22 pages

WRITER: David Michelinie

ARTIST: Todd McFarlane

VILLAIN: Venom

#318: AUGUST 1989

"STING YOUR PARTNER": 22 pages

WRITER: David Michelinie

ARTIST: Todd McFarlane

VILLAINS: Scorpion, Justin Hammer

#319/#320: SEPTEMBER 1989

"THE SCORPION'S TAIL OF WOE": 22 pages

"LICENSE INVOKED": 22 pages

WRITER: David Michelinie

ARTIST: Todd McFarlane

VILLAIN: The Scorpion

#321/#322: OCTOBER 1989

"UNDERWAR": 22 pages

"CEREMONY": 22 pages

WRITER: David Michelinie

ARTIST: Todd McFarlane

VILLAINS: Protectors, Ultimatum

#323/#324/#325: NOVEMBER 1989

"ASSAULT RIVALS": 22 pages

"TWOS DAY": 22 pages

"FINALE IN RED"

WRITER: David Michelinie

ARTIST: Todd McFarlane

VILLAINS: Ultimatum, Sabretooth, Red Skull

#326/#327: DECEMBER 1989

"GRAVITY STORM": 22 pages

WRITER: David Michelinie

ARTIST: Colleen Doran

VILLAIN: Graviton

"CUNNING ATTRACTIONS": 22 pages

WRITER: David Michelinie

ARTIST: Erik Larsen

VILLAINS: Magneto, Wizard, Doctor Doom, Kingpin

#328: JANUARY 1990

"SHAW'S GAMBIT": 23 pages

WRITER: David Michelinie

ARTIST: Todd McFarlane

VILLAIN: Sebastian Shaw

#329: FEBRUARY 1990

"POWER PREY": 22 pages

WRITER: David Michelinie

ARTIST: Erik Larsen

VILLAINS: Tri-Sentinel, Sebastian Shaw, Loki

#330: MARCH 1990

"THE POWDER CHASE": 22 pages

WRITER: David Michelinie

ARTIST: Erik Larsen

GUEST STARS: Punisher, The Black Cat

#331: APRIL 1990

"THE DEATH STANDARD": 22 pages

WRITER: David Michelinie

ARTIST: Erik Larsen

VILLAIN: Venom

#332: MAY 1990

"SUNDAY IN THE PARK WITH VENOM": 22 pages

WRITER: David Michelinie

ARTIST: Erik Larsen

VILLAINS: Venom, Styx & Stone

#333: JUNE 1990

"STALKING FEAT": 22 pages
WRITER: David Michelinie
ARTIST: Erik Larsen
VILLAINS: Venom, Styx & Stone

#334/#335: JULY 1990

"SECRETS, PUZZLES AND LITTLE FEARS":
    22 pages
"SHOCKS": 22 pages
WRITER: David Michelinie
ARTIST: Erik Larsen
VILLAINS: Sinister Six

#336/#337: AUGUST 1990

"THE WAGES OF SIN": 22 pages
"RITES AND WRONGS": 22 pages
WRITER: David Michelinie
ARTIST: Erik Larsen
VILLAINS: Sinister Six

#338/#339: SEPTEMBER 1990

"DEATH FROM ABOVE": 23 pages
"THE KILLING CURE": 22 pages
WRITER: David Michelinie
ARTIST: Erik Larsen
VILLAINS: Sinister Six

#340: OCTOBER 1990

"THE HERO SUBTRACTER": 22 pages
WRITER: David Michelinie
ARTIST: Erik Larsen
VILLAINS: Femme Fatales

#341: NOVEMBER 1990

"WITH (OUT) GREAT POWER": 22 pages
WRITER: David Michelinie
ARTIST: Erik Larsen
VILLAIN: The Tarantula II

#342: DECEMBER 1990

"THE JONAH TRADE": 22 pages
WRITER: David Michelinie
ARTIST: Erik Larsen
VILLAINS: Scorpion, Dr. Elias Wirtham
    (Cardiac)

#343: JANUARY 1991

"WAR GARDEN": 22 pages
WRITER: David Michelinie
ARTIST: Erik Larsen
VILLAINS: Scorpion, Tarantula II, Femme
    Fatales, Chameleon, Dr. Elias Wirtham
    (Cardiac)

#344: FEBRUARY 1991

"HEARTS AND POWERS": 22 pages
WRITER: David Michelinie
ARTIST: Erik Larsen
VILLAINS: Cletus Kasady (Carnage), Eddie
    Brock (Venom), Cardiac, Rhino

#345: MARCH 1991

"GUN FROM THE HEART": 22 pages
WRITER: David Michelinie
ARTIST: Mark Bagley
VILLAINS: Cletus Kasady (Carnage), Venom,
    Cardiac, Boomerang

#346: APRIL 1991

"ELLIPTICAL PURSUIT": 22 pages
WRITER: David Michelinie
ARTIST: Erik Larsen
VILLAIN: Venom

#347: MAY 1991

"THE BONEYARD HOP": 22 pages
WRITER: David Michelinie
ARTIST: Erik Larsen
VILLAIN: Venom

#348: JUNE 1991

"RIGHTEOUS STAND": 22 pages
WRITER: David Michelinie
ARTIST: Erik Larsen
VILLAIN: Black Fox

#349: JULY 1991

"MAN OF STEAL": 22 pages
WRITER: David Michelinie
ARTIST: Erik Larsen
VILLAINS: Black Fox, Doctor Doom

#350: AUGUST 1991

"DOOM SERVICE": 33 pages
WRITER: David Michelinie
ARTIST: Erik Larsen
VILLAINS: Black Fox, Doctor Doom,
    Arcane

#351: SEPTEMBER 1991

"THE THREE FACES OF EVIL": 23 pages
WRITER: David Michelinie

ARTIST: Erik Larsen
VILLAIN: Tri-Sentinel

#352: OCTOBER 1991

"DEATH WALK": 22 pages
WRITER: David Michelinie
ARTIST: Mark Bagley
VILLAIN: Tri-Sentinel

#353/#354: NOVEMBER 1991

"WHEN MIDNIGHT STRIKES": 22 pages
WRITER: David Michelinie
ARTIST: Mark Bagley
"WILDE AT HEART": 22 pages
WRITER: Al Milgrom
ARTIST: Mark Bagley
VILLAINS: Secret Empire, Midnight

#355/#356: DECEMBER 1991

"TOTAL ECLIPSE OF THE MOON KNIGHT":
    22 pages
"AFTER MIDNIGHT": 22 pages
WRITER: Al Milgrom
ARTIST: Mark Bagley
VILLAINS: Secret Empire, Midnight, The
    Seekers

#357/#358: JANUARY 1992

"A BAGEL WITH NOVA": 22 pages
"OUT ON A LIMB": 22 pages
WRITER: Al Milgrom
ARTIST: Mark Bagley
VILLAINS: Secret Empire, Midnight, Wrecker,
    Silhouette, The Seekers

#359: FEBRUARY 1992

"TOY DEATH": 22 pages
WRITER: David Michelinie
ARTIST: Mark Bagley
VILLAINS: Cardiac, Cletus Kasady (Carnage)

#360: MARCH 1992

"DEATH TOY": 22 pages
WRITER: David Michelinie
ARTIST: Chris Marrinan
VILLAINS: Cardiac, Carnage

#361: APRIL 1992

"SAVAGE GENESIS"
WRITER: David Michelinie
ARTIST: Mark Bagley
VILLAIN: Carnage

#362: MAY 1992

"SAVAGE ALLIANCE": 22 pages
WRITER: David Michelinie
ARTIST: Mark Bagley
VILLAINS: Carnage, Venom

#363: JUNE 1992

"SAVAGE GRACE": 22 pages
WRITER: David Michelinie
ARTIST: Mark Bagley
VILLAINS: Carnage, Venom

#364: JULY 1992

"THE PAIN OF FAST AIR": 22 pages
WRITER: David Michelinie
ARTIST: Mark Bagley
VILLAIN: Shocker

#365: AUGUST 1992

"FATHERS AND SINS": 31 pages
WRITER: David Michelinie
ARTIST: Mark Bagley
VILLAIN: The Lizard

#366: SEPTEMBER 1992

"SKULLWORK": 22 pages
WRITER: David Michelinie
ARTIST: Jerry Bingham
VILLAIN: Red Skull, Viper, Taskmaster

#367: OCTOBER 1992

"SKULLDUGGERY": 22 pages
WRITER: David Michelinie
ARTIST: Jerry Bingham
VILLAINS: Red Skull, Viper, Taskmaster,
    Death-Shield, Jagged Bow, Blood Spider

#368/#369: NOVEMBER 1992

"ON RAZORED WINGS": 16 pages
WRITER: David Michelinie
ARTIST: Mark Bagley
"CASHING IN": 6 pages
WRITER: David Michelinie
ARTIST: Aaron Lopresti
"ELECTRIC DOOM": 16 pages
WRITER: David Michelinie
ARTIST: Mark Bagley
"MORE BAD NEWS"
WRITER: David Michelinie
ARTIST: Tod Smith
VILLAINS: Spider-Slayer Alien, Spider-Slayer
    "Birdy", Alistaire Smythe, Electro, Terrible
    Tinkerer

#370/#371: DECEMBER 1992

"LIFE STINGS": 16 pages
WRITER: David Michelinie
ARTIST: Mark Bagley
"THE WEB": 6 pages
WRITER: David Michelinie
ARTIST: Aaron Lopresti
"ONE CLUE OVER THE CUCKOO'S NEXT"
    16 pages
WRITER: David Michelinie
ARTIST: Mark Bagley
"STRAINED RELATIONS": 6 pages
WRITER: Al Milgrom
ARTIST: Aaron Lopresti
VILLAIN: Spider-Slayer, Scorpion, Terrible
    Tinkerer

#372/#373: JANUARY 1993

"ARACHNOPHOBIA TOO": 17 pages
WRITER: David Michelinie
ARTIST: Mark Bagley
"PUNCH . . . COUNTER-PUNCH": 6 pages
WRITER: Al Milgrom
ARTIST: Aaron Lopresti
"THE BEDLAM PERSPECTIVE": 16 pages
WRITER: David Michelinie
ARTIST: Mark Bagley
"THE GETAWAY SCREAM": 6 pages
WRITER: David Michelinie
ARTIST: Tod Smith
VILLAINS: Spider Slayer, Alistaire Smythe,
    Venom II

#374: FEBRUARY 1993

"MURDER ON PARADE": 22 pages
WRITER: David Michelinie
ARTIST: Mark Bagley
VILLAIN: Venom

#375: MARCH 1993

"THE BRIDE OF VENOM": 28 pages
WRITER: David Michelinie
ARTIST: Mark Bagley
"TRUE FRIENDS": 8 pages
WRITER: Tom DeFalco
ARTIST: Pat Olliffe
VILLAINS: Venom, Kraven the Hunter (ghost),
    Chameleon

#376: APRIL 1993

"GUILT BY ASSOCIATION": 22 pages
PLOTTER: David Michelinie
WRITER: Steven Grant
ARTIST: Jeff Johnson
VILLAINS: Cardiac, Styx & Stone

#377: MAY 1993

"DUST TO DUST": 22 pages
PLOTTER: David Michelinie
WRITER: Steven Grant
ARTIST: Jeff Johnson
VILLAINS: Cardiac, Styx & Stone

#378: JUNE 1993

"DEMONS ON BROADWAY": 23 pages
WRITER: David Michelinie
ARTIST: Mark Bagley

VILLAINS: Carnage, Venom, Shriek,
    Doppelganger, Demogoblin

#379: JULY 1993

"THE GATHERING STORM": 23 pages
WRITER: David Michelinie
ARTIST: Mark Bagley
VILLAINS: Carnage, Venom, Shriek,
    Doppelganger, Demogoblin, Carrion

#380: AUGUST 1993

"SOLDIERS OF HOPE": 23 pages
WRITER: David Michelinie
ARTIST: Mark Bagley
VILLAINS: Carnage, Venom, Shriek,
    Doppelganger, Demogoblin, Carrion

#381: SEPTEMBER 1993

"SAMSON UNLEASHED"
WRITER: David Michelinie
ARTIST: Mark Bagley
GUEST STAR: The Hulk

#382: OCTOBER 1993

"EMERALD RAGE": 22 pages
WRITER: David Michelinie
ARTIST: Mark Bagley
GUEST STARS: The Hulk, Doc Samson

#383: NOVEMBER 1993

"JUDGMENT NIGHT": 22 pages
WRITER: David Michelinie
ARTIST: Mark Bagley
VILLAIN: Jury

#384: DECEMBER 1993

"DREAMS OF INNOCENCE": 22 pages
WRITER: David Michelinie
ARTIST: Mark Bagley
VILLAIN: Jury

#385: JANUARY 1994

"ROUGH JUSTICE": 23 pages
WRITER: David Michelinie
ARTIST: Mark Bagley
VILLAIN: Jury

#386: FEBRUARY 1994

"THE WINGS OF AGE": 22 pages
WRITER: David Michelinie
ARTIST: Mark Bagley
VILLAIN: The Vulture

#387: MARCH 1994

"THE THIEF OF YEARS": 22 pages
WRITER: David Michelinie
ARTIST: Mark Bagley
VILLAIN: The Vulture

#388: APRIL 1994

"THE SADNESS OF TRUTH": 30 pages
WRITER: David Michelinie
ARTIST: Mark Bagley
"THE LOST BOYS": 12 pages
WRITER: David Michelinie
ARTIST: Ron Lim
"MY ENEMY'S ENEMY": 12 pages
WRITER: David Michelinie
ARTIST: Larry Alexander

VILLAINS: The Vulture, Chameleon, Venom, Cardiac, Solo

#389: MAY 1994

"THE FACELESS MAN"

WRITER: David Michelinie

ARTIST: Mark Bagley

VILLAIN: Chameleon

#390: JUNE 1994

"BEHIND THE WALLS": 22 pages

WRITER: J. M. DeMatteis

ARTIST: Mark Bagley

VILLAINS: Shriek, Carrion

#391: JULY 1994

"THE BURNING FUSE": 22 pages

WRITER: J. M. DeMatteis

ARTIST: Mark Bagley

VILLAINS: Shriek, Carrion

#392: AUGUST 1994

"THE COCOON": 23 pages

WRITER: J. M. DeMatteis

ARTIST: Mark Bagley

VILLAINS: Shriek, Carrion

#393: SEPTEMBER 1994

"MOTHER LOVE, MOTHER HATE": 22 pages

WRITER: J. M. DeMatteis

ARTIST: Mark Bagley

VILLAINS: Shriek, Carrion

#394: OCTOBER 1994

"BREAK DOWN": 23 pages

WRITER: J. M. DeMatteis

ARTIST: Mark Bagley

VILLAINS: Dr. Judas Traveller, The Host, Scrier, Vermin, Chameleon, Carnage, Jackal

#395: NOVEMBER 1994

"OUTCASTS": 23 pages

WRITER: J. M. DeMatteis

ARTIST: Mark Bagley

VILLAIN: Puma

#396: DECEMBER 1994

"DEADMEN": 23 pages

WRITER: J. M. DeMatteis

ARTIST: Mark Bagley

VILLAINS: The Vulture, Owl

#397: JANUARY 1995

"TENTACLES": 22 pages

WRITER: J. M. DeMatteis

ARTIST: Mark Bagley

VILLAINS: Doctor Octopus, Stunner, Kaine

#398: FEBRUARY 1995

"BEFORE I WAKE": 23 pages

WRITER: J. M. DeMatteis

ARTIST: Mark Bagley

VILLAINS: Doctor Octopus, Stunner, Kaine

#399: MARCH 1995

"RESURRECTION": 23 pages

WRITER: J. M. DeMatteis

ARTIST: Mark Bagley

VILLAINS: Scrier, Kaine, Jackal, Death Guardian

#400: APRIL 1995

"THE GIFT": 37 pages

WRITER: J. M. DeMatteis

ARTIST: Mark Bagley

VILLAINS: Jackal, Dr. Judas Traveller, The
Host, Burglar

#401: MAY 1995

"DOWN IN THE DARKNESS": 22 pages

WRITER: J. M. DeMatteis

ARTIST: Mark Bagley

VILLAINS: Kaine, Dr. Judas Traveller, The
Host, Scrier

#402: JUNE 1995

"CROSSFIRE": 22 pages

WRITER: J. M. DeMatteis

ARTIST: Mark Bagley

VILLAINS: Dr. Judas Traveller, Scrier

#403: JULY 1995

"JUDGMENT AT BEDLAM": 23 pages

WRITER: J. M. DeMatteis

ARTIST: Mark Bagley

VILLAINS: Dr. Judas Traveller, Carnage, Shriek,
Chameleon, Kaine, Vermin, Stunner

#404: AUGUST 1995

"IN THE NAME OF THE FATHER": 22 pages

PLOTTER: J. M. DeMatteis

WRITER: Todd Dezago

ARTIST: Mark Bagley

VILLAINS: Jackal, Spidercide, Kaine, Scrier

#405: SEPTEMBER 1995

"THE WORTH OF A MAN": 22 pages

PLOTTER: J. M. DeMatteis

WRITER: Todd Dezago

ARTIST: Darick Robertson

GUEST STAR: Scarlet Spider

#406: OCTOBER 1995

"CROSSROADS": 22 pages

WRITER: J. M. DeMatteis

ARTIST: Angel Medina

VILLAIN: Doctor Octopus II

#407: JANUARY 1996

"BLASTS FROM THE PAST": 22 pages

WRITER: Tom DeFalco

ARTIST: Mark Bagley

VILLAIN: Mysterio

#408: FEBRUARY 1996

"IMPOSSIBLE, BE MY DREAM": 22 pages

WRITER: Tom DeFalco

ARTIST: Mark Bagley

VILLAINS: Mysterio, Armada

#409: MARCH 1996

"OF WAGERS AND WAR": 22 pages

WRITER: Tom DeFalco

ARTIST: Mark Bagley

VILLAINS: Kaine, Muse, Rhino, Joystick,
Polestar, Doctor Octopus II

#410: APRIL 1996

"AND NOW, SPIDER-CARNAGE": 22 pages

WRITER: Tom DeFalco

ARTIST: Mark Bagley

VILLAIN: Carnage

#411: MAY 1996

"TARGETS": 22 pages

WRITER: Tom DeFalco

ARTIST: Mark Bagley

VILLAINS: Gaunt, Cell-12

#412: JUNE 1996

"THE FACE OF MY ENEMY": 22 pages

WRITER: Tom DeFalco

ARTIST: Mark Bagley

VILLAIN: Gaunt

#413: JULY 1996

"BUG STORY": 22 pages

WRITER: Tom DeFalco

ARTIST: Mark Bagley

VILLAINS: Mysterio, Armada

#414: AUGUST 1996

"DEADLY IS DELILAH": 22 pages

WRITER: Tom DeFalco

ARTIST: Mark Bagley

VILLAINS: Delilah, Rose

#415: SEPTEMBER 1996

"SEIGE": 22 pages

WRITER: Tom DeFalco

ARTIST: Mark Bagley

VILLAIN: Sentinel

#416: OCTOBER 1996

"THE ROAD BACK": 22 pages

WRITER: Tom DeFalco

ARTIST: Ron Garney

VILLAINS: Delilah, Rose, Scrier, Gaunt, Dr. Judas Traveller, The Host

#417: NOVEMBER 1996

"SECRETS": 22 pages

WRITER: Tom DeFalco

ARTIST: Ron Garney

VILLAINS: Delilah, Rose, Scrier, Gaunt, Dr. Judas Traveller, The Host

#418: DECEMBER 1996

"TORMENT": 22 pages

WRITER: Tom DeFalco

ARTIST: Steve Skroce

VILLAIN: Gaunt

#419: JANUARY 1997

"BEWARE THE BLACK TARANTULA": 22 pages

WRITER: Tom DeFalco

ARTIST: Steve Skroce

VILLAINS: Rose, Deliliah, El Uno

#420: FEBRUARY 1997

" 'TWAS THE NIGHT BEFORE CHRISTMAS": 22 pages

WRITER: Tom DeFalco

ARTIST: Steve Skroce

VILLAINS: Rose, Delilah, El Uno

#421: MARCH 1997

"AND DEATH SHALL FLY LIKE A DRAGON":
22 pages

WRITER: Tom DeFalco

ARTIST: Steve Skroce

VILLAINS: Dragonfly, Rose, Delilah

#422: APRIL 1997

"EXPOSED WIRING": 22 pages

WRITER: Tom DeFalco

ARTIST: Joe Bennett

VILLAINS: Electro, Fortunato, Dragonfly,
Rose, Delilah

#423: MAY 1997

"CHOICES": 22 pages

WRITER: Tom DeFalco

ARTIST: Joe Bennett

VILLAINS: Electro, Dragonfly, Rose, Delilah

#424: JUNE 1997

"THEN CAME . . . ELEKTRA": 22 pages

WRITER: Tom DeFalco

ARTIST: Joe Bennett

VILLAINS: Electro, Dragonfly, Rose, Delilah

#425: AUGUST 1997

"THE CHUMPS, THE CHALLENGE AND THE
CHAMPION": 39 pages

WRITER: Tom DeFalco

ARTIST: Steve Skroce

VILLAINS: Electra, Rose, Delilah, Doctor
Octopus II

#426: SEPTEMBER 1997

"ONLY THE EVIL RETURNS": 22 pages

WRITER: Tom DeFalco

ARTIST: Steve Skroce

VILLAINS: Doctor Octopus II, Rose, Delilah,
Stunner, Master Programmer, Doctor
Octopus

#427: OCTOBER 1997

"SACRIFICE PLAY": 22 pages

WRITER: Tom DeFalco

ARTIST: Steve Skroce

VILLAINS: Doctor Octopus II, Rose, Delilah,
Stunner, Doctor Octopus

#428: NOVEMBER 1997

"LIVING LARGE": 23 pages

WRITER: Tom DeFalco

ARTIST: Steve Skroce

VILLAINS: Doctor Octopus, Doctor Octopus
II, Rose, Delilah, Stunner

#429: DECEMBER 1997

"THE PRICE": 23 pages

WRITER: Tom DeFalco

ARTIST: Joe Bennett

VILLAINS: Absorbing Man, Titania, Doctor
Octopus, Doctor Octopus II

#430: JANUARY 1998

"SAVAGE REBIRTH": 22 pages

WRITER: Tom DeFalco

ARTIST: Joe Bennett

VILLAIN: Carnage

#431: FEBRUARY 1998

"THE CARNAGE COSMIC": 23 pages

WRITER: Tom DeFalco

ARTIST: Joe Bennett

VILLAIN: Carnage

#432: MARCH 1998

"THE HUNTED": 22 pages

WRITER: Tom DeFalco

ARTIST: John Romita, Jr.

VILLAINS: Black Tarantula, Rose,
Fortunato

#433: APRIL 1998

"THE LONG FAREWELL"

WRITER: Tom DeFalco

ARTIST: Tom Lyle

VILLAIN: Mister Hyde

#434: MAY 1998

"ROUND AND ROUND WITH RICOCHET":
22 pages

WRITER: Tom DeFalco

ARTIST: Joe Bennett

VILLAINS: Rose, Black Tarantula, Delilah,
Scrier, Fortunato

#435: JUNE 1998

"FUN 'N' GAMES WITH THE FOUR STAR
SQUAD": 22 pages

WRITER: Tom DeFalco

ARTIST: Joe Bennett

VILLAINS: Rose, Black Tarantula, Delilah,
Scrier, Fortunato, Roughhouse,
Bloodscream, Kaine

#436: JULY 1998

"IN FINAL BATTLE WITH THE BLACK
TARANTULA": 22 pages

WRITER: Tom DeFalco

ARTIST: Joe Bennett

VILLAINS: Rose, Black Tarantula, Fortunato

#437: AUGUST 1998

"I, MONSTER": 22 pages

WRITER: Tom DeFalco

ARTIST: Rafael Kayanan

VILLAIN: Plantman

#438/#439: SEPTEMBER 1998

"SEEING IS DISBELIEVING": 22 pages

WRITER: Tom DeFalco

ARTIST: Scott Kolins

"THERE ONCE WAS A SPIDER": 22 pages

WRITER: Tom DeFalco

ARTIST: Rafael Kayanan

VILLAIN: Synario

#440: OCTOBER 1998

"A HOT TIME IN THE OLD TOWN": 22 pages

WRITER: John Byrne

ARTIST: Rafael Kayanan

VILLAIN: Molten Man

#441: NOVEMBER 1998

"AND WHO SHALL CLAIM A KINGLY CROWN?":
22 pages

WRITER: John Byrne

ARTIST: Rafael Kayanan

VILLAINS: Override, Molten Man

The Amazing Spider-Man: Volume 2

#1 (#442): JANUARY 1999

"WHERE R U SPIDER-MAN?": 30 pages

WRITER: Howard Mackie

ARTIST: John Byrne

VILLAIN: The Scorpion

#2 (#443): FEBRUARY 1999

"I CAN'T (AND I DON'T WANT TO), BUT I
MUST": 22 pages

WRITER: Howard Mackie

ARTIST: John Byrne

VILLAIN: Shadrac

#3 (#444): MARCH 1999

"OFF TO A FLYING START": 22 pages

WRITER: Howard Mackie

ARTIST: John Byrne

VILLAIN: Shadrac

#4 (#445): APRIL 1999

"BETRAYALS": 23 pages

WRITER: Howard Mackie

ARTIST: John Byrne

VILLAINS: Sandman, Senator Ward, Trapster,
Wizard

#5 (#446): MAY 1999

"AND THEN THERE WAS ONE": 22 pages

WRITER: Howard Mackie

ARTIST: John Byrne

VILLAIN: Evil Spider-Woman

#6 (#447): JUNE 1999

"TRUTH BE TOLD (OR NOT)": 22 pages

WRITER: Howard Mackie

ARTIST: John Byrne

VILLAINS: Evil Spider-Woman, Doctor
Octopus

#7 (#448): JULY 1999

"HEROES AND VILLAINS": 22 pages

WRITER: Howard Mackie

ARTIST: John Byrne

VILLAINS: Illusions of Dr. Doom, Blastaar,
Annihilus

#8 (#449): AUGUST 1999

"THE MAN BEHIND THE CURTAIN":
22 pages

WRITER: Howard Mackie

ARTIST: John Byrne

VILLAINS: Mysterio, Illusions of Kingpin, Red
Skull, Doctor Octopus

#9 (#450): SEPTEMBER 1999

"THE LIST": 22 pages

WRITER: Howard Mackie

ARTIST: John Byrne

VILLAIN: Doctor Octopus

#10 (#451): OCTOBER 1999

"AND THEN THERE WERE . . .": 22 pages

WRITER: Howard Mackie

ARTIST: John Byrne

VILLAINS: Doctor Octopus, Captain Power,
Stalker

#11 (#452): NOVEMBER 1999

"BRIGHT LIGHTS, BIGGER CITY": 22 pages

WRITER: Howard Mackie

ARTIST: John Byrne

VILLAIN: Blob

#12 (#453): DECEMBER 1999

"ANOTHER RETURN OF THE SINISTER SIX":
32 pages

WRITER: Howard Mackie

ARTIST: John Byrne

"LET THERE BE LIGHT": 5 pages

WRITER: Howard Mackie

ARTIST: Sean Philips

VILLAINS: Sinister Six, Vulture, Sandman,
Kraven II, Electro, Venom, Senator Ward,
Doctor Octopus, Mysterio

#13 (#454): JANUARY 2000

"TIME ENOUGH?": 22 pages

WRITER AND ARTIST: John Byrne

VILLAINS: Rocket Racer II, Stalker

#14 (#455): FEBRUARY 2000

"A SURFEIT OF SPIDERS": 22 pages

WRITER AND ARTIST: John Byrne

VILLAIN: Evil Spider-Woman

#15 (#456): MARCH 2000

"WE'RE ALL DOOMED . . . AGAIN": 22 pages

WRITER: Howard Mackie

ARTIST: John Byrne

VILLAIN: Doctor Doom

#16 (#457): APRIL 2000

"COMINGHOME": 22 pages

WRITER: Howard Mackie

ARTIST: John Byrne

VILLAIN: The Ghost

#17 (#458): MAY 2000

"DUST IN THE WIND": 22 pages

WRITER: Howard Mackie

ARTIST: John Byrne

VILLAINS: Sandman, Mysterio, Electro

#18 (#459): JUNE 2000

"HOMEWARD BOUND": 23 pages

WRITER: Howard Mackie

ARTIST: John Byrne

VILLAIN: Green Goblin V

#19 (#460): JULY 2000

"MIRROR MIRROR": 22 pages

WRITER: Howard Mackie

ARTIST: Erik Larsen

VILLAIN: Venom

#20 (#461): AUGUST 2000

"SET UP": 22 pages

WRITER: Howard Mackie

ARTIST: Erik Larsen

VILLAINS: Alistaire Smythe, Spider-Slayer, Senator Ward

#21 (#462): SEPTEMBER 2000

"SLAYERS TO THE LEFT OF ME": 22 pages

WRITER: Howard Mackie

ARTIST: Erik Larsen

VILLAINS: Alistaire Smythe, Spider-Slayer, Senator Ward

#22 (#463): OCTOBER 2000

"DISTINGUISHED GENTLEMEN FROM NEW YORK": 22 pages

WRITER: Howard Mackie

ARTIST: John Romita, Jr.

VILLAINS: Venom, Senator Ward

#23 (#464): NOVEMBER 2000

"DISTINGUISHED GENTLEMEN FROM NEW YORK, PART 2": 23 pages

WRITER: Howard Mackie

ARTIST: John Romita, Jr.

VILLAINS: Senator Ward, Green Goblin, Z'Nox

#24 (#465): DECEMBER 2000

"DISTINGUISHED GENTLEMEN FROM NEW YORK, PART 3": 24 pages

WRITER: Howard Mackie

ARTIST: John Romita, Jr.

VILLAINS: Senator Ward, Z'Nox, Badoon, Green Goblin

#25 (#466): JANUARY 2001

"DARKNESS CALLING": 41 pages

WRITER: Howard Mackie

ARTIST: John Romita, Jr.

VILLAIN: Green Goblin

#26 (#467): FEBRUARY 2001

"THE MASK": 22 pages

WRITER: Howard Mackie

ARTIST: John Romita, Jr.

VILLAIN: Squid

#27 (#468): MARCH 2001

"THE STRAY": 22 pages

WRITER: Howard Mackie

ARTIST: John Romita, Jr.

VILLAIN: AIM

#28 (#469): APRIL 2001

"DISTRACTIONS": 22 pages

WRITER: Howard Mackie

ARTIST: Joe Bennett

VILLAINS: Stalker, Enforcers, Giacomo, Fortunato

#29 (#470): MAY 2001

"MARY JANE": 22 pages

WRITER: Howard Mackie

ARTIST: Lee Weeks

VILLAIN: Stalker

#30 (#471): JUNE 2001

"TRANSFORMATIONS, LITERAL AND OTHERWISE": 22 pages

WRITER: J. Michael Straczynski

ARTIST: John Romita, Jr.

VILLAIN: Morlun

#31 (#472): JULY 2001

"COMING HOME": 22 pages

WRITER: J. Michael Straczynski

ARTIST: John Romita, Jr.

VILLAIN: Morlun

Marvel Team-Up Checklist

Marvel Team-Up

#1: MARCH 1972

"HAVE YOURSELF A SANDMAN LITTLE
    CHRISTMAS": 21 pages
WRITER: Roy Thomas
ARTIST: Ross Andru
GUEST STAR: Human Torch
VILLAIN: Sandman

#2: MAY 1972

"AND SPIDEY MAKES FOUR": 21 pages
WRITER: Gerry Conway
ARTIST: Ross Andru
GUEST STAR: Human Torch
VILLAINS: Frightful Four

#3: JULY 1972

"THE POWER TO PURGE": 21 pages
WRITER: Gerry Conway
ARTIST: Ross Andru
GUEST STARS: Human Torch, Mister Fantastic,
    Invisible Girl, Martine
VILLAIN: Morbius

#4: SEPTEMBER 1972

"AND THEN . . . THE X-MEN": 20 pages
WRITER: Gerry Conway
ARTIST: Gil Kane
GUEST STARS: The X-Men
VILLAIN: Morbius

#5: NOVEMBER 1972

"A PASSION OF THE MIND": 20 pages
WRITER: Gerry Conway
ARTIST: Gil Kane
GUEST STAR: The Vision
VILLAINS: Puppet Master, Monstroid

#6: JANUARY 1973

"AS THOSE WHO WILL NOT SEE":
    20 pages
WRITER: Gerry Conway
ARTIST: Gil Kane
GUEST STAR: The Thing
VILLAINS: Puppet Master, Mad Thinker,
    Awesome Android

#7: MARCH 1973

"A HITCH IN TIME": 20 pages
WRITER: Gerry Conway
ARTIST: Ross Andru
GUEST STARS: Thor, The Watcher
VILLAIN: Kryllk

#8: APRIL 1973

"THE MAN-KILLER MOVES AT MIDNIGHT":
    20 pages
WRITER: Gerry Conway
ARTIST: Jim Mooney
GUEST STAR: The Cat
VILLAIN: Man-Killer

#9: MAY 1973

"THE TOMORROW WAR": 20 pages

WRITER: Gerry Conway

ARTIST: Ross Andru

GUEST STAR: Iron-Man

VILLAIN: Zaarko the Tomorrow Man, Kang

#10: JUNE 1973

"TIME BOMB": 20 pages

WRITER: Gerry Conway

ARTIST: Ross Andru

GUEST STAR: Human Torch

VILLAINS: Zarko the Tomorrow Man, Kang

#11: JULY 1973

"THE DOOMSDAY GAMBIT": 20 pages

WRITER: Len Wein

ARTIST: Jim Mooney

GUEST STARS: The Inhumans

VILLAINS: Maximum, Kang

#12: AUGUST 1973

"WOLF AT BAY": 19 pages

WRITER: Len Wein

ARTIST: Ross Andru and Don Perlin

GUEST STAR: Werewolf by Night

VILLAIN: Moondark

#13: SEPTEMBER 1973

"THE GRANITE SKY"

WRITER: Len Wein

ARTIST: Gil Kane

GUEST STAR: Captain America

VILLAINS: Gray Gargoyle, AIM

#14: OCTOBER 1973

"MAYHEM IS THE MEN-FISH": 19 pages

WRITER: Len Wein

ARTIST: Gil Kane

GUEST STAR: Sub-Mariner

VILLAINS: Men-Fish, Tiger Shark, Dr. Dorcas

#15: NOVEMBER 1973

"IF AN EYE OFFEND THEE . . .": 19 pages

WRITER: Len Wein

ARTIST: Ross Andru

GUEST STAR: Ghost Rider

VILLAIN: Orb

#16: DECEMBER 1973

"BEWARE THE BASILISK MY SON": 19 pages

WRITER: Len Wein

ARTIST: Gil Kane

GUEST STAR: Captain Marvel

VILLAIN: Basilisk

#17: JANUARY 1974

"CHAOS AT THE EARTH'S CORE": 19 pages

WRITER: Len Wein

ARTIST: Gil Kane

GUEST STAR: Mister Fantastic

VILLAINS: Mole Man, Basilisk

#18: FEBRUARY 1974

Spider-Man does not appear

#19: MARCH 1974

"THE COMING OF STEGRON THE DINOSAUR
MAN": 19 pages

WRITER: Len Wein
ARTIST: Gil Kane
GUEST STAR: Ka-Zar
VILLAIN: Stegron

#20: APRIL 1974

"DINOSAURS ON BROADWAY": 19 pages
WRITER: Len Wein
ARTIST: Sal Buscema
GUEST STAR: Black Panther
VILLAIN: Stegron

#21: MAY 1974

"THE SPIDER AND THE SORCERER":
  19 pages
WRITER: Len Wein
ARTIST: Sal Buscema
GUEST STAR: Doctor Strange
VILLAIN: Xandu

#22: JUNE 1974

"THE MESSIAH MACHINE": 19 pages
WRITER: Len Wein
ARTIST: Sal Buscema
GUEST STAR: Hawkeye
VILLAIN: Quasimodo

#23: JULY 1974

Spider-Man does not appear

#24: AUGUST 1974

"MOONDOG IS ANOTHER NAME FOR MURDER":
  19 pages
WRITER: Len Wein
ARTIST: Jim Mooney

GUEST STAR: Brother Voodoo
VILLAIN: Moondog

#25: SEPTEMBER 1974

"THREE INTO TWO WON'T GO": 18 pages
WRITER: Len Wein
ARTIST: Jim Mooney
GUEST STAR: Daredevil
VILLAIN: Unholy Trio

#26: OCTOBER 1974

Spider-Man does not appear

#27: NOVEMBER 1974

"A FRIEND IN NEED": 18 pages
WRITER: Len Wein
ARTIST: Jim Mooney
GUEST STAR: The Hulk
VILLAIN: Chameleon

#28: DECEMBER 1974

"THE CITY STEALERS": 18 pages
WRITER: Gerry Conway
ARTIST: Jim Mooney
GUEST STAR: Hercules
VILLAINS: City Stealers

#29: JANUARY 1975

Spider-Man does not appear

#30: FEBRUARY 1975

"ALL THAT GLITTERS IS NOT GOLD":
  18 pages
WRITER: Gerry Conway
ARTIST: Jim Mooney

GUEST STAR: Falcon

VILLAIN: Midas

#31: MARCH 1975

"FOR A FEW FISTS MORE": 18 pages

WRITER: Gerry Conway

ARTIST: Jim Mooney

GUEST STAR: Iron Fist

VILLAIN: Drom the Backwards Man

#32: APRIL 1975

Spider-Man does not appear

#33: MAY 1975

"ANYBODY HERE KNOW A GUY NAMED METEOR
     MAN?": 18 pages

WRITER: Gerry Conway

ARTIST: Sal Buscema

GUEST STAR: Nighthawk

VILLAINS: Meteor Man, Jeremiah

#34: JUNE 1975

"BEWARE THE DEATH CRUSADE": 18 pages

WRITER: Gerry Conway

ARTIST: Jim Mooney

GUEST STAR: Valkyrie

VILLAINS: Meteor Man, Jeremiah

#35: JULY 1975

Spider-Man does not appear

#36: AUGUST 1975

"ONCE UPON A TIME IN A CASTLE": 17 pages

WRITER: Gerry Conway

ARTIST: Sal Buscema

GUEST STAR: Frankenstein's Monster

VILLAINS: Baron Ludwig Van Shtupf,
     Man-Wolf

#37: SEPTEMBER 1975

"SNOW DEATH": 18 pages

WRITER: Gerry Conway

ARTIST: Sal Buscema

GUEST STAR: Frankenstein's Monster

VILLAINS: Baron Ludwig von Shtupf,
     Man-Wolf

#38: OCTOBER 1975

"NIGHT OF THE GRIFFIN": 18 pages

WRITER: Bill Mantlo

ARTIST: Sal Buscema

GUEST STAR: Beast

VILLAIN: Griffin

#39: NOVEMBER 1975

"ANY NUMBER CAN SLAY": 18 pages

WRITER: Bill Mantlo

ARTIST: Sal Buscema

GUEST STAR: Human Torch

VILLAINS: Enforcers, Crime Master II,
     Sandman

#40: DECEMBER 1975

"MURDER'S BETTER THE SECOND TIME
     AROUND": 19 pages

WRITER: Bill Mantlo

ARTIST: Sal Buscema

GUEST STAR: Sons of the Tiger

VILLAINS: Enforcers, Death Big Man II,
     Crime-master II, Sandman

#41: JANUARY 1976

"A WITCH TIME": 18 pages

WRITER: Bill Mantlo

ARTIST: Sal Buscema

GUEST STAR: Scarlet Witch

VILLAIN: Cotton Mather

#42: FEBRUARY 1976

"VISIONS OF HATE": 18 pages

WRITER: Bill Mantlo

ARTIST: Sal Buscema

GUEST STAR: The Vision

VILLAINS: Cotton Mather, Dark Rider, Doctor Doom

#43: MARCH 1976

"A PAST GONE MAD": 17 pages

WRITER: Bill Mantlo

ARTIST: Sal Buscema

GUEST STAR: Doctor Doom

VILLAINS: Cotton Mather, Dark Rider

#44: APRIL 1976

"DEATH IN THE YEAR BEFORE YESTERDAY": 17 pages

WRITER: Bill Mantlo

ARTIST: Sal Buscema

GUEST STAR: Moondragon

VILLAINS: Cotton Mather, Dark Rider, Doctor Doom

#45: MAY 1976

"FUTURE SHOCK": 17 pages

WRITER: Bill Mantlo

ARTIST: Sal Buscema

GUEST STAR: Killraven

VILLAINS: Cotton Mather, Overlords

#46: JUNE 1976

"AM I NOW OR HAVE I EVER BEEN": 17 pages

WRITER: Bill Mantlo

ARTIST: Sal Buscema

GUEST STAR: Deathlok

VILLAIN: Ryker

#47: JULY 1976

"I HAVE TO FIGHT THE BASILISK": 17 pages

WRITER: Bill Mantlo

ARTIST: Ron Wilson

GUEST STAR: The Thing

VILLAIN: Basilisk

#48: AUGUST 1976

"A FINE NIGHT FOR DYING": 17 pages

WRITER: Bill Mantlo

ARTIST: Sal Buscema

GUEST STAR: Iron-Man

VILLAIN: Wraith

#49: SEPTEMBER 1976

"MADNESS IS ALL IN THE MIND": 17 pages

WRITER: Bill Mantlo

ARTIST: Sal Buscema

GUEST STAR: Iron-Man

VILLAIN: Wraith

#50: OCTOBER 1976

"THE MYSTERY OF THE WRAITH": 17 pages

WRITER: Bill Mantlo

ARTIST: Sal Buscema

GUEST STAR: Doctor Strange

VILLAIN: Wraith

#51: NOVEMBER 1976

"THE TRIAL OF THE WRAITH": 17 pages

WRITER: Bill Mantlo

ARTIST: Sal Buscema

GUEST STAR: Iron-Man

VILLAIN: Wraith

#52: DECEMBER 1976

"DANGER: DEMON ON A RAMPAGE": 17 pages

WRITER: Gerry Conway

ARTIST: Sal Buscema

GUEST STAR: Captain America

VILLAIN: Batroc

#53: JANUARY 1977

"NIGHTMARE IN NEW MEXICO": 17 pages

WRITER: Bill Mantlo

ARTIST: John Byrne

GUEST STAR: The Hulk

#54: FEBRUARY 1977

"SPIDER IN THE MIDDLE"

WRITER: Bill Mantlo

ARTIST: John Byrne

GUEST STAR: The Hulk

VILLAIN: Del Tremens

#55: MARCH 1977

"SPIDER, SPIDER ON THE MOON": 17 pages

WRITER: Bill Mantlo

ARTIST: John Byrne

GUEST STAR: Warlock

VILLAIN: The Stranger

#56: APRIL 1977

"DOUBLE DANGER AT THE DAILY BUGLE":
    17 pages

WRITER: Bill Mantlo

ARTIST: Sal Buscema

GUEST STAR: Daredevil

VILLAINS: Electro, Blizzard

#57: MAY 1977

"WHEN SLAYS THE SILVER SAMURAI":
    17 pages

WRITER: Chris Claremont

ARTIST: Sal Buscema

GUEST STAR: Black Widow

VILLAIN: Silver Samurai

#58: JUNE 1977

"PANIC ON PIER ONE": 17 pages

WRITER: Chris Claremont

ARTIST: Sal Buscema

GUEST STAR: Ghost Rider

VILLAIN: Trapster

#59: JULY 1977

"SOME SAY SPIDEY WILL DIE BY FIRE":
    17 pages

WRITER: Chris Claremont

ARTIST: John Byrne

GUEST STARS: Yellow Jacket, Wasp

VILLAIN: Equinox

#60: AUGUST 1977

"A MATTER OF LOVE . . . AND DEATH":
17 pages
WRITER: Chris Claremont
ARTIST: John Byrne
GUEST STARS: Yellow Jacket, Wasp
VILLAIN: Equinox

#61: SEPTEMBER 1977

"NOT ALL THY POWERS CAN SAVE THEE":
17 pages
WRITER: Chris Claremont
ARTIST: John Byrne
GUEST STAR: Human Torch
VILLAIN: Super Skrull

#62: OCTOBER 1977

"ALL THIS AND THE QE2": 17 pages
WRITER: Chris Claremont
ARTIST: John Byrne
GUEST STAR: Ms. Marvel
VILLAIN: Super Skrull

#63: NOVEMBER 1977

"NIGHT OF THE DRAGON": 17 pages
WRITER: Chris Claremont
ARTIST: John Byrne
GUEST STAR: Ironfist
VILLAINS: Steel Serpent, Bushmaster

#64: DECEMBER 1977

"IF DEATH BE MY DESTINY": 17 pages
WRITER: Chris Claremont
ARTIST: John Byrne

GUEST STAR: Daughters of the Dragon
VILLAIN: Steel Serpent

#65: JANUARY 1978

"IF DEATH BE MY DESTINY": 17 pages
WRITER: Chris Claremont
ARTIST: John Byrne
GUEST STAR: Captain Britain
VILLAIN: Arcade

#66: FEBRUARY 1978

"MURDER WORLD": 17 pages
WRITER: Chris Claremont
ARTIST: John Byrne
GUEST STAR: Captain Britain
VILLAIN: Arcade

#67: MARCH 1978

"TIGRA, TIGRA, BURNING BRIGHT": 17 pages
WRITER: Chris Claremont
ARTIST: John Byrne
GUEST STAR: Tigra
VILLAIN: Kraven the Hunter

#68: APRIL 1978

"THE MEASURE OF A MAN": 17 pages
WRITER: Chris Claremont
ARTIST: John Byrne
GUEST STAR: Man-Thing
VILLAIN: D'Spayre

#69: MAY 1978

"NIGHT OF THE LIVING GOD": 17 pages
WRITER: Chris Claremont
ARTIST: John Byrne

GUEST STAR: Havok

VILLAIN: Living Monolith

#70: JUNE 1978

"WHOM GODS DESTROY": 17 pages

WRITER: Chris Claremont

ARTIST: John Byrne

GUEST STAR: Thor

VILLAIN: Living Monolith

#71: JULY 1978

"DEATHGARDEN": 18 pages

WRITER: Bill Kunkel

ARTIST: Dave Wenzel

GUEST STAR: Falcon

VILLAIN: Plantman

#72: AUGUST 1978

"CRACK OF THE WHIP": 17 pages

WRITER: Bill Mantlo

ARTIST: Jim Mooney

GUEST STAR: Iron Man

VILLAIN: Whiplash, Wraith

#73: SEPTEMBER 1978

"A FLUTTERING OF WINGS MOST FOUL":
17 pages

WRITER: Gary Friedrich

ARTIST: Kerry Gammil

GUEST STAR: Daredevil

VILLAIN: Owl

#74: OCTOBER 1978

"LIVE FROM NEW YORK IT'S SATURDAY NIGHT":
18 pages

WRITER: Chris Claremont

ARTIST: Bob Hall

GUEST STARS: The Not Ready for Prime Time
Players

VILLAIN: Silver Samurai

#75: NOVEMBER 1978

"THE SMOKE OF THAT GREAT BURNING":
17 pages

WRITER: Chris Claremont

ARTIST: John Byrne

GUEST STAR: Power-Man

VILLAIN: Rat Pack

#76: DECEMBER 1978

"IF NOT FOR LOVE": 17 pages

WRITER: Chris Claremont

ARTIST: Howard Chaykin

GUEST STAR: Dr. Strange

VILLAINS: Silver Dagger, Marie LaVeau the
Witch-Queen

#77: JANUARY 1979

"IF I'M TO LIVE . . . MY LOVE MUST DIE":
18 pages

WRITER: Chris Claremont

ARTIST: Howard Chaykin

GUEST STAR: Ms. Marvel

VILLAIN: Silver Dagger, Marie LaVeau the
Witch-Queen

#78: FEBRUARY 1979

"CLAWS": 17 pages

WRITER: Bill Kunkel

ARTIST: Don Perlin

GUEST STAR: Wonder Man

VILLAIN: Griffin

#79: MARCH 1979

"SWORD OF THE SHE-DEVIL": 17 pages

WRITER: Chris Claremont

ARTIST: John Byrne

GUEST STAR: Red Sonja

VILLAIN: Kulan Gath

#80: APRIL 1979

"A SORCERER POSSESSED": 17 pages

WRITER: Chris Claremont

ARTIST: Mike Vosburg

GUEST STAR: Dr. Strange and Clea

#81: MAY 1979

"LAST RITES": 17 pages

WRITER: Chris Claremont

ARTIST: Mike Vosburg

GUEST STAR: Santana

VILLAIN: Basilisk

#82: JUNE 1979

"NO WAY TO TREAT A LADY": 17 pages

WRITER: Chris Claremont

ARTIST: Sal Buscema

GUEST STAR: Black Widow

#83: JULY 1979

"SLAUGHTER ON 10TH AVENUE": 17 pages

WRITER: Chris Claremont

ARTIST: Sal Buscema

GUEST STAR: Nick Fury

VILLAIN: Boomerang, Silver Samurai

#84: AUGUST 1979

"CATCH A FALLING HERO": 17 pages

WRITER: Chris Claremont

ARTIST: Sal Buscema

GUEST STAR: Master of Kung Fu

VILLAINS: Boomerang, Silver Samurai, Viper

#85: SEPTEMBER 1979

"THE WOMAN WHO NEVER WAS": 17 pages

WRITER: Chris Claremont

ARTIST: Sal Buscema

GUEST STARS: Shang Chi, the Black Widow,
Nick Fury

VILLAINS: Boomerang, Silver Samurai, Viper

#86: OCTOBER 1979

"STORY OF THE YEAR": 17 pages

WRITER: Chris Claremont

ARTIST: Bob McLeod

GUEST STARS: Guardians of the Galaxy

VILLAINS: Hammer and Anvil

#87: NOVEMBER 1979

"THE RAZOR'S EDGE": 17 pages

WRITER: Steven Grant

ARTIST: Gene Colan

GUEST STAR: Black Panther

VILLAIN: Hellrazor

#88: DECEMBER 1979

"A CHILD IS WAITING": 17 pages

WRITER: Chris Claremont

ARTIST: Sal Buscema

GUEST STAR: Invisible Girl

#89: JANUARY 1980

"SHOOT-OUT OVER CENTER RING": 17 pages

WRITER: Chris Claremont

ARTISTS: Michael Nassar and Rich Buckler

GUEST STAR: Nightcrawler

VILLAINS: Arcade, Cutthroat

#90: FEBRUARY 1980

"DEATH ON THE AIR": 17 pages

WRITER: Steven Grant

ARTIST: Mike Vosburg

GUEST STAR: Beast

VILLAINS: Killer Shrike, Modular Man

#91: MARCH 1980

"CARNIVAL OF SOULS": 18 pages

WRITER: Steven Grant

ARTIST: Pat Broderick

GUEST STAR: Ghost Rider

VILLAIN: Moondark

#92: APRIL 1980

"FEAR": 17 pages

WRITER: Steven Grant

ARTIST: Carmine Infantino

GUEST STAR: Hawkeye

VILLAIN: Mister Fear

#93: MAY 1980

"RAGS TO RICHES": 17 pages

WRITER: Steven Grant

ARTIST: Tom Sutton and Carmine Infantino

GUEST STAR: Werewolf by Night

VILLAIN: Tattermedalion

#94: JUNE 1980

"DARKNESS, DARKNESS": 17 pages

WRITER: Steven Grant

ARTIST: Mike Zeck

GUEST STAR: The Shroud

#95: JULY 1980

"AND NO BIRDS SING": 17 pages

WRITER: Steven Grant

ARTIST: Jimmy Janes

GUEST STAR: Mocking Bird

VILLAIN: Delandan

#96: AUGUST 1980

"PANIC IN THE PARK": 17 pages

WRITER AND ARTIST: Alan Kupperberg

GUEST STAR: Howard the Duck

#97: SEPTEMBER 1980

Spider-Man does not appear

#98: OCTOBER 1980

UNTITLED: 17 pages

WRITER: Roger McKenzie

ARTIST: Will Meugniot

GUEST STAR: Black Widow

VILLAIN: Owl

#99: NOVEMBER 1980

"AND SPIDER-MAN MAKES 3": 22 pages

WRITER: Tom DeFalco

ARTIST: Jerry Bingham

GUEST STAR: Machine Man

VILLAINS: Baron Brimstone, Sandman

#100: DECEMBER 1980

"KARMA": 30 pages

WRITER: Chris Claremont

ARTIST: Frank Miller

"CRY VENGEANCE": 10 pages

WRITER: Chris Claremont

ARTIST: John Byrne

GUEST STAR: Fantastic Four

VILLAIN: Tran

#101: JANUARY 1981

"TO JUDGE A NIGHTHAWK": 17 pages

WRITER: J. M. DeMatteis

ARTIST: Jerry Bingham

"DON'T LET THE SUN COME UP ON ME":
    5 pages

WRITER: Mike W. Barr

ARTIST: Steve Ditko

GUEST STAR: Nighthawk

#102: FEBRUARY 1981

"SAMSON AND DELILAH": 22 pages

WRITER: Mike W. Barr

ARTIST: Frank Springer

GUEST STAR: Doc Samson

VILLAINS: Rhino, AIM

#103: MARCH 1981

"THE ASSASSIN ACADEMY": 22 pages

WRITER: David Michelinie

ARTIST: Jerry Bingham

GUEST STAR: Ant-man

VILLAIN: Taskmaster

#104: APRIL 1981

Spider-Man does not appear

#105: MAY 1981

Spider-Man does not appear

#106: JUNE 1981

"A SAVAGE STING HAS THE SCORPION": 22 pages

WRITER: Tom DeFalco

ARTIST: Herb Trimpe

GUEST STAR: Captain America

VILLAIN: The Scorpion

#107: JULY 1981

"THIS RUMOR OF REVOLUTION": 22 pages

WRITER: Tom DeFalco

ARTIST: Herb Trimpe

GUEST STAR: She-Hulk

VILLAIN: Man-Killer

#108: AUGUST 1981

"SOMETHING WICKED THIS WAY KILLS":
    22 pages

WRITER: David Michelinie

ARTIST: Herb Trimpe

GUEST STAR: Paladin

VILLAIN: Thermo

#109: SEPTEMBER 1981

"CRITICAL MASS": 22 pages

WRITER: David Kraft

ARTIST: Herb Trimpe

GUEST STAR: Dazzler

VILLAIN: Thermo

#110: OCTOBER 1981

"MAGMA FORCE": 22 pages
WRITER: David Michelinie
ARTIST: Herb Trimpe
GUEST STAR: Iron Man
VILLAIN: Magma

#111: NOVEMBER 1981

"OF SPIDERS AND SERPENTS": 21 pages
WRITER: J. M. DeMatteis
ARTIST: Herb Trimpe
GUEST STARS: Devil-Slayer, The Defenders
VILLAINS: Serpent Men

#112: DECEMBER 1981

"A KING COMES RIDING": 21 pages
WRITER: J. M. DeMatteis
ARTIST: Herb Trimpe
GUEST STARS: Kull, Doctor Strange
VILLAIN: Ju-Lak

#113: JANUARY 1982

"THE RESURRECTION OF EDWARD LANSKY":
21 pages
WRITER: Mark Gruenwald
ARTIST: Herb Trimpe
GUEST STAR: Quasar
VILLAINS: Lightmaster, Nitro

#114: FEBRUARY 1982

"THE HEAT IN HARLEM": 21 pages
WRITER: J. M. DeMatteis
ARTIST: Herb Trimpe
GUEST STAR: Falcon
VILLAIN: Stone-Face

#115: MARCH 1982

"DICHOTOMIES": 21 pages
WRITER: J. M. DeMatteis
ARTIST: Herb Trimpe
GUEST STAR: Thor
VILLAINS: Meru the Mind-Bender; Dalia the
　　　Shape Changer

#116: APRIL 1982

"BEWEEN SWORD AND HAMMER": 21 pages
WRITER: J. M. DeMatteis
ARTIST: Herb Trimpe
GUEST STARS: Thor, Valkyrie

#117: MAY 1982

"SCENTS AND SENSES": 23 pages
WRITER: J. M. DeMatteis
ARTIST: Herb Trimpe
GUEST STAR: Wolverine
VILLAIN: Professor Power

#118: JUNE 1982

"MEETING OF THE MINDS": 22 pages
WRITER: J. M. DeMatteis
ARTIST: Herb Trimpe
GUEST STARS: Wolverine, Professor X,
　　　Colossus, Kitty Pryde
VILLAINS: Professor Power, Mentallo

#119: JULY 1982

"TIME, RUN LIKE A FREIGHT TRAIN": 22 pages
WRITER: J. M. DeMatteis
ARTIST: Kerry Gammill
GUEST STAR: Gargoyle

#120: AUGUST 1982

"OLD SOLDIERS": 22 pages
WRITER: J. M. DeMatteis
ARTIST: Kerry Gammill
GUEST STAR: Dominic Fortune
VILLAIN: Turner D. Century

#121: SEPTEMBER 1982

"LOOK BEFORE YOU LEAP": 22 pages
WRITER: J. M. DeMatteis
ARTIST: Kerry Gammill
GUEST STAR: Human Torch, Leap Frog
VILLAIN: Speed Demon

#122: OCTOBER 1982

"A SIMPLE TWIST OF FATE": 22 pages
WRITER: J. M. DeMatteis
ARTIST: Kerry Gammill
GUEST STAR: Man-Thing
VILLAIN: Fate

#123: NOVEMBER 1982

"RIVERS OF BLOOD": 22 pages
WRITER: J. M. DeMatteis
ARTIST: Kerry Gammill
GUEST STAR: Daredevil
VILLAIN: Solarr

#124: DECEMBER 1982

"THE TIES THAT BIND": 22 pages
WRITER: J. M. DeMatteis
ARTIST: Kerry Gammill
GUEST STAR: Beast
VILLAIN: Professor Power

#125: JANUARY 1983

"YESTERDAY AND TODAY": 16 pages
WRITER: J. M. DeMatteis
ARTIST: Kerry Gammill
"CROSS FIRE": 6 pages
WRITER: Jo Duffy
ARTIST: Kerry Gammill
GUEST STARS: Tigra, Doctor Strange,
    Scarlet Witch
VILLAINS: Zabo, Fire Beast of Beliath

#126: FEBRUARY 1983

"A FIRM OFFER": 12 pages
(Starring Spider-Man and The Hulk)
WRITER: J. M. DeMatteis
ARTIST: Bob Hall
"THE OBLIGATION": 10 pages
Spider-Man does not appear

#127: MARCH 1983

"SMALL MIRACLES": 2 pages
WRITER: J. M. DeMatteis
ARTIST: Kerry Gammill
GUEST STARS: The Watcher, Captain
    America

#128: APRIL 1983

"SWEET TEMPTATION": 17 pages
WRITER: J. M. DeMatteis
ARTIST: Kerry Gammill
GUEST STARS: Captain America, Bernie
    Rosenthal
VILLAIN: Vermin

#129: MAY 1983

"AND MUCH TO PONDER BEFORE THE DAWN":
22 pages

WRITER: J. M. DeMatteis

ARTIST: Kerry Gammill

GUEST STARS: The Vision, Scarlet Witch

VILLAIN: Alpha Android

#130: JUNE 1983

"TILL DEATH DO US PART": 22 pages

WRITER: J. M. DeMatteis

ARTIST: Sal Buscema

GUEST STARS: The Vision, Scarlet Witch

VILLAIN: Necrodamus

#131: JULY 1983

"THE BEST THINGS IN LIFE ARE FREE . . . BUT
EVERYTHING ELSE COSTS MONEY": 22 pages

WRITER: J. M. DeMatteis

ARTIST: Kerry Gammill

GUEST STAR: Frog-Man

VILLAIN: White Rabbit

#132: AUGUST 1983

"THE COMMON DENOMINATOR": 22 pages

WRITER: J. M. DeMatteis

ARTIST: Sal Buscema

GUEST STAR: Mister Fantastic

VILLAIN: Everyman

#133: SEPTEMBER 1983

"THE WORLD ACCORDING TO FAUSTUS":
22 pages

WRITER: J. M. DeMatteis

ARTIST: Sal Buscema

GUEST STARS: The Fantastic Four

VILLAIN: Doctor Faustus

#134: OCTOBER 1983

"THE BOY'S NIGHT OUT": 22 pages

WRITER: Bill Mantlo

ARTIST: Ron Frenz

GUEST STARS: Jack of Hearts, S.H.I.E.L.D.

#135: NOVEMBER 1983

"DOWN DEEP IN DARKNESS": 22 pages

WRITER: Bill Mantlo

ARTIST: Ron Frenz

GUEST STARS: Kitty Pryde, X-Men

VILLAINS: Morlocks

#136: DECEMBER 1983

"WEBS": 22 pages

WRITER: David Micheline

ARTIST: Ron Frenz

GUEST STAR: Wonder Man

VILLAIN: Mauler

#137: JANUARY 1984

"TWINKLE, TWINKLE": 22 pages

WRITER: Michael Carlin

ARTIST: Greg LaRocque

GUEST STARS: Franklin Richards, The Fantastic
Four

VILLAIN: Galactus

#138: FEBRUARY 1984

"STARTING OVER": 22 pages

WRITER: Tom DeFalco

ARTIST: Greg LaRocque

GUEST STAR: Sandman

VILLAINS: New Enforcers, Arranger

#139: MARCH 1984

"EVERYBODY LOVES SOMEBODY SOMETIME":
  22 pages

WRITER: Carl Buckett

ARTIST: Brian Postman

GUEST STARS: Nick Fury, Dum Dum Dugan,
  Dino Manelli

VILLAIN: Dreadnought

#140: APRIL 1984

"WHERE WERE YOU WHEN THE LIGHTS WENT
  OUT?": 21 pages

WRITER: Bill Mantlo

ARTIST: Ron Frenz

GUEST STARS: Black Widow, Daredevil

#141: MAY 1984

"BLIND JUSTICE": 22 pages

WRITER: Jim Owsley

ARTIST: Greg LaRocque

GUEST STARS: Black Widow, Daredevil,
  Foggy Nelson

VILLAIN: Kingpin

#142: JUNE 1984

"FOILED": 22 pages

WRITER: David Michelinie

ARTIST: Greg LaRocque

GUEST STARS: Captain Marvel, Starfox

VILLAIN: Burglars

#143: JULY 1984

"SHIFTS AND PLANES": 22 pages

WRITER: David Michelinie

ARTIST: Greg LaRocque

GUEST STARS: Captain Marvel, Starfox

VILLAIN: Will-killer

#144: AUGUST 1984

"MY SWORD I LAY DOWN": 22 pages

WRITER: Cary Burkett

ARTIST: Greg LaRocque

GUEST STAR: Moonknight

VILLAIN: White Dragon

#145: SEPTEMBER 1984

"HOMETOWN BOY": 22 pages

WRITER: Tony Isabella

ARTIST: Greg LaRocque

GUEST STAR: Iron Man

VILLAIN: Blacklash

#146: OCTOBER 1984

"HERO WORSHIP": 22 pages

WRITER: Cary Burkett

ARTIST: Greg LaRocque

GUEST STAR: Nomad

VILLAINS: Black Abbott, Taskmaster

#147: NOVEMBER 1984

"A DEBT REPAID": 24 pages

WRITER: Cary Burkett

ARTIST: Greg LaRocque

GUEST STAR: Human Torch

VILLAIN: Black Abbott

#148: DECEMBER 1984

"A CHILD SHALL LEAD THEM": 23 pages
WRITER: Cary Burkett
ARTIST: Greg LaRocque
GUEST STARS: Thor, Human Torch
VILLAIN: Black Abbott

#149: JANUARY 1985

"THE INCANDESCENT MAN": 23 pages
WRITER: Louise Simmons
ARTIST: Bret Blevins
GUEST STAR: Cannonball
VILLAIN: Incandescent Man

#150: FEBRUARY 1985

"'TIS BETTER TO GIVE": 38 pages
GUEST STARS: X-Men
VILLAINS: Juggernaut, Black Tom
    Cassidy

PART TWO

Web TV

Apart from Superman and Batman, one would be hard-pressed to find another comic book superhero who has been reincarnated on television as many times as Spider-Man.

At this point, the Man of Steel holds the record with four live-action series (George Reeves's classic fifties show *The Adventures of*

Superman, the syndicated *Adventures of Superboy, Lois & Clark: The New Adventures of Superman*, and the WB's *Smallville*) and seven animated series (the self-titled *Superman* from the 1960s and the 1980s, *Superfriends, Galactic Guardians, Challenge of the Superfriends, Superman: The Animated Series*, and Cartoon Network's *Justice League*), followed by the Caped Crusader in one live-action show (the sixties series starring Adam West) and eight animated series (*Batman and Robin* from the sixties, seventies, and nineties, *Superfriends, Galactic Guardians, Challenge of the Superfriends, Batman: The Animated Series*, and *Batman Beyond*). Spider-Man, however, is coming up strong with a total of six series on the air since the mid-sixties, with a seventh following on the heels of the live-action movie.

Spider-Man Animated: 1967–70

Few may realize it, given the pathetically unimaginative state of Saturday-morning programming today, but back in the 1960s, Saturday television was nearly as competitive as the networks' prime-time schedule. Each fall, ABC, CBS, and NBC—long before there was a Cartoon Network or Nickelodeon—would load the hours of 8 A.M. to 12 noon with a variety of programming designed to entice kids to nag their parents to buy them whatever products were being advertised.

Considering the popularity of the Spider-Man comic book at the time and the way it was eclipsing the competition in sales, it hardly seems surprising that one of the big three desperately wanted to get their hands on the web-slinger. The honor ultimately went to ABC, which debuted the show in September of 1967.

Marvel Comics had previously entered the medium with the syndicated *Marvel Superheroes*, which featured a number of short animated adventures of such heroes as Iron Man, the Incredible Hulk, the Mighty Thor, the Sub-Mariner and Captain America. In truth, the word *animated* overstates the situation. A better description might be filmed comic-book panels with lips that occasionally moved. It was abysmal. We might see Captain America leap into action (literally) and then we would *hear* the battle

itself before we finally got a new image, usually showing the good Cap standing triumphantly over his opponents—not very inspiring at that, and an attempt that makes *South Park* look like a Disney animated feature by comparison. In its favor, though, the series did offer a number of theme songs that have endured quite well, in a campy sort of way.

Spider-Man, on the other hand, featured a slightly more traditionally fluid animation style—this despite the fact that the show was being produced by Grantray-Lawrence, the animation house behind *Marvel Superheroes*. Although an improvement, there still wasn't much in the way of detail provided to the characters in general and the backgrounds in particular during year one. Overall, there was a definite sense of getting the job done as quickly and affordably as possible, which is pretty evident in the finished product.

Cast on the show was Bernard Cowan as the voice of Peter Parker, Paul Soles as Spider-Man, Peg Dixon as Betty Brant, and Paul Kligman as J. Jonah Jameson, all of whom made up the show's core group of characters. Indeed, right from the commencement of the first year, the show's formula was set in stone: a crime is committed, Peter Parker finds out about it during some interplay with his coworkers at the *Daily*

Bugle, and he sets out as Spider-Man to stop that week's bad guy, who was usually someone from the comic books—Doctor Octopus, the Green Goblin, Mysterio, or any number of others.

Although a ratings hit, *Spider-Man* didn't have an easy go of it during that first season, particularly because Grantray-Lawrence went bankrupt shortly after production of the first twenty episodes, leaving thirty-two shows yet to be produced for ABC. Desperate to live up to their contractual obligation to the network, Krantz Films (the company that had hired the animators) turned to animator Ralph Bakshi to take over the show and move its production to New York City. The result was a series that offered more attention to detail, with considerably richer backgrounds and more effective character animation, despite an annoying reliance on stock footage of Spidey swinging through New York City. Additionally, whereas year one had featured two stories in each half-hour episode, year two for the most part focused on single scenarios, thus allowing for greater emphasis on character and plot-line, and year three featured a combination of single and dual stories.

Born on October 29, 1938, in Brooklyn, New York, Bakshi has often said that he was raised on the streets of the borough, a point one can sense from his edgy creations, which tended to push the envelope whether or not Hollywood was ready for it to be pushed.

His career began at the age of eighteen, when he went to work for Terrytoons, eventually becoming an animator and, by his early twenties, an animation director. In that position he oversaw the production of a number of Terrytoon animated shorts (among them the TV cartoons of Deputy Dawg) before creating the much-loved *Mighty Heroes*, a lighthearted parody of the genre featuring such characters as Strongman, Tornado Man, and Diaper Man. Following his work on Grantray-Lawrence's *Rocket Robin Hood* and *Spider-Man*, he would go on to a number of animated features, including the first X-rated cartoon, *Fritz the Cat* (1972), as well as *Heavy Traffic* (1973), *Coonskin* (1974), *Wizards* (1977), *The Lord of the Rings* (1978), *American Pop* (1981), *Hey Good Lookin'* (1982), *Fire and Ice* (1983), and *Cool World* (1992).

The impression one gets from Bakshi is that many of his experiences simply weren't enjoyable (*Lord of the Rings* included), though for some reason *Spider-Man* is a show he seems to hold in some esteem.

"At the time, I had just left Paramount Pictures as a producer/director," says Bakshi. "Basically, I wanted to do adult animation at that point in my life and they promised that I could. But when I showed them what that was, they freaked. So I left the studio and got a job with Steve Krantz, who was doing *Spider-Man* and *Rocket Robin Hood* with Grantray-Lawrence, but then they were going bankrupt. I went back to Steve Krantz, who I had already told about *Fritz the Cat*. He loved the idea, but he said, 'You have to do my Spider-Man show for me.' I finally said yes, because I was twenty-something years old and it was a chance to open a studio in New York, so I could get ready to do *Fritz*. I had a lot of friends who came with me from Paramount who needed jobs, so for me it was also, 'How do I get my friends jobs?' Not just myself, but my New York guys who would eventually go on to do *Fritz* with me."

Bakshi's first step upon taking over the Spidey reins was to hire a number of comic-book artists to create designs for him, among them such veterans as Gray Morrow, Jim Steranko, Joe Kubert, and Wally Wood.

"What I tried to do with those guys and my animators was to make it more realistic," he explains. "I should also point out that my distaste for comic-book publishers and editors rose vehemently at that point. Marvel Comics could care less what the guys on the Coast were doing and they could care less what I was doing. In other words, they didn't give a shit what I did with the show as long as they got their weekly stipend from ABC. They couldn't care less. I had to show them nothing. I could have done anything. My whole fight was to try and make the show more adult, and they were no help at all. A lot of the things the network came back with—they would give you notes like, 'Do this, you can't do this'—I abhorred. Marvel at that

point was no help at all. They didn't care. They were making their money and they wanted to keep it running as long as the network wanted it. So I was on my own trying to get some of the realism that Ditko and those guys had gotten into the comic that I loved so much.

"I remember," he adds, "that I used to go to Marvel with ABC's notes and say, 'Can't you do something?' and they wouldn't. Every time I came up to argue that the network was killing the show, Stan Lee kept saying, 'What else can we sell them?' That was my impression."

One of his proudest achievements, despite the ongoing problems with the network and Marvel, was that he was able to add a bit more depth to the show in terms of the animation and backgrounds.

"To me," Bakshi points out, "it was utterly amazing in those days to achieve anything realistic. It was all such crap, and Spider-Man, to me, was real. Marvel Comics, Simon and Kirby and Ditko were great. I broke my heart to do the show, which is why I was so angry at Marvel Comics, because if they had been even a little helpful, the show would have been so much better. You see, ABC wanted me to turn it into a kids' show. They kept wanting me to turn it younger and younger, so it became almost like a six-year-old would dig it. My whole thing was that teenagers would dig it, too. So we were at odds with that all the way. I wasn't there to sell

Spider-Man toys, I was there to sell the characters as I loved them in the comic books, with all these hang-ups that were in Peter Parker's head."

So determined was Bakshi to make the show realistic that there were a couple of episodes in which Spidey went through what could only be described as an acid trip.

"I was trying to do what Marvel was doing in the comic books, which was to be relevant to what was happening around you," he says. "The whole thing about me and animation was for animation to be relevant. In other words, not a fantasy but part of the time you were in. When you spoke to Wally Wood and the rest of the comic-book artists, that was their battle, too. So we were all beatniks trying to do what's happening, and there was tremendous resistance against that.

"The scripts were usually pretty bad," Bakshi adds with a laugh. "I remember sitting down with the guys and saying, 'We've got to change this stuff.' A lot was changed in layouts, but because the script might have been recorded already by the cast, it caused great difficulties in terms of how much you could change. The best you could do was throw out lines. You couldn't *add* lines. I think I gave the guys carte blanche to re-layout the script and get away from some of the bullshit that wasn't working, and I think they did very well with that. That's when the network screaming started; that's when the notes and the fights

started, because I would ignore them. So the cartoonists were let go to the best of their abilities. That was my frustration, because it showed we had started to rewrite stuff and how much better it would have been. There was an awful lot of fighting, but that's always the way in television. If you do it, you know you're going to fight. I try not to do it as much as possible, because who wants to fight their whole life? It's not like you ever win."

One falsehood about the show is that all of the attention to detail resulted in higher costs and a show that frequently went over budget.

"If you do something right," offers Bakshi, "it's cheaper. It's really quite extraordinary. If you have your heart in something, it moves along faster than if you don't have your heart in it. With the old guys, nobody cared and the thing just moped along. We were excited, we worked hard and fast because we loved what we were doing. Our show prices didn't go up. We were probably cheaper. Animation has to do with the amount of love the animator pours into it. If he likes what he's doing, he flies. If he hates what he's doing, he goes slowly. It was so different for our guys, and they liked the idea that I was fighting the network. It was a very good unit."

Despite all the heartache involved, Bakshi enjoyed the opportunity to not only get prepared for a feature film career, but to work with a character he genuinely enjoyed.

"There are actually very few comic-book characters that have gotten to the screen in original condition," he offers. "Most of the Hanna-Barbera superhero stuff was material originated by them. There were very few successful comics brought to the screen. I remember Max Fleischer's animated Superman shorts, which were brilliant. I would love to have done Superman. That was the excitement about Spider-Man. I think he was one of the first characters that came out that had social consciousness. He was a superhero that thought about problems that teenagers really had. That was very unusual in those days."

Spider-Man was cancelled by ABC after its third season, though it enjoyed years of popularity through syndication. Overall, there were some fine episodes produced, as well as a number of creative disappointments. Probably most memorable about the show was its "Spider-Man, Spider-Man, does whatever a spider can" theme song, which has withstood the passage of the decades, and has even been re-recorded a number of times, most notably by the Ramones.

Episode Guide

SEASON ONE: 1967–68

EPISODE 1: *"The Power of Doctor Octopus"* / *"Sub-Zero for Spidey"*
Mysterious lights in the sky lead Peter Parker to a hidden cave in which he, as Spider-Man, finds the headquarters of Doc Ock.

Ice creatures are living in New York Harbor aboard their damaged spacecraft. Spider-Man, with the help of propulsion expert Dr. Smartyr, must do what he can to get them home.

EPISODE 2: *"Where Crawls the Lizard"* / *"Electro the Human Lightning Bolt"*
In an experiment gone awry, Dr. Curt Connors is transformed into the Lizard, and quickly develops a plan that will turn other reptiles into intelligent beings intent on enslaving humanity.

Electro robs J. Jonah Jameson's wall safe, and ultimately goes *mano a mano* with Spider-Man in an amusement park.

EPISODE 3: *"The Menace of Mysterio"*
Disguising himself as Spider-Man in an attempt to discredit him, Mysterio pulls off a museum robbery and then collaborates with J. Jonah Jameson to make sure that old webhead is captured by the police.

EPISODE 4: *"The Sky Is Falling"* / *"Captured by J. Jonah Jameson"*
Utilizing a device that allows him to control the minds of birds, the Vulture launches a series of attacks on New York City.

Jameson apparently steps a bit over the line when he hires scientist Henry Smythe to create a killer robot that speaks in Jameson's voice and has his image projected on the robot's faceplate. His goal: to rid the world of Spider-Man once and for all.

EPISODE 5: *"Never Step on a Scorpion"* / *"Sands of Crime"*
Jameson hires the Scorpion to kill Spider-Man, but the villain decides that the *Daily Bugle* publisher himself deserves to die more than Spidey.

Able to transform any part of his body into sand, the Sandman steals a priceless diamond and demands two million dollars for its return.

EPISODE 6: *"Diet of Destruction"* / *"The Witching Hour"*
A fiery creature leaves a path of destruction in its wake. Utilizing a tugboat, Spider-Man comes up with a unique way of extinguishing this particular problem.

The Green Goblin attempts to bring to life a plan to conjure up the spirits of underworld demons, utilizing Jameson as a pawn in his plans.

EPISODE 7: *"Kilowatt Kaper" / "The Peril of Parafino"*

Escaping from jail, Electro takes control of the New York City power station, demanding that the city make him absolute ruler.

His pursuit of an escaped prisoner leads Spider-Man to Parafino's Wax Museum. There he finds himself the intended victim of the madman Parafino, who plans on coating Spidey in wax to add him to his collection of living exhibits.

EPISODE 8: *"Horn of the Rhino"*

As the components of a new military weapon begin to arrive in New York City, the Rhino unleashes his seemingly unstoppable strength to steal them. Spider-Man must go into battle against this larger-than-life being while simultaneously fighting a cold and his Aunt May, who has forbidden Peter Parker from leaving the house until he feels better.

EPISODE 9: *"The One-Eyed Idol" / "Fifth Avenue Phantom"*

Pretending to be a great fan of his work, Australian hunter Harley Clivendon pays a visit to J. Jonah Jameson. Completely won over by the praise, Jameson doesn't even realize he's being hypnotized to rob his own wall safe.

A hooded villain known as the Phantom uses a trio of female robots and a shrinking ray to pull off an unprecedented crime wave.

EPISODE 10: *"The Revenge of Dr. Magneto"/"The Sinister Prime Minister"*

Spider-Man must stop Dr. Magneto from using his magnetic ray to destroy New York City.

Actor Charles Cameo alters his appearance to look like the prime minister of Rutania so that he can perpetrate a fraud that will be worth millions.

EPISODE 11: *"The Night of the Villains" / "Here Comes Trubble"*

When Jesse James, the Executioner of Paris, and Blackbeard the Pirate arrive in modern-day New York City to carry out a new crime wave, Spider-Man tracks them back to Parafino's Wax Museum.

Spider-Man sets his sights on used book store–owner Miss Trubble, an expert in mythology who has obtained a magic chest that allows her to unleash mythological beasts on an unsuspecting world.

EPISODE 12: *"Spider-Man Meets Dr. Noah Boddy" / "The Fantastic Fakir"*

Seeking vengeance for a story in the *Daily Bugle* that ruined his career, Dr. Noah Boddy uses his invisibility machine to destroy Jameson's life.

An Arabian jewel thief uses a magic flute to control animals, which he commands to destroy Spider-Man.

EPISODE 13: *"Return of the Flying Dutchman"* / *"Farewell Performance"*
Sightings of the ghostly Flying Dutchman turn out to be the machinations of the returning Mysterio.

A Dr. Jekyll-and-Mr. Hyde-like creature seems to come to life at a condemned theater. Upon further investigation, Spider-Man learns that this "creature" is actually an actor trying to have the theater preserved as an historic landmark.

EPISODE 14: *"The Golden Rhino"* / *"Blueprint for Crime"*
The Rhino returns with a bizarre plan: to steal all the gold bullion he needs to create a solid gold tribute to himself.

Spider-Man has to recover the blueprint for a top-secret weapon from the Plotter and his two moronic henchmen, Cowboy and Ox.

EPISODE 15: *"The Spider and the Fly"* / *"The Slippery Doctor Von Schlick"*
Spider-Man nearly meets his match when he goes up against a pair of people identifying themselves as the Fly.

Doctor Von Schlick plans on using the world's oil reserves to consolidate power for himself.

EPISODE 16: *"The Vulture's Prey"* / *"The Dark Terrors"*
Jameson is taken hostage by the Vulture in a scheme involving a visiting diamond merchant.

Shadows of vicious creatures are being used to allow the Phantom to rob a panicked populace.

EPISODE 17: *"The Terrible Triumph of Doctor Octopus"* / *"Magic Malice"*
Doc Ock obtains a newly designed "destructor" missile, which he plans on using to gain worldwide control.

The Green Goblin uses stolen magic books to try to destroy Spider-Man.

EPISODE 18: *"Mountain of Terror"* / *"Fiddler on the Loose"*
Spider-Man heads back to Florida to investigate the disappearance of Dr. Curt Connors, who has apparently discovered the Fountain of Youth and is being held prisoner by Ponce de Leon.

An insane fiddler decides to extract revenge on the world for choosing rock 'n' roll over classical music.

EPISODE 19: *"To Catch a Spider"* / *"Double Identity"*
Dr. Noah Boddy unites the Green Goblin, the Vulture, and Electro in an effort to extract vengeance upon Spider-Man.

Actor Charles Cameo uses makeup and

disguises to commit a series of art gallery robberies.

EPISODE 20: *"Sting of the Scorpion" / "Trick or Treachery"*

The Scorpion, seeking vengeance on both Spider-Man and Jameson, uses a scientific device to grow giant-size.

When the Human Fly twins are paroled, they immediately set about trying to frame Spider-Man for a series of crimes.

SEASON TWO: 1968–69

EPISODE 21: *"The Origin of Spider-Man"*

Back to basics as we see Spider-Man's origin, from the moment Peter Parker is bitten by a radioactive spider to the realization that he is indirectly responsible for the death of his Uncle Ben.

EPISODE 22: *"King Pinned"*

Spider-Man goes after the gang leader known as the Kingpin, after he learns that the villain's organization is taking control of the pharmaceutical market with cheaper (and inferior) drugs.

EPISODE 23: *"Swing City"*

Manhattan is hoisted into the clouds by a madman who has developed an anti-gravity ray. Spider-Man attempts to stop him and is struck by "anti-radiation" which, it's believed, will neutralize his powers.

EPISODE 24: *"Criminals in the Clouds"*

No sooner has Peter Parker decided to use his spider powers to try out for the school football team than star player Roy Robinson is kidnapped by the Sky Master. The villain's intention is to hold Roy captive until his father hands over a potion for invisibility. Putting his selfish concerns aside, Peters changes to Spider-Man to unravel Sky Master's plan.

EPISODE 25: *"Menace from the Bottom of the World"*

Banks around New York City are sinking underground without a trace. Spider-Man discovers that the people in those banks are being turned into slaves by a city of molemen, who are intent on conquering the surface dwellers.

EPISODE 26: *"Diamond Dust"*

Criminals unleash a plan to cause panic at a city zoo by releasing a gorilla from its cage, and then using that distraction as a means of stealing a nearby priceless diamond. Naturally, Spider-Man refuses to allow anyone to make a monkey out of him.

EPISODE 27: *"Spider-Man Battles the Molemen"*

A sequel of sorts to "Menace from the Bottom of the World," but, in reality, an excuse to save money and utilize a tremendous amount of footage from that episode. Spidey goes back underground to take on the molemen—again.

EPISODE 28: *"Rhino" / "The Madness of Mysterio"*

The Rhino story is little more than a pastiche of elements from the previous two Rhino episodes, while in the second segment, thanks to Mysterio's efforts, Spider-Man is convinced that he's been shrunk in size and is battling to survive in a miniature amusement park that is anything but amusing.

EPISODE 29: *"The Evil Sorcerer"*

A sorcerer from ancient Egypt is resurrected and immediately attacks New York with its demon henchmen. Spider-Man must stop Kotep before he is whisked to another dimension.

EPISODE 30: *"Vine"*

Spider-Man finds himself drawn back to prehistoric times as he searches for a means of stopping a sentient plant that threatens New York in the present.

EPISODE 31: *"Pardo Presents"*

A sorcerer named Pardo, who can transform himself into a giant cat equipped with hypnotic abilities, attempts to rob New York's richest. It all culminates in a battle atop the Brooklyn Bridge.

EPISODE 32: *"Cloud City of Gold"*

A plane crash in South America forces exchange student Peter Parker to assume his Spider-Man persona and lead the survivors to safety. Completely unexpected is the discovery of a lost city and its inhabitants.

EPISODE 33: *"Neptune's Nose Cone"*

While on assignment, Peter Parker and a *Daily Bugle* pilot named Penny crash on an island, where they become the target of a primitive culture that demands they be sacrificed to their gods.

EPISODE 34: *"Home"*

Spider-Man goes up against a woman who has similar powers. This ultimately leads to the discovery of a race of spider-people who are attempting to repair their vessel so they can go home.

EPISODE 35: *"Blotto"*

A movie producer named Clive nurses a festering hatred toward the critics and audiences who have dismissed his theory that the darker aspects of the human soul can be captured on film and brought to life. Once he discovers the means of doing so, he unleashes these cinematic terrors in an effort to claim revenge against those who doubted him. Spider-Man and the military take on Clive's inventions.

EPISODE 36: *"Thunder Rumble"*
Spider-Man takes on a giant Martian who has come to earth in an attempt to steal all of our gold (though why a Martian wants to bring gold back to Mars is never addressed).

EPISODE 37: *"Spider-Man Meets Skyboy"*
Spider-Man must rescue Dr. Irving Caldwell and his son, Jan, from the evil Dr. Zap, who has captured the duo in an effort to possess Caldwell's levitation helmet.

EPISODE 38: *"Cold Storage"*
When Dr. Cool and his gang attempt to smuggle a large quantity of stolen diamonds within ice from an ice factory, Spider-Man must do whatever he can to defrost the good doctor's plans.

EPISODE 39: *"To Cage a Spider"*
After being rendered unconscious while attempting to stop a robbery, Spider-Man finds himself arrested and his true identity about to be exposed. Desperate to keep the truth hidden, he pretends to join up with prisoners attempting to escape, but ultimately begins to stop them one by one before they can break out.

SEASON THREE: 1969–70

EPISODE 40: *"The Winged Thing"* / *"Conner's Reptiles"*

Spidey goes up first against the Vulture and then the Lizard in a pair of stories largely made up of footage from earlier encounters between hero and villains.

EPISODE 41: *"Trouble With Snow"* / *"Spider-Man vs. Desperado"*
A combination of industrial chemicals and electricity somehow brings a snowman to life, and it continues to grow with each new snowfall. On a murderous rampage, Spider-Man must figure out a way to stop it.

Using an electronic horse, a modern-day cowboy named Desperado embarks on a New York crime wave, with Spider-Man trying to lasso him in.

EPISODE 42: *"Sky Harbor"* / *"The Big Brainwasher"*
Spider-Man challenges a German baron who launches an attack on New York with a number of World War I fighter planes.

The Kingpin returns, and this time he's armed with a device that will allow him to brainwash city officials into obeying his every command.

EPISODE 43: *"The Vanishing Doctor Vespasian"* / *"Scourge of the Scarf"*
A number of robberies are committed by a green-skinned scientist and his dog after the scientist creates an invisibility formula.

An artistic genius known as the Scarf

makes the moon look psychedelic, which disorients the people of Manhattan long enough for them to be robbed blind.

EPISODE 44: *"Super Swami"* / *"The Birth of Microman"*
A number of extremely realistic illusions panics the city of New York. These illusions are being used by the Super Swami, who is demanding the populace obey his every word or he will destroy them.

Spider-Man must allow himself to be shrunken down in size to combat Prof Pretories, who has shrunken himself in an attempt to construct a microscopic atomic detonator.

EPISODE 45: *"Knights Must Fall"* / *"The Devious Dr. Dumpty"*
This time Spider-Man's foe is a motorcycle-riding knight in armor who is committing a series of robberies.

Spidey takes to the sky as he battles Dr. Dumpty, a villain who uses hot-air balloons to launch attacks on the people of New York.

EPISODE 46: *"Up from Nowhere"*
Dr. Atlantian, sole survivor of the lost city of Atlantis, arises from the ocean floor with the power to conquer the surface world.

EPISODE 47: *"Rollarama"*
Essentially a remake of the episode "Vine," with the primary difference that the vicious plant has been replaced by a series of rolling pods. Beyond that, it's the same story.

EPISODE 48: *"The Phantom from the Depths of Time"*
Giant mechanical beetles arrive on an island and force the inhabitants to mine a rare and valuable ore they need. This episode uses a large amount of animation from the *Rocket Robin Hood* series, which Ralph Bakshi also worked on.

EPISODE 49: *"Revolt in the Fifth Dimension"*
Rocket Robin Hood strikes again as an alien scientist crashes on earth and passes on to Spider-Man an incredible wealth of knowledge, including information about a dimension in which every thought becomes reality.

EPISODE 50: *"Specialists and Slaves"*
Manhattan is once again hoisted into the sky and a deranged scientist uses a device to turn the residents of New York City into millions of mindless drones.

EPISODE 51: *"Down to Earth"*
"Neptune's Nose Cone" lives on, as once again Spidey fights for survival against primitives in a similar hostile environment.

EPISODE 52: *"Trip to Tomorrow"*
Spider-Man attempts to talk a young runaway out of becoming a superhero by
recounting some of his most harrowing
adventures. Needless to say, the episode
consists largely of footage from other
episodes.

The Electric Company

Generally speaking, most of Spider-Man's television incarnations were created with one goal in mind: to garner audience ratings and, in turn, to sell products (notably toys) based on the character. Despite this, there was one effort designed to do little more than use the character's ever-burgeoning popularity to reach children who might otherwise be unreachable. To this end, Spidey began to appear in small education vignettes on the Public Television series *The Electric Company.*

Designed as a more hip companion piece to *Sesame Street, The Electric Company*'s ensemble cast included Jim Boyd, Judy Graubart, Ship Hinnant, Rita Moreno, and Morgan Freeman, who, like Moreno, has had a long and varied acting career. While the series itself premiered in 1971 and ran until 1977, Spider-Man didn't become a member of the show until the 1974–75 season.

Portrayed by Danny Seagren, this particular version of the web-crawler was a silent player, never uttering a single word—quite a contrast to the original comic-book incarnation, which basically couldn't keep his mouth shut for more than a panel or two at a time. In each segment, Spider-Man would stop some villain while always teaching the viewer something, usually about vocabulary.

What follows is an episode guide to Spider-Man's appearances on the show (for a more detailed look at these episodes, check out *www.spiderfan.org*). In truth, it's difficult to critically assess a show such as this, when its only intention is to teach young viewers.

Episode Guide

SEASON ONE FEATURING SPIDER-MAN: 1974–75

EPISODE 1: *"Spidey Meets the Spoiler"*
The web-crawler has to stop the Spoiler from ruining everyone's day, whether it be wrecking their ice-cream treat or trying to rid the world of Spider-Man once and for all.

EPISODE 2: *"A Night at the Movies"*
Count Dracula tries to put the bite on a couple of moviegoers, but is stopped by Spider-Man.

EPISODE 3: *"Dr. Fly"*
A human-fly hybrid plans on making everyone else in the world look just like him.

EPISODE 4: *"The Can Crusher"*
A costumed man invades supermarkets and opens cans of tomato soup, hoping to find his lost frog who "was disappeared" years earlier in a soup factory.

EPISODE 5: *"Spidey Up against the Wall"*
Spidey attends a Mets baseball game, but finds things interrupted by a criminal known as the Wall, who's intent on wrecking everybody's day.

EPISODE 6: *"The Funny Bunny"*
Because a bully crushed her Easter basket, a little girl grows up to steal treats from other kids' baskets.

EPISODE 7: *"Dr. Fright"*
This evil mastermind is going to use his horrible face to freeze Spider-Man in his tracks, until Spidey uses a mirror to reverse the situation.

EPISODE 8: *"Meet Mr. Measles"*
Can Spidey stop this madman from inflicting thousands of children with measles? What do you think?

EPISODE 9: *"The Queen Bee"*
A human-bee hybrid plans on using her colony to take over the world.

EPISODE 10: *"The Thumper"*
Dressed like Napoleon Bonaparte, a spoiled woman thumps people in the head because she's not getting her way.

EPISODE 11: *"The Bookworm"*
Worms under the command of the Bookworm start destroying books in the New York Public Library, and it's up to Spider-Man to stop this planned illiteracy.

EPISODE 12: *Untitled*
Spidey stops the spider that's been terrifying Little Miss Muffet.

SEASON TWO FEATURING SPIDER-MAN: 1975–76

EPISODE 13: *"The Birthday Bandit"*
Spidey must thwart the plans of a villain who is ruining the birthday parties of little boys and girls.

EPISODE 14: *"Spidey Meets the Prankster"*
Students and children at a public school find themselves the victims of numerous pranks, such as snakes popping out of textbooks and chocolate pies being replaced by mud.

EPISODE 15: *"Who Stole the Show?"*
A former child star named Winky Goodyshoes tries to disrupt a school play.

EPISODE 16: *"Spidey Meets the Mouse"*
When his McDonalds Big Mac comes without cheese, a teenager dresses as a giant mouse and begins stealing cheese from others.

EPISODE 17: *"Spidey Meets the Sitter"*
Posing as an elderly baby-sitter, this villain is able to rob the homes she is supposedly working for.

EPISODE 18: *"Spidey Meets the Yeti"*
Spider-Man has to help an abominable snowman find his way home.

Spider-Man: The Live-Action Series

When Dean Devlin and Roland Emmerich created the epic feature film *Independence Day*, many critics dismissed the project—no matter how entertaining it might be in its own right—as little more than a pastiche of past sci-fi efforts, most notably the television miniseries "*V*" and George Lucas's *Star Wars*. But then, Lucas himself finally released a new *Star Wars* film in the form of *The Phantom Menace*, and all of a sudden *Independence Day* started to look much better by comparison.

The same could be said of Spider-Man's previous incarnations as compared to the live-action effort produced by CBS in 1977. While criticism could be leveled at the 1967–70 animated series and the character's mimelike performances on *The Electric Company*, at least there was some effort to get things right. In the former, much of the character's charm and nonstop commentary was retained from the comics, becoming a highlight of a series that, generally speaking, offered average animation. In the latter, the costume was really quite effective, and far superior to the higher-budgeted one created for the prime-time drama.

Stan Lee, who always dreamed of the kind of success achieved by Superman and Batman's reincarnations in different mediums, was determined to allow Spider-Man to leap off the comic panel into a live-action drama. George Reeves's *The Adventures of Superman* had been a television staple of the 1950s, and the live-action *Batman*, which starred Adam West in the title role, assumed the mantle a decade later. In the days just prior to Christopher Reeve's donning the Man of Steel's red-and-blue costume for *Superman: The Movie*, Lee had hoped that Spidey could be *the* quintessential comic hero brought to life in the seventies. Unfortunately, he didn't get his wish.

It should, however, be pointed out that things certainly began with the proper intentions, as writer Alvin Boertz was hired in 1977 to write a two-hour Spider-Man telefilm. Having built his reputation writing for the medium during its Golden Age, he initially was insulted when the network asked him to get involved with this project. "I don't think of myself as a comic-book writer," he says. "I've written over one thousand shows, so when CBS asked me to do this, I kind of blanched and said, 'What's the matter with you? I don't write about cockroaches and spiders. What are you giving me this shit for?' Then I thought about it and I realized that if this thing goes, it will be a pilot and I'll make a couple of dollars. So, quite frankly, that's why I did it. But I also had a lot of fun writing it, because we decided that it wasn't just an adventure show, but it was a way to have some fun, which is what we did. I worked with some very nice people."

Among these "nice people" was Spider-Man creator Stan Lee, who provided Boertz with all the research he needed, as the writer had never studied the comic books. "Stan did a very good job," he offers. "He really had that character pinned to the mat; he knew what he was doing. In talking to him, I got a lot of ideas about how it should go. I didn't want it to be ridiculous, I didn't want the character to be laughed at, but at the same time I would do a couple of things that people would say, 'What the hell was that about?' People enjoyed it. The network loved the show."

Apparently so did the audience, as the original *Spider-Man* TV movie was a ratings winner, striking a nice balance between the standard superhero TV show of the time (*The Six Million Dollar Man*, *The Bionic Woman*, *Wonder Woman*, etc.) and a taste of the comic books with a plotline that involved a scientist who devises a mind-controlling device. Guest star Thayer David, who portrayed Mr. Byron, brought the proper sense of menace to *Spider-Man* and was a worthy adversary.

Cast in the lead role was Nicholas Hammond, a young actor who was (and still is) best remembered for his role as one of the Von Trapp children in the Julie Andrews movie, *The Sound of Music* (1965). Two years earlier he had made his debut as one of the kids in the adaptation of *Lord of the Flies*. Although he would go on to other roles, it's *The Sound of Music* and his Spider-Man portrayal that he's best remembered for. It should be noted, however, that much of Spidey's on-camera time featured stuntman Fred Waugh in the famous red-and-blue costume.

David White, who epitomized the word *smarm* as Darren Stevens's boss, Larry Tate, on *Bewitched*, was cast as *Daily Bugle* publisher J. Jonah Jameson, nicely capturing the character's continuously stressed-out nature. Chip Fields portrayed Jameson's assistant, Rita Conway, while veteran character actor Michael Pataki took on the role of Captain Barbera of the NYPD. Eventually White would be out, replaced by Robert F. Simon in the role of Jameson, Pataki would only last a few episodes, and Ellen Bry was added as Julie Masters, a photographer who offers a challenge to Peter in getting the best pics for the *Bugle*.

The order from CBS to turn Spider-Man into a weekly series came about fairly abruptly. Unfortunately, while the first film managed fairly well to walk the line between standard television and capturing the essence of the comics, the subsequent series most definitely lost its balance altogether. The show was, in a word, bland, maintaining none of the character or edge that had distinguished Spidey as a hero in the first place. Gone were the machinations of Doc Ock or the Green Goblin, and in their place was a series of ordinary bad guys, one more mundane than the next. There were bad guys trying to obtain a student-built atomic bomb; commandos who take a group of people—including Peter Parker—hostage; attempts to steal top-secret NATO defense plans; a prison break that must be thwarted, a fake ghost, a chemical that makes people open to suggestion, and the framing of a Chinese foreign minister. When the show did venture into larger-than-life scenarios—a man who has acquired the gift of telekinesis, a geneticist who creates evil clones of, among other things, Peter Parker—they were usually

clumsily handled, leaving the viewer with one question: Why did they bother?

Again, bland.

Stan Lee, who had dreamed of this moment for so long, didn't exactly let the show go down without a fight. In the excellent reference work *Science Fiction Television Series* (1996, McFarland), he explained, "After I read the scripts, I called a meeting at CBS. The director was there, the producer was there, and the network executives were there. I spent twenty minutes telling them what was wrong with the show, they listened politely and then they

Stan Lee with Batman and Spider-Man

left and paid no attention to what I had told them."

In the same book, producer Daniel Goodman added, "My concept was to make *Spider-Man* more acceptable to a general audience than just to kiddies, and perhaps there was a clash of ideologies. We had to compromise, as CBS was sold on my original sales presentation of a prime-time, *general* audience show."

General, in the mind of writer Gregory Dinallo, whose credits at the time included *Quincy* and *The Six Million Dollar Man*, did not mean childish. "Nothing was ever a young children's show," he emphasizes. "Whether it was *The Six Million Dollar Man*, *Spider-Man*, or any show we were doing in those days, it had to appeal to everybody. That was the whole point of it. The kids had something that they could latch on to, but you have to have character development, you had to have a plot that made sense so that you could get the family. This stuff was on at an hour where you weren't going to have five-year-olds sitting down by themselves. It's eight o'clock and there was a certain amount of violence on the show. I don't think I ever wrote anything that was targeted at kids. If anything, the kids were there because of the basic concept, but you had to have an adult audience or you were out of business."

As to the lack of super-villains, he notes, "There may have been a conscious effort not to do a Saturday-morning cartoon. By using credible adversaries, credible to adults as opposed to using super-villains, that's how you got the adult audience. However cleverly your incredible hero dealt with them was acceptable. In truth, we tried to have a certain level of moral issues and a certain amount of overall credibility. It had to make sense from a plot point of view. What people did had to make sense, and even within the powers of the hero, there were constraints. It had to be not so off the deep end that you'd dismiss it as ridiculous. All powers have limits that kept them within a realm of believability."

Unfortunately, by sticking to that desire for believability, *The Amazing Spider-Man* never had the opportunity to soar in the way that it inherently had the potential to do.

Episode Guide

EPISODE 1: *"Spider-Man"*
ORIGINAL AIRDATE: *September 14, 1977*
Written by Alvin Boertz
Directed by E. W. Swackhamer
Guest stars: David White (J. Jonah Jameson),
Lisa Eilbacher (Judy Taylor), Thayer
David (Mr. Byron)

Spider-Man's origin is detailed as Peter Parker is bitten by a radioactive spider and finds himself endowed with the proportionate powers of a spider. No sooner does he become Spidey than he goes up against one Mr. Byron, a criminal genius using a newly developed mind-controlling device to make ordinary citizens commit robberies and then kill themselves so that the crimes can't be traced back to him.

Casting note: The late Thayer David, who portrayed Mr. Byron, is probably best known by genre fans for a variety of roles on the 1960s horror soap opera, *Dark Shadows*. Additionally, in this TV movie, the role of J. Jonah Jameson was played by David White, known to a number of generations as Larry Tate on *Bewitched*.

EPISODES 2 AND 3: *"The Deadly Dust"*
ORIGINAL AIRDATES: *Part 1, April 5, 1978;*
Part 2, April 12, 1978
Written by Robert Janes

Directed by Ron Satlof
Guest stars: Joanna Cameron (Gale
Hoffman), Robert Alda (Mr. White)

Spider-Man must recover a stolen atomic bomb, which was constructed by a number of college students who are protesting plutonium being stored at the college. It was their intention to prove the ease with which such a device can be constructed, not expecting that it would be seen as a valuable prize to criminals.

Casting note: Actress Joanna Cameron spent two season in the 1970s as the star of the live-action Saturday morning series *Isis*.

EPISODE 4: *"The Curse of Rava"*
ORIGINAL AIRDATE: *April 19, 1978*
Written by Dick Nelson and Robert Janes
Directed by Michael Caffrey
Guest stars: Theodore Bikel (Mr. Mandak),
Adrienne LaRussa (Trina Pandit), Byron
Webster (Professor Ruston), David Ralphe
(Dr. Keller)

The Kalistan cult protests the fact that a New York museum has set on display a statue of Rava, their god. Spider-Man ultimately goes up against the cult's leader, Mandak, who has acquired a number of telekinetic abilities.

EPISODE 5: *"Night of the Clones"*
ORIGINAL AIRDATE: *April 26, 1978*
Written by John W. Bloch
Directed by Fernando Lamas
Guest stars: Morgan Fairchild (Lisa Benson),
Lloyd Bochner (Dr. Moon), Rich Traeger
(Dr. Reichman)

Jameson assigns Peter Parker to interview Dr. Moon, an American geneticist who claims to have discovered the secrets behind cloning—which he demonstrates for Parker and others by cloning a frog. Moon, resentful of being overlooked by the TOVAL awards committee for years, attempts to extract revenge, inadvertently getting a sample of blood from Spider-Man, which he uses to clone an evil version of Peter Parker. Spider-Man has to stop his evil clone and discover the truth about Moon's identity.

EPISODE 6: *"Escort to Danger"*
ORIGINAL AIRDATE: *May 3, 1978*
Written by Duke Standefur
Directed by Dennis Donnelly
Guest stars: Barbara Luna (Lisa Alvarez),
Alejandro Rey (President Caldrone),
Madeline Stowe (Maria Caldrone),
Harold Sakata (Matsu)

No sooner has the daughter of the Tavilia president arrived to compete in an international beauty contest than she is kidnapped. The culprits demand that her father resign from his office in front of a live worldwide audience by making the announcement at the beauty contest. Spider-Man tries to intercede, though the task is made more difficult by the power of a martial arts master named Matsu.

Casting note: Matsu is portrayed by the late Harold Sakata, best known as the mute Oddjob in the James Bond thriller *Goldfinger*, with Sean Connery.

EPISODE 7: *"The Captive Tower"*
ORIGINAL AIRDATE: *September 5, 1978*
Written by Gregory S. Dinallo
Directed by Cliff Bole
Guest stars: David Sheiner (Major Forester),
Todd Sussman (Mr. Farnum), Fred
Lerner (Duke), Barry Cutler (Barry)

At the unveiling of a new super high-tech building, terrorists take control and hold a number of people hostage, including Jameson and Parker. Naturally, Parker's challenge is being able to slip away and change into Spider-Man.

EPISODE 8: *"A Matter of State"*
ORIGINAL AIRDATE: *September 12, 1978*
Written by Howard Dimsdale
Directed by Larry Stewart
Guest stars: Nicholas Coster (Andre), John
Crawford (Mr. Evans), Michael Santiago
(Carl), Barry Cutler (Barry)

When Spider-Man thwarts thieves from getting their hands on a top-secret NATO defense plan, the criminals kidnap an innocent woman and bring her to the top of the Empire State Building, threatening to kill her if Spidey doesn't let them go. Knowing he hasn't much time, Spider-Man scales the building, to arrive at the last possible moment.

EPISODE 9: *"Con Caper"*
ORIGINAL AIRDATE: *November 11, 1978*
Written by Brian McKay and George S. Dinallo
Directed by Tom Blank
Guest stars: William Smithers (James Colbert), Fred Downs (Warden Richer), Ramon Bieri (Mr. Cates), Andrew Robinson (Mr. McTeague)
Recent prison parolee James Colbert—a politician convicted of breaking political campaign rules—seems to be making great strides in working with other convicts, most notably by quelling a prisoner uprising. It's all a ruse, however, as he plans on freeing two other convicts so that the trio can commit a daring bank robbery.

EPISODE 10: *"The Kirkwood Haunting"*
ORIGINAL AIRDATE: *December 30, 1978*
Written by Michael Michaelian
Directed by Don McDougall
Guest stars: Marilyn Mason (Lisa Kirkwood), Peter MacLean (Dr. Polarsky), Paul Carr (Mr. Ganz), Peggy McCay (Dr. Davis)
The elderly Mrs. Kirkwood fears that she is being haunted by the spirit of her late husband. Peter is sent to investigate, ultimately discovering that Mrs. Kirkwood is the victim of con men who are attempting to

frighten her into turning over the estate to them.

EPISODE 11: *"Photo Finish"*
ORIGINAL AIRDATE: *February 7, 1979*
Written by Howard Dimsdale
Directed by Tony Ganz
Guest stars: Geoffrey Lewis (Weldon Gray), Charles Haid (Police Lieutenant), Jennifer Billingsley (Mrs. Gray)
While photographing a collection of rare and expensive coins, Peter is knocked unconscious. Awakening, he finds all evidence (taken from film shot at the scene) pointing to the collector's wife, Mrs. Gray. Not believing this, Peter refuses to turn the film over to the police, which results in his being thrown in jail for contempt of court. Using his spider-powers to escape, Spidey must uncover the truth—if he doesn't die first!

EPISODE 12: *"Wolf Pack"*
ORIGINAL AIRDATE: *February 21, 1979*
Written by Stephen Kandel
Directed by Joseph Manduke
Guest stars: Gavin O'Herlihy (David), Wil Setzler (Art), Allan Arbus (George Hansen)
A friend of Peter's named David is working on developing a relaxation serum. Through accidental circumstances, the makeup of this serum is altered, leaving test subjects completely open to suggestion. Overcome with greed, David decides to order these people to steal a rare item from a museum.

EPISODE 13: *"The Chinese Web" (2 hours)*
ORIGINAL AIRDATE: *July 6, 1979*
Written by Lionel E. Siegel
Directed by Don McDougall
Guest stars: Benson Fong (Min Lo Chan),
*   Rosalind Chao (Emily Chan), Richard*
*   Erdman (Mr. Zeider), John Milford*
*   (Professor Dent)*

In a nutshell, Peter/Spider-Man must prove the innocence of Min Lo Chan, China's minister of Industrial Development, who is accused of selling military secrets during World War II.

Spider-Man: The Japanese Series

The success of Spider-Man was never a purely domestic one, with the character garnering popularity in a wide variety of countries, most notably Japan. In fact, in 1978 the Toei production company produced forty-one episodes of a television series simply called *Spider-Man*, which ran on Japanese television from May 1978 through March 1979.

A strange entry in the Spidey canon, the series had more in common with the Power Rangers than with Marvel Comics. In this take on the character, Spidey's alter-ego, Yamashiro Takuya (Kagawa Kousuke), is a motocross racer, who, while on a mountain hike with his family, loses his father in a battle with a strange creature. Before he can help, Yamashiro is attacked by a mysterious woman and a number of gray soldiers, who believe they have killed him. Barely alive, he manages to escape to a cave, where he meets the sole survivor of the Spider Planet, Garia. Dying, Garia (Nishizawa Toshiaki) explains that he has come to earth to battle the warriors of the Iron Cross Group. To ensure that the battle will continue, he gives Yamashiro a mysterious bracelet and then dies, transforming himself into a giant spider. As he does so, Spider-venom is abruptly pumped into Yamashiro's veins, giving him the appropriate powers.

Beyond super strength, the ability to stick to walls, and the spider-sense, this Spider-Man gets much from the alien bracelet which, when activated, causes his costume to magically fly onto him and also provides the ability to shoot out a rope and nets. Then there's his high-tech car, the GP-7; the Marveller, a flying fortress equipped with a number of weapons; and a pair of robots—one giant-size, the other fitted for him—which he enters to battle the creatures he goes up against.

Other characters featured in the series include Yamashiro's father (Ooyama Izumi), who is killed by the Iron Cross monster Bokun, and basically serves as this show's version of Uncle Ben and one of the main reasons that Yamashiro decides to become a superhero; his sister, Niiko; girlfriend Hitome Sakuma (Miura Rika), a photographer for *Weekly Woman* magazine; and his younger brother, Takuji (Yabuki Yoshiharu).

The villains of the show (and it should be noted that not a single villain from the comics appeared on this show) all belong to the Iron Cross, the criminal group that has destroyed the Spider Planet and has now set its sights on earth. They are more or less after earth's resources, but are happy to cause as much chaos in getting them as they can. Given this goal, it is admittedly strange that they spend so much time involved in crimes such as loan-sharking and illegal gambling.

The Iron Cross is led by Professor Monster (Andou Mitsuo), who has created the BEMs (bug-eyed-monsters), which go after Spider-Man on a weekly basis. He is equipped with a laser in his mechanical eye, though he never seems able to hit the target he's after. Amazoness (Kagawa Yukie) is the field commander of the Iron Cross, and she often uses disguises so that she can spy on Spider-Man. Her "day" job is serving as editor of *Weekly Woman*, where she also happens to be Hitome's boss.

Week after week, Spider-Man goes up against the soldiers of the Iron Cross, who are known as Ninders. Their job is to basically get Spidey in a weakened state so that the BEM of the week can do him in—naturally, they're never quite successful in their efforts.

What follows is an episode guide to the series, featuring title, airdate, and BEM of the week. Some of Spider-Man's opponents in this show were so ludicrous that it was difficult to include them with any sort of seriousness. Some of the episode titles are intriguing, and one wonders if there might have been more depth to some of the individual shows than the premise suggests.

Episode Guide

EPISODE 1: *"The Time of Revenge Hath Come! Strike the Iron Cross"*

ORIGINAL AIRDATE: *May 17, 1978*

A mutant dinosaur—wielding sword blades and a sickle in place of its hands—terrorizes Tokyo.

EPISODE 2: *"World of the Weird! A Man Who Lives Out His Destiny"*

ORIGINAL AIRDATE: *May 24, 1978*

A double-headed demon is able to launch its head at its enemies (hey, you can't make this stuff up!). Its brain emits "destructo-beams" and its arms, which can cut through virtually anything, sit on its body, praying-mantis–like.

EPISODE 3: *"Strange Thief 001 vs. the Spider Man"*

ORIGINAL AIRDATE: *May 31, 1978*

A mutant cicada known as the Phantom Bug uses a hypnotic sound in its quest to destroy humanity.

EPISODE 4: *"The Fearsome Half-Fish Man! A Silver Thread That Summons a Miracle"*

ORIGINAL AIRDATE: *June 7, 1978*

A giant man/fish hybrid—able to function either on land or in the sea—launches an attack on civilization.

EPISODE 5: *"Collision with Machine GP-7! Vow of the Brothers"*

ORIGINAL AIRDATE: *June 14, 1978*

The Bird-God Beast—a giant man with the beak of a parrot—takes to the skies and plans on firing rockets from its left hand at an unsuspecting populace.

EPISODE 6: *"Laboratory of Terror! The Demonic Professor Monster"*

ORIGINAL AIRDATE: *June 21, 1978*

Beings known as Killer Donkeys (due to their extremely large, hypersensitive ears) have rockets locked into their forearms that they're preparing to launch.

EPISODE 7: *"A Scary Hit Song! Sing and Dance to Murder Rock"*

ORIGINAL AIRDATE: *June 28, 1978*

The Scorpler, a scorpion-like creature equipped with poison needles that kill whoever they come into contact with, takes on Spider-Man.

EPISODE 8: *"A Truly Bizarre Folktale! The Cursed Cat Mound"*

ORIGINAL AIRDATE: *July 5, 1978*

The Cat Beast is equipped with iron claws and black hair that can be used as a whip.

EPISODE 9: *"The Moving Accessory: The Beetle Spy's Tragic Romance"*

ORIGINAL AIRDATE: *July 12, 1978*

Beetlon is a beetle-like creature that can shoot lasers from its eyes and ram objects with its head, which is horned.

EPISODE 10: *"I Saw the Snake Woman's Tears in a Flaming Hell"*

ORIGINAL AIRDATE: *July 19, 1978*

The Snake Woman, like the legendary Medusa, can turn anyone who looks at her into stone. Adding to the fun is the fact that one of her snake heads can shoot fire from its mouth.

EPISODE 11: *"Professor Monster's Ultra Poison Killing"*

ORIGINAL AIRDATE: *July 26, 1978*

The Deep Sea King is a shell-headed creature armed with a trident.

EPISODE 12: *"Transformation into a Beautiful Killing Machine"*

ORIGINAL AIRDATE: *August 2, 1978*

Villain unknown

EPISODE 13: *"The Skull Gang vs. the Demonic Hearse"*

ORIGINAL AIRDATE: *August 9, 1978*

The Runaway Beast is a reptile-like demon that shoots a fluid from its mouth, melting its target.

EPISODE 14: *"For Father: A Song of a Brave Man Who Wouldn't Fight"*

ORIGINAL AIRDATE: *August 16, 1978*

The opponent is Bat Man, a creature equipped with bat-wing ears and missiles that it can fire from its arms.

EPISODE 15: *"The Promise of Our Lives"*

ORIGINAL AIRDATE: *August 23, 1978*

The Killer Unicorn is a dragon creature that fires machine guns from its head (don't ask us!).

EPISODE 16: *"O Fine Dog, Run to Father"*

ORIGINAL AIRDATE: *August 30, 1978*

A giant centipede protected by iron spines on its body sets out to destroy Tokyo.

EPISODE 17: *"The Tears of Pro Wrestler Samson"*

ORIGINAL AIRDATE: *September 6, 1978*

Professor Monster transforms a wrestler into a creature that is somewhat similar to the Thing from Marvel Comics' the Fantastic Four.

EPISODE 18: *"The Boy Who Returned to Life in His Mother's Heart"*

ORIGINAL AIRDATE: *September 13, 1978*

A human-carnivorous plant hybrid starts chowing down on human beings.

EPISODE 19: *"The Phantom Boy: The Unmapped Village"*

ORIGINAL AIRDATE: *September 20, 1978*

The Turtlenger features a metal jaw on its left hand and can fire a pair of machine guns from its chest.

EPISODE 20: *"The Secret of My Birth: Mysteries upon Mysteries"*
ORIGINAL AIRDATE: *September 27, 1978*
Primordial is an ape-man that has a powerful club, night vision, and a robotic arm.

EPISODE 21: *"A Father's Love That Perished in the Sky"*
ORIGINAL AIRDATE: *October 4, 1978*
Tank Buffalo, a being with tank treads, can transform itself into a tank.

EPISODE 22: *"Cry for Dark Destiny: Father and Son"*
ORIGINAL AIRDATE: *October 11, 1978*
A skeleton-like vampire known as Skull Monster attempts to gather blood for Professor Monster.

EPISODE 23: *"A School of Love for Homeless Children"*
ORIGINAL AIRDATE: *October 18, 1978*
Witch Monkey is a blond-haired sorceress who happens to have the face of an ape.

EPISODE 24: *"The Great Cockroach Boys' War"*
ORIGINAL AIRDATE: *October 25, 1978*
The Cockroach Combine, a hybrid of a cockroach and a businessman, performs a number of daring robberies.

EPISODE 25: *"The Secret Treasure, the Dog and the Clone"*
ORIGINAL AIRDATE: *November 1, 1978*
The Crab Demon is armored, has a laser canon on its head, and decapitates its opponents with a claw on its left hand.

EPISODE 26: *"In Deep Trouble: A Fake Hero"*
ORIGINAL AIRDATE: *November 8, 1978*
The Eruption Beast is a walking volcano who can set off explosions whenever he wants.

EPISODE 27: *"Farewell Comrade-in-Arms, Beloved Shepherd Dog"*
ORIGINAL AIRDATE: *November 15, 1978*
No creature of the week

EPISODE 28: *"Boy Detectives of Stationfront Alley"*
ORIGINAL AIRDATE: *November 22, 1978*
Magnicatfish uses its body to burrow underground and create massive earthquakes.

EPISODE 29: *"Hurry, GP-7! Stop Time"*
ORIGINAL AIRDATE: *November 29, 1978*
The Bomb Wolf is basically a Wolfman who has a pair of missile launchers on its shoulders.

EPISODE 30: *"Do Your Best, Pretty Patrolwoman"*
ORIGINAL AIRDATE: *December 6, 1978*

Anger Pat is an anglerfish that can transform into a patrol car, which causes a great deal of problems for Spider-Man.

EPISODE 31: *"No Future for the Lone Cop and Kid"*
ORIGINAL AIRDATE: *December 13, 1978*
The Mushroommonger creates hallucinogenic mushrooms that it uses against its enemies.

EPISODE 32: *"The Evil Woman Who Whispers Sweetly"*
ORIGINAL AIRDATE: *December 20, 1978*
The Electric Earthworm has the power to electrocute anyone who comes up against it.

EPISODE 33: *"The Boy-Bullying, Incredibly Wild Girl"*
ORIGINAL AIRDATE: *December 27, 1978*
Flame Fox is a foxlike being that is able to shoot fire from its mouth.

EPISODE 34: *"The Candid Camera Murders"*
ORIGINAL AIRDATE: *January 10, 1979*
The Scrapman is created from the remains of a number of old cars, and has the power to reduce anything it attacks to a pile of junk.

EPISODE 35: *"The Mummified Beauty from the Unexplored Amazon"*
ORIGINAL AIRDATE: *January 17, 1979*
The Tiger Pump is armed with machine guns attached to its waist.

EPISODE 36: *"Onion Iron Mask and the Boy Detectives"*
ORIGINAL AIRDATE: *January 24, 1979*
The Iron Masked Miracle, who can turn onions into drugs (!) begins a crime wave.

EPISODE 37: *"King Yama, Secret Emissary from Hell"*
ORIGINAL AIRDATE: *February 7, 1979*
King Yama, who has come to earth from hell, has the power to raise the dead and control the reborn.

EPISODE 38: *"Tin Planet No. 1 and the Boy Detectives"*
ORIGINAL AIRDATE: *February 14, 1979*
Tooth-Decayed Gator is a being that loses teeth when it attacks, but comes back stronger after it gets dentures.

EPISODE 39: *"The World Hand-to-Hand Combat Championship"*
ORIGINAL AIRDATE: *February 21, 1979*
The Great Strongman Fighter is an armor-wearing human warrior, while the Great Birdman Fighter has the power to grow giant-sized.

EPISODE 40: *"The Zero Fighter Farewell Mystery"*
ORIGINAL AIRDATE: *March 7, 1979*
Bomber Ray is a flying manta ray that shoots missiles from horns on its head. It also has the power to fight underwater.

EPISODE 41: *"Shine On, Hot-Blooded Hero"*
ORIGINAL AIRDATE: *March 14, 1979*
Professor Monster is the BEM as he enlarges to giant-size and takes on Spider-Man himself in this final episode of the series.

Spider-Man and His Amazing Friends

The 1970s proved to be an odd period for Marvel as far as animation was concerned, with only two series based on their properties produced, both of which were based to differing degrees on the Fantastic Four.

The first appeared in 1978 and was simply called *The Fantastic Four*. A more apt title might have been "Three Superheroes and a Robot," because the Human Torch was nowhere to be found, with the "lovable" Herbie the Robot taking his place. The reasons for Herbie's existence, despite the outcry of FF fans, were twofold: first of all, there was some concern on NBC's part that children might try to emulate the Human Torch by setting themselves on fire (not difficult to imagine, as in the fifties there were kids who tied towels around their necks and tried to fly out a window like Superman); and the other, more practical explanation is that the Torch had been licensed as a feature film and therefore was not legally available to the animated series.

The second Marvel project was *Fred and Barney Meet the Thing*—as in Fred Flintstone and Barney Rubble from *The Flintstones*. This series alternated adventures of Fred and Barney with tales of a teenage Ben Grimm, who turned into the Thing by using his "Thing Ring" and uttering the classic phrase, "Thing Ring, Do Your Thing!" Needless to say, the series was aimed at a *very* young audience, though one would love to have been a fly on the wall of the programming meeting that came up with *that* particular idea.

Writer/story editor Christy Marx, whose credits include the TV series *Jem*, *Captain Power and the Soldiers of the Future*, *Babylon 5*, and *Hypernauts*, got her professional start as a television writer on *Spider-Man and His Amazing Friends*. She has vivid memories of the restrictions placed on children's television at the time.

"You can understand that business about the Human Torch," she remarks, "but I do recall being amazed at all the restrictions, some of which seemed just so excruciatingly silly to me at the time. I remember one in particular because, to me, it was just so classic. I can't remember if it was a scene that I wrote or the story editor added, but there was a scene in one of the scripts where one of the characters was going to throw a cream pie into the face of another character. The network note was that we couldn't have the pie thrown directly, but what we could do was have the pie levitate in the air and *then* hit the person in the face. I'm serious. They felt it was imitable behavior, which was the big thing in children's television, and it hasn't changed all that much. When I wrote *Teenage Mutant Ninja Turtles*, it was the same thing. You've got these four characters that are martial artists with weapons, and they can't use them directly on anybody. It all has to be indirect action, and that was years after *Spider-Man*."

These restrictions, she adds, certainly complicated things creatively. "It throws a wrinkle into things." She laughs. "It means that sometimes you have to tie yourself into knots to do something. It means you have to be very inventive and try to find ways to write around things or find indirect ways to accomplish something you otherwise might accomplish very directly. When I did *Conan the Adventurer*, I had a big barbarian with a sword and I couldn't use his sword on anybody. Instead, I had to invent an evil race of lizard men who weren't actually killed by being hit by the sword, but as soon as the magical sword came close to them—poof, they went to another dimension. I also remember that I wrote a kiss between Medusa and Spider-Man, which had to be—here's another incident of concern—a situation where you didn't actually have an on-screen kiss. Instead you have them together and then her hair comes around and conceals them. You know the kiss happened, but you don't see it. It was another one of those silly things.

"So you have to go to extremes to accomplish these things," she elaborates. "There's certainly a long and complex debate you can have concerning what's right to show to children and what isn't. There must be some basis behind the worry about imitable behavior, otherwise it wouldn't be an issue. So it is something to think about, and I think it gets into a much larger debate about children's television. I think that hiding such topics as death and the real consequences of violence from children is not necessarily beneficial. On the other hand, I don't know how great it is to put that stuff in front of children. It's something that I've had to think about an awful lot in recent years and I haven't come to any definite conclusions, to tell you the truth.

"One of my big bugaboos all along," Marx continues, "and this seems to be true everywhere I've worked—whether it be for a toy company, an animation company or even people who have hired me to write comic strips for newspapers—invariably I run into this attitude of having to dumb things down and it drives me absolutely crazy. I just hate to simplify or dumb things down for kids. This is especially true in terms of the use of vocabulary. 'Kids wouldn't know that word.' 'Fine, but how do you think they learn words? By being exposed to them.' I have had this over and over throughout my entire career, and it's one of my hot buttons, it just drives me crazy."

Dumbing down television? Have we mentioned *Fred and Barney Meet the Thing*?

The 1980s saw a return to a slightly older demographic target audience in Marvel's animation efforts and a genuine treat for Spidey fans across the country. The new decade was ushered in by no less than *two* new Spider-Man series produced concurrently: one for first-run syndication and the other for network television. Both series used the same character designs and had similar animation and music. But personality-wise—if such a phrase is applicable to a cartoon—they were worlds apart. *The Amazing Spider-Man*, which didn't premiere until 1982, focused itself squarely on Spider-Man as the main character with Peter Parker's life revolving around his job at the *Daily Bugle*. Unfortunately, the series was pretty formulaic, following the same basic plot each week: Peter Parker is sent to cover a news story, he finds himself embroiled in events (which more often than not involved FF villain Doctor Doom); he changes to Spider-Man and puts an end to the nefarious deeds of that week's villain. Generally speaking, there was nothing setting it apart from any other superhero animated series that had preceded it.

Conversely, the Spider-Man series developed for NBC proved itself to be considerably more intriguing. Premiering a year before the Spider-Man solo series, *Spider-Man and His Amazing Friends* dealt with a slightly younger Peter Parker, who is still going to college while simultaneously working for the *Bugle*. As with the Fantastic Four series from 1978, the network had creative input and set certain parameters for the show. This time, however, the suits weren't looking to exorcise a main character as they had with the Torch, but instead wanted to add superhero characters, perhaps hoping to duplicate ABC's ratings success with the long-running *Super Friends* in its various incarnations. To this end, Bobby Drake (a.k.a. Iceman), an original member of the X-Men team who would later become part of the Defenders in the comic book of the same name, was the first addition to the new Spidey-team. To complement Iceman's power over ice and cold, the character Angelica Jones (a.k.a. Firestar) was created. Angelica was said to be a former member of the X-Men, but that character background does not fit within comic-book continuity. Peter Parker/Spider-Man served as team leader.

The series premise established that the three heroes attend Empire State University in their "civilian" lives and live at Aunt May's house. Also residing with them is the team's mascot, Angelica's pet dog, Ms. Lion (who was intended as the show's comic relief, but quickly became a stereotypical cartoon pet who seems to understand everything spoken to her). Unbeknownst to Aunt May (somehow), Peter managed to rig the room he and Bobby share so that at the flick of a trophy on the mantel, the furniture slides into the walls and floor and is replaced by a "high-tech" crime lab complete with those lumbering eighties computers with the huge tape reels. Not quite stated was that poor Aunt May must have been hit with a severe case of senility, as she failed to stumble across the crime lab or notice the half-disintegrated webbing residue and slowly melting ice slides that must have frequented her property as the team made a hasty departure from the house in pursuit of the villain of the week.

For Christy Marx—a self-proclaimed comic-book "fanatic" who has been reading comics since she began reading—who worked on both of the Spidey series, *Amazing Friends* was a more enjoyable experience due to the fact that there was more than one hero to develop.

"One of the big problems you have with a solo series," she muses, "is having someone there for him to have a conversation with. For a solo Spider-Man that becomes a problem. Mainly you just have Spidey tossing off his own little smart-ass comments when he's fighting with someone or talking to himself a lot. People have different attitudes about that. There are some story editors who absolutely hate having characters talk to themselves, but sometimes you just have to. You can just do so much more when you have the other characters around; you just get so much more mileage out of them when they can bounce stuff off of each other."

The series premiered on September 12, 1981, and was an instant hit with comic book fans and children of all ages. Even up against other Saturday-morning animated shows like *Blackstar, The Fonz and the*

Happy Days Gang (an odd spinoff of *Happy Days* in which the gang stumbles across a time machine from the future that is piloted by a girl named Cupcake, who allows them to have a series of historical adventures), and *The Kid Super Power Hour with Shazam, Spider-Man and His Amazing Friends* was the buzz on the playground and in high school hallways. The show excelled beyond the previous on-screen adventures of the web-slinger, including its sister syndicated series, due to its above-average (for cartoons of the time) writing.

While the basic story lines weren't particularly original, the character interaction was the high point of the show. The constant banter among the three friends was so well scripted that it made the viewer feel extremely comfortable with this group. Admittedly, the teenage angst that was so prevalent in the original comics was gone, replaced by three well-adjusted college buddies who were enjoying themselves—even when in the midst of fighting yet another super-villain hellbent on taking over the world. Believe it or not, there was also an element of sexual tension (relatively speaking) as the characters of Peter Parker and Bobby Drake vied for Angelica's attention. Undoubtedly her skintight costume that left little to the imagination was the constant cause of their teenage testosterone rising to superpowered levels. Yet another highlight was the writers' predilection for incorporating guest superheroes from the

Marvel Universe in an effort to spice up the show and stay away from formulaic storytelling.

Season one of *Spider-Man and His Amazing Friends* comprised a dozen episodes, which offered a healthy mix of story types—some effective and some not. Things started off with the relatively strong "The Return of the Green Goblin," which featured one of Spider-Man's most recognizable arch-villains from the comic books, although slightly repurposed for the show. Things begin as though we haven't been privy to previous battles between Spidey and the Goblin. Norman Osborn is unable to remember his adventures in green, until a near-fatal plane crash not only jolts his memory but allows him to physically transform once again into the Goblin. In the original comic-book series, Norman (and later Harry) Osborn does not transform into the Green Goblin, but instead dons a Goblin mask. This relatively minor change makes Norman a somewhat sympathetic character, more akin to Curt Connors (the Lizard), who is as much a victim of his alter ego as anyone else. The comic-book version of Osborn features a man who is plagued with numerous psychological problems. These result in a personality split between himself and the Green Goblin, which proves considerably more interesting. It's probably safe to assume that this particular notion was considered too complex for the show's intended audience, which is why the

writers went for a simple Jekyll-and-Hyde–type transformation.

This being said, the episode effectively establishes the main characters and their strong friendships with each other. There is one scene in particular that serves as a genuine treat for Marvel Comics fans: a costume party in which everyone is dressed as a different Marvel superhero; a dozen "characters" are represented. This was something that was to happen quite frequently. Guest heroes and villains made the rounds throughout the run of the show.

Doctor Doom, the primary recurring villain of the solo Spider-Man show, appeared in the episode "The Fantastic Mr. Frump." While hardly one of the best episodes in the series, the good doctor proved to be as menacing as ever. That, in itself, is a worthwhile point to make, as it often seems impossible for villains to be true to themselves in these types of settings. Of course, Doom is the complete antithesis to the character of Frump—an old man who finds himself imbued with superpowers when he discovers an amulet Doom had been planning to use to conquer the world. The story focuses primarily on Frump's use and misuse of his powers. Attempts to use this premise as the basis for a series of comedic scenes fell a bit flat.

Another well-known Spider-Man villain, Mysterio, makes his appearance in "Spidey Goes Hollywood" as the Spider-Friends get caught up with his machinations on the set of a movie they are consulting on. Another Marvel character who gets involved is Bruce Banner, better known as the Incredible Hulk. In fact, the entire episode serves as a vehicle for a spinoff starring the Hulk, and when feedback on the episode proved positive, NBC approved a separate half-hour show starring that character to debut the following season.

The Mighty Thor, along with his half-brother and arch-nemesis, Loki, show up in "The Vengeance of Loki," an enjoyable romp through Asgard as Thor and Iceman struggle to return to earth, free Spider-Man and Firestar from Loki's imprisonment, and stop the evil Asgardian trickster from destroying New York disguised as Thor.

One episode that carried a little more substance beyond mere action sequences is "Sunfire," in which Firestar finds herself falling for Sunfire, a mutant whose powers nearly mirror her own. Peter and Bobby instantly distrust Sunfire and do a little investigating to determine if his intentions are honorable. They uncover a plot by Sunfire's uncle to create a fire monster he intends to use to take over the world (a recurring theme on the show, which begs the question, just what in hell would these guys do with the world once they take it over?).

Undoubtedly inspired by Irwin Allen's 1979 disaster film of the same name, was "Swarm." In this episode, a meteor housing an alien intelligence crashes on earth, the being within taking control of a swarm of bees, which it uses to create a body for itself. Swarm was visually exciting as the bees continually buzz about while retaining a basic humanoid outline that gives the character a ghostlike appearance. Unfortunately, the plotline deteriorates into yet another world-conquest scenario.

"Seven Little Superheroes" proved to be the high point of the season. The Chameleon, Spider-Man's oldest enemy (he appeared in the first issue of *Amazing Spider-Man*), concocts a plan to trap seven superheroes on an island in order to dispose of them. In addition to the three Spider-Friends, Chameleon traps Captain America, Doctor Strange, the Sub-Mariner and Shannah the She-Devil. While the latter was an odd choice as she was never a very popular character in the comics, the other three guest heroes made the episode something special. Naturally, the seven prisoners figure out what's going on, but before they can, the Chameleon uses his powers to impersonate them one by one so that they will go into battle against each other. The episode's denouement, unfortunately, is a major disappointment. Spidey ends up being the only one to evade the Chameleon's traps, and he ultimately defeats the shape-changing villain with the help of Ms. Lion, Firestar's dog. The episode serves as a perfect example of how the "cute" Ms. Lion is portrayed in the series as a super-intelligent dog who serves as an integral character. It's painful to watch and difficult to stomach.

Over a decade prior to *Jurassic Park*, Kraven the Hunter grew his own dinosaurs in order to hunt them and test his mettle in the episode "The Crime of All Centuries." Kraven, another well-known villain from the Spider-Man comics, makes his transition to the world of animation with a little adjustment. The episode is interesting in that Firestar proves to be the one who evades capture and saves the day, a nice move away from Spider-Man serving his usual role. This particular story is a good example of the healthy mix of action, humor, and character development that made this series stand apart from the majority of animated superhero shows on television at the time.

Magneto, the master of magnetism and arch-nemesis of the X-Men, makes an appearance in "The Prison Plot" as he attempts to free fellow Brotherhood of Evil Mutant members Toad and Mastermind from incarceration. The Spider-Friends find themselves caught up in the middle of Magneto's prison break and manage to put an end to his plans. Unfortunately, Magneto is reduced to a parody of the character that gave the X-Men comic books such depth. Gone is the self-proclaimed champion of mutant rights who seeks to free his fellow mutants from persecution by mankind. Also absent is any ambiguity of the character's personal moral code. Here,

Magneto is reduced to yet another power-hungry megalomaniac.

Captain America makes another appearance, as does his archenemy, the Red Skull. But instead of playing off of their longtime relationship dating back to World War II, which saw the Skull working for Hitler while Cap fought to keep America free, the decision was made to have them appear in two completely separate episodes. "Pawns of the Kingpin" saw Spider-Man's old foe using a mind-control device to instruct Captain America to steal a powerful military weapon. "The Quest of the Red Skull" turned out to be a slightly more interesting story, involving the Skull's attempt to locate a secret Nazi storehouse containing deadly experimental weapons. The character of Hiawatha Smith in this episode could easily have been rewritten for Captain America, thus adding much more depth to the Skull's character. Nonetheless, it stands as a decent adventure featuring a chase through the jungles of Africa and climaxes with our heroes strapped to rockets, about to be launched in an effort to trigger World War III (a very 1930s Saturday-morning serial-style cliffhanger).

The first season also introduced the only villain destined to pop up in all three years of the series—Video Man. In an effort to capitalize on the growing interest in arcade video games and home video game systems like Atari and Intellivision, the writers invented a villain who literally steps out of a video game to fight our heroes. In the story, Electro, another longtime Spidey adversary, uses his powers of electricity to draw Video Man out of an arcade game and into the "real" world. Admittedly, there's never an explanation as to how he manages to pull this off or how Video Man obtains the power to transport people into video games, but that's par for the course in the world of children's cartoons. Interestingly, Video Man himself was given a "two-dimensional" look in that he had height and width but no depth. He also seems to be constructed of the same large, blocky pixels that Atari used to create images in its video games (which never turned out looking anything like the original game versions). An interesting subplot in the episode had Flash Thompson (Peter's eternal rival) discovering Firestar's true identity as Angelica Jones. Naturally, in typical soap-opera fashion, this plotline was wrapped up with a convenient bout of amnesia on Flash's part.

Spider-Man and His Amazing Friends' second season began in September 1982 and found itself paired up with the newly created Hulk series. Instead of airing them as two distinct shows, NBC opted for a combined one-hour program titled *The Incredible Hulk and the Amazing Spider-Man.* This allowed them to air a full season of thirteen Hulk episodes while only commissioning four new *Spider-Man and His Amazing Friends* episodes, which were alternated with recycled shows from year one. At the same time, Stan Lee was hired to do voice-over narration for the new episodes in his traditional over-the-top style that hadn't changed one bit in over two decades of involvement with Marvel Comics. While the Hulk series turned out to be rather bland and ultimately was not renewed for another season, these four Spider-Man episodes proved to be the best in the series' three-year run.

Early on, a decision was made that since there would be so few episodes produced in year two, a little more would be spent on the animation (which is very obvious to the viewers' eyes) and the stories would each be a little more special. Three of the four focused on the origins of one of the Spider-Friends, beginning with Iceman, whose story was told in the aptly titled "The Origin of Iceman." When Bobby Drake finds that he is losing his powers, the gang heads for the Empire State University science lab where they just happen to have a nifty memory probe with which Peter and Angelica can look back through Bobby's memories to see if they hold any clues as to why his powers are failing him. The probe doesn't turn up anything, but does allow the viewer to quickly look at how Bobby discovered his powers and learned to use them. By far the most interesting clip is the one showing Iceman as part of the X-Men, all wearing the old black-and-yellow costumes that adorned the team when the comic book began in the early sixties (although Iceman did *not* look like a snowman as he had in those comic books). Things deteriorate drama-wise when the team discovers that Video Man is behind the loss of power, which is achieved by draining the electrical energy from Bobby's brain. This nonsensical plot device is used against Firestar as well, who begins experiencing a similar loss of power. A quick jaunt to the video world by Bobby allows him to defeat the computer villain using his own video creations.

"A Firestar Is Born" followed, delving into Angelica's past and detailing her origin. This particular episode is generally considered the best the series had to offer, and with good reason. Not only was the audience entertained by another origin story, but the writers cleverly utilized the ever-growing popularity of the X-Men by having Firestar turn out to be a former member of that team as well. The episode actually begins with Firestar and Iceman attending an X-Men reunion, and we are introduced to Professor Xavier, Wolverine, Storm, Cyclops, and Angel. The villain of the story is X-Men nemesis Juggernaut, who is also Professor X's half-brother. For once (thankfully) the villain is *not* concerned with world domination; he merely wants revenge. Firestar's personal tale, which she shares with Peter and Bobby, is one of teenage angst, in which Angelica's struggle to control her powers results in her becoming an outcast among her peers. She ulti-

mately manages to gain control of her powers and, in the process, develops the self-confidence she needs to overcome the adversity she faces. The X-Men, as portrayed in this episode, look great. They left viewers screaming for an X-Men spinoff, which eventually came to pass.

The third new episode of year two was "Along Came a Spidey," which retold the character's familiar origin story, with a few minor updates and changes. Peter's recounting of the events leading up to his assuming the identity of Spider-Man is brought on by feelings of guilt when the Shocker, another villain stripped from the pages of the comic-book, causes Aunt May to be injured. Peter finally realizes that his initial reason for becoming Spider-Man— the axiom that with great power comes great responsibility—still holds true to this day, and he proceeds to stop the Shocker. Aunt May, of course, recovers. While most comic-book fans were already familiar with Spider-Man's origin, the episode lent a much more updated feel to the story and rounded out the origin trilogy of episodes.

"Knights and Demons" was the final new episode of the season. It had none of the distinction of its predecessors. The animation maintained year two's high quality, but the plot was a thinly veiled attempt to capitalize on the popularity of Dungeons and Dragons (even the title was similar). A Marvel character called Black Knight was the guest star du jour as he helps the Spider-

Friends put a stop to the evil sorcerer, Modred.

The show returned for a third and final season in 1983, once again retitled. Now the show was called *The Amazing Spider-Man and The Incredible Hulk*. No new Hulk episodes were produced that year, though there were eight new *Spider-Man and His Amazing Friends* shows. While that number was twice that of the year before, the quality, both in scripting and animation, was considerably lower. The majority of these new episodes were hardly memorable and begged the question: Why bother?

Among the low-level episodes was "Mission: Save the Guardstar," in which the Spider-Friends find themselves caught in a plot by a S.H.I.E.L.D. agent who is controlling the mind of an ex-agent called Lightwave (who turns out to be Bobby's half-sister). The agent is attempting to gain control of a powerful satellite called the Guardstar, with which he can control the world (of course). In "Spider-Man Unmasked," the Sandman learns Spidey's true identity only to be fooled later into thinking he was mistaken, when the gang arranges for Sandman to see Peter Parker alongside Spider-Man (who is, in reality, Flash Thompson in a Spidey costume).

One of the worst episodes of the series was "Spidey Meets the Girl from Tomorrow." Peter falls in love with an alien from a distant galaxy in the future named Ariel. Together they try to stop Doctor Octopus from gaining control of her timeship. Peter returns with Ariel to her time period, only to find out that the "Earth germs" he carries would be deadly to her people. Peter is given the temporal boot back to his own time; he is brokenhearted. Surprisingly, this is the first episode of the series to feature Doctor Octopus.

"Attack of the Arachnoid" finds Spider-Man being impersonated by an evil scientist named Zoltan, who has used a spider-serum he created to give him similar powers to Spider-Man. A slew of Spider-Man's villains appear in cameos when Spidey is locked up in prison. The most ridiculous moment here is that Spider-Man is not unmasked when he's thrown in jail, nor are any of his adversaries, who are in their cells in full super-villain regalia. Matt Murdock (Daredevil) makes an appearance representing Spider-Man in court. Zoltan's formula eventually transforms him into a human-spider hybrid, which is only stopped by a handy antidote that Peter whips up.

"The Transylvania Connection" (later renamed "The Bride of Dracula" in reruns) has Firestar falling for a charming stranger who turns out to be Count Dracula himself. Unfortunately, the story degrades into a poor parody of *Abbott & Costello Meet Frankenstein* when the Spider-Friends are forced not only to fight Dracula, but also the Wolfman and Frankenstein's Monster. Ugh!

There were only three episodes worth noting in the show's last year. The first was "The X-Men Adventure," which was planned to serve as the pilot for an X-Men spinoff series in much the same way that the season one episode "Spidey Goes Hollywood" led to the Hulk series. This time out, the X-Men are revamped, consisting of Professor X, Cyclops, Colossus, Storm, Sprite, and Thunderbird (a character who appeared twice in the comics before being killed off, and who has powers completely altered for this episode). While having the X-Men in the story garnered it much attention by comics fans, the actual story line was abysmal. The Spider-Friends are hanging out with the X-Men when a cyborg attacks. He turns out to be Nathan Price, a former love of Angelica's who has gone mad due to an accident that transformed him. The teams split up in an attempt to stop Price's villainy, but it is ultimately Firestar who defeats him. The character of Price is poorly developed and never comes across as sympathetic, which completely undermines the emotional angst that Angelica is supposedly going through when she confronts her former lover.

"Education of a Superhero" is another sub-par episode, worth noting only because it played a part in the proposed X-Men spinoff series. In this episode, a video game fanatic named Francis Byte gets so far in playing the Video Man arcade game that it brings Video Man to life (by far the most bizarre superhero origin story in the series). Video Man is now a superhero fighting alongside the Spider-Friends. He ultimately joins the X-Men in order to learn how to better utilize his powers. The original plan was to have Video Man serve as a team member on the new X-Men series. Unfortunately (or fortunately, depending on your point of view), the X-Men series did not get the green light. In fact, five years later a new pilot, "Pryde of the X-Men," was produced, which featured beautiful animation (done in Japan) and a decent story. That, too, was not developed into a series. The X-Men finally did get their own show in 1992, which ran 76 episodes stretched out over six years. This series, however, was horribly animated (with only a few exceptions) and ranged from mediocre stories adapted from the comic books to horrendous original tales.

The final episode of the series, "Origin of the Spider-Friends," was another origin story, detailing how the three heroes first teamed up and began their combined fight against crime. Another Spider-Man villain from the comics, the Beetle, steals a new invention by Tony Stark (Iron Man). The three heroes get involved with the events that ultimately result in a new friendship and partnership and a reward from Stark— a crime-fighting lab that can be hidden neatly in Peter's room (finally explaining how that complex setup found its way into Aunt May's house).

Over the course of its run, *Spider-Man and His Amazing Friends* turned out a few gems along with the clunkers. Overall, it was an entertaining series with true characters—something that always seemed to be lacking from previous animated superhero endeavors. The series is, on the whole, fondly remembered by comic-book fans to this day. Undoubtedly, the Spider-Man feature will rekindle nostalgic interest on the part of Spidey fans around the globe.

In assessing the character's enduring popularity—and the fondness people have for *Amazing Friends*—Christy Marx notes, "Probably the most unique thing about Spider-Man, certainly when he started out, was that he departed very much from the standard superhero. He wasn't extremely powerful, but he had sort of quirky powers. He didn't have the Superman problem of being too powerful. He was a more down-to-earth kind of character. The fact that he was basically a kid, inexperienced, a smart-ass and a loner, I think made him the perfect anti-hero for the times. Although he was a hero, he wasn't part of a group, he wasn't somebody that spouted platitudes, he was just more like your regular person who has gained powers, and this is what he ends up doing with them. Basically, he wasn't a cookie-cutter character.

"I think we were pretty true to the character," she emphasizes. "It seemed to me that we were. Now, currently, it seems that there are huge departures from what was originally there in an attempt to update them. But certainly at the time, there was no feeling of needing to update it. He was still very contemporary and worked the way he was."

Episode Guide

VOICE CAST: Dan Gilvezan (Peter Parker/Spider-Man), Frank Welker (Iceman), Kathy Garver (Firestar), June Foray (Aunt May), Dennis Marks (Green Goblin), Michael Bell (Doctor Octopus), Hans Conried (the Chameleon), Peter Cullen (Bruce Banner/the Hulk), Jerry Dexter (Sunfire), George Dicenzo (Captain America), Stanley Jones (Professor X), Sally Julian (Mona Osborne), Chris Latta (the Sandman), Keye Luke (Sunfire's uncle, Jin Ju), William Marshall (Juggernaut), Alan Melvin (Video Man), Shepard Menkin (Doctor Doom), Robert Rigley (Kraven), Neil Ross (Cyclops, Norman Osborn), Michael Rye (Magneto), John Stephenson (Colossus, Thunderbird, Uncle Ben), Frank Welker (the Vision, Flash Thompson, Ms. Lion), William Woodson (J. Jonah Jameson), Alan Young (Mr. Frump)

SEASON ONE

EPISODE 1: *"Triumph of the Green Goblin"*
Written by Dennis Marks
Reverting to his alter ego of the Green Goblin, Norman Osborn hatches a plan to poison the New York reservoir with his goblin serum to create a race of people just like him.

EPISODE 2: *"The Fantastic Mr. Frump"*
Written by Christy Marx
When an old man named Mr. Frump discovers an amulet on the streets of New York, he suddenly finds himself endowed with incredible powers. Doctor Doom, who has planned on using the amulet for himself, essentially manipulates Frump into doing his bidding.

EPISODE 3: *"Sunfire"*
Written by Christy Marx
Shortly after Firestar meets a mutant with similar powers to hers named Sunfire, the two of them team up with Iceman and Spider-Man to battle a bizarre fire creature.

EPISODE 4: *"Spidey Goes Hollywood"*
Written by Christy Marx
Spider-Man is hired by a Hollywood producer to star in a movie about himself. Unfortunately, production is disrupted by a series of accidents and the lives of the Spider-Friends are in danger, thanks to the machinations of Mysterio, who also pulls the Incredible Hulk into the mix.

EPISODE 5: *"Quest of the Red Skull"*
Written by Dennis Marks
The Spider-Friends go after Captain Amer-

ica's archenemy the Red Skull to stop him from locating a hidden cache of high-tech weapons that had been developed by Nazi scientists.

EPISODE 6: *"Seven Little Superheroes"*
Written by Doug Booth
The Spider-Friends find themselves as well as Captain America, Doctor Strange, Sub-Mariner, and Shanna the She-Devil on a mysterious island where they are being manipulated by the Chameleon.

EPISODE 7: *"Swarm"*
Written by Dennis Marks
When a meteor crashes on earth, an entity from within it takes physical form by using a swarm of bees. From there he begins using his mysterious powers to transform other innocents into bee people.

EPISODE 8: *"Pawns of the Kingpin"*
Written by Donald F. Glut
The Spider-Friends go up against the King-pin, who's attempting to get his hands on a new military weapon known as the Omni-Blaster.

EPISODE 9: *"The Vengeance of Loki"*
Written by Donald F. Glut
When the mighty Thor shows up, the god of thunder teams up with Spider-Man, Firestar, and Iceman to stop Thor's half-brother, Loki, from obtaining a gem that will make him all-powerful.

EPISODE 10: *"The Crime of All Centuries"*
Written by Donald F. Glut
Kraven the Hunter tries to use Firestar's power combined with a sacred ruby to regenerate a dinosaur army that he will have complete control over.

EPISODE 11: *"Prison Plot"*
Written by Francis Peighan and Jack Hanrahan
The Spider Trio must do whatever they can to thwart Magneto's plans to free a number of evil mutants from prison.

EPISODE 12: *"Videoman"*
Written by Christy Marx
Electro's creation, Video Man, uses his powers to imprison Iceman and Firestar in an arcade game, and it's up to Spider-Man to free them before it's too late.

SEASON TWO

EPISODE 13: *"The Origin of Iceman"*
Written by Donald F. Glut
The title says it all (see discussion of this episode in main section on *Spider-Man and His Amazing Friends*).

EPISODE 14: *"A Firestar Is Born"*
Written by Christy Marx
The origin of Firestar (see discussion of this episode in main section on the series).

EPISODE 15: *"Along Came a Spider"*
Written by Donald F. Glut
A framing story involving the Shocker serves as a means of retelling Spider-Man's origin.

EPISODE 16: *"Knights and Demons"*
Written by Donald F. Glut
The Spider-Friends travel to another dimension to stop a sorcerer known as Modred from coming to earth.

SEASON THREE

EPISODE 17: *"Mission: Save the Guardstar"*
Written by Dennis Marks
A mutant named Lightwave is attempting to obtain control of a satellite, known as Guardstar, with which she can dominate the world. There is also an enigmatic relationship between her and Iceman that Spidey and Firestar are desperate to figure out.

EPISODE 18: *"Spider-Man Unmasked"*
Written by Michael Reaves
Shortly after the Spider-Friends save swimmers from a school of sharks, they find themselves going up against the Sandman.

EPISODE 19: *"Girl from Tomorrow"*
Written by Dennis Marks
When a pair of time travelers arrive on earth, Doctor Octopus plans on stealing their vehicle so he can manipulate history to suit his own means.

EPISODE 20: *"Attack of the Arachnoid"*
Written by Michael Reaves
Spider-Man finds himself arrested for crimes committed by a scientist named Zoltan, who has developed a spider-serum that gives him powers similar to that of the web-crawler.

EPISODE 21: *"The X-Men Adventure"*
Written by Michael Reaves
The Spider-Friends and the X-Men team up to battle Cyberiad, a cyborg that is intent on killing them all.

EPISODE 22: *"The Education of a Superhero"*
Written by Dennis Marks
Video Man becomes a good guy as he teams up with the Spider-Friends to stop Gamesman, a being determined to hypnotize young people and use them to carry out crimes for him.

EPISODE 23: *"The Transylvania Connection"*
Written by Jack Mendelsohn
In a nutshell, the Spider-Friends take on the king of the undead, Dracula.

EPISODE 24: *"Origin of the Spider-Friends"*
Written by Donald F. Glut
An exploration of how the team came together for the first time.

Spider-Man: The Animated Series

Every so often it becomes obvious that creative personnel have gotten their endeavor—whatever form it might take—absolutely right. In 1964, it was the James Bond thriller *Goldfinger* that seemed to lock onto a film-making formula that successfully paved the way for a film series that continues to this day. In 1978, it was the moment that an unknown actor named Christopher Reeve made you believe that a man could fly in *Superman: The Movie*. In the mid-1990s, it was *Spider-Man: The Animated Series*, the finest adaptation of the wall-crawler ever attempted.

"I was very proud of *Spider-Man*, because my goal was to create the kind of experience that I had when I first read the comics in the 1960s," explains John Semper, who served as producer and story editor (i.e., "head writer") of the series. "Then when I went back and reread the comics, I realized that the storytelling, which had worked for the comic books, wasn't going to work for television once you brought them to screen verbatim. The real trick for me was to try and create the same feeling you got from reading those comics, while telling different stories. I didn't want people to feel that we were really deviating from the essence of what had happened with Spider-Man in the sixties. Consequently, a lot of people came to me and said, 'You really did a great job of adapting

that comic.' Most of those stories were original when you get right down to it, especially when you get past season one. But it still captured the right feeling. It worked for the kids and it worked for the grown-ups. I was happy with the end results, though I was not happy working on the show."

By the time *Spider-Man: The Animated Series* debuted in November 1994, the landscape of Saturday-morning children's television had changed. Indeed, all one has to do is compare *Spider-Man and His Amazing Friends* to the newer show to see the differences. Gone for the most part were childish plotlines, and *Super Friends*–like shows, in which Superman, Batman, and Wonder Woman were joined by the Wonder Twins and their oh-so-funny dog. Things had grown somewhat grittier and arguably more adult thanks to *Batman: The Animated Series*, which, ironically, eventually touched off a call for less violence in children's television.

"When *Spider-Man* came along, there really was a preexisting standard, which was *Batman*," Semper reflects. "*Batman* had kind of gone through a very painful birth to get itself to the point of being what it was. When a show is trying to be something that no one has ever seen before, that's a hard birth, and there was a lot of blood spilled on that show. There were a lot of people hired and fired, who felt that they had put a lot of time and effort into that show but were not with it when it finally got going. I think that's the hard birth of anything that truly tries to break new ground. I say break new ground, but they did have the Tim Burton movie, which was the inspiration for everything that they did. They also had Frank Miller's comics as a template and the comic book itself from the early years as a template. But for Saturday morning, they were really trying to do something pretty unique and different." And they were successful, ushering in a new (albeit short-lived) era of edgy animation that led to some innovative programming, among them HBO's animated version of *Spawn*, and the Warner Brothers efforts *Superman: The Animated Series* and *Batman Beyond*, and Cartoon Network's *Justice League*.

One person who took fiscal interest in these successes—particularly the merchandising bonanza that greeted the Batman features as well as its animated spinoffs—was Avi Arad, whose company, Toy Biz, had acquired Marvel Comics. It was Arad's opinion that Marvel, given its library of characters, should be enjoying equal opportunity in the marketplace. To this end, he began putting together the latest animated incarnation of Spider-Man, which Fox Broadcasting—the home of *Batman: The Animated Series* until it was brought "home" by Warner Brothers to the WB—expressed interest in.

In an effort to hedge his bets, Arad brought in Emmy Award–winning writer Martin Pasko, who was coming off of the animated Batman and who had made a name for himself in comics. It was Pasko's job to essentially write the show's bible and bring its scripts together.

"This writer," who Semper himself doesn't mention by name, "was hired with plenty of time to develop the show and given the mandate to just go out there and do the best show possible. He was the guy who was going to bring them to Superhero Valhalla. Now this guy might have done a perfectly wonderful Spider-Man show. The problem is that in this business, when you are placed in charge of a show—and so many people don't realize that this is why so many shows suck—the majority of your time is spent dealing with politics. If you're not a political animal, you can't do this work, because the creative stuff only begins *after* the politics have ended. So you spend all of your day dealing with people and their egos and their insanity, and *then* you have to go home and do the creative stuff. Basically you have three hours of politics and one hour of creativity. So I'd have to fight with people a lot, but do it in such a way that I could continue to work with them. Then I'd go in my room with my writers and we'd beat out a story. If you can't do both, then you can't run a show. It's that simple. Especially a show as dysfunctional as *Spider-Man*. Well, my predecessor apparently could not do both. He was probably an extremely talented, wonderful writer, but my guess is that politically he might have been in way over his head."

During *Spider-Man*'s earliest days of development, Semper, a writer with an extensive background in comedy (*Scooby Doo, Fraggle Rock*, the live-action feature *Class Act*), was working on the PBS series *Puzzle Palace* when he read an item in *Variety* about the Spider-Man series going into production.

"When you read something like that," he muses, "you always experience that whole pang of, 'God, that's what I always wanted to do.' I went through that and I read who it was that was going to do it. I had met this person many years earlier when he was riding high, prior to doing *Batman*. In fact, he had a fairly extensive live-action career and I thought to myself, 'I don't know if that person is actually a very political animal. I don't know if he's going to be able to handle actually running a high-profile show like that all by himself.' That was my first thought. My second was, 'Wouldn't it be great if he failed miserably?'—because that's the way writers *really* think."

Semper nearly got the gig at that time. Stan Lee called him shortly thereafter, explaining that things might not be working out with the writer they'd hired, and that Semper was someone he'd like on the show. Managing to keep his excitement in check,

Semper did not end up disappointed when he learned that the other writer actually was staying with the series, though as it turned out his tenure wouldn't last all that long.

"What happened," says Semper, "and I understand this now, which is why I say he can't be blamed, is that the people working on the show were horrible. They were insane. Please quote me. They were simply nasty people. There was so much fighting going on between them that, quite honestly, I think they drove him close to a nervous breakdown."

Eventually, Semper's phone started to ring, and it was Lee on the other end, stating that things hadn't worked out with the other guy and that they wanted to bring him in. Although he was weary of the obvious political machinations taking place, he nonetheless decided to take the offer.

"So I walk in, sort of dumb and happy, ready to do this show," he says. "The reality about me is that if you ask me to do anything, I can do anything. If you ask me tomorrow to do a script for *The West Wing*, I'd watch a bunch of episodes and write a *West Wing*. That's how I've kept myself alive in this business. But you can't ever tell anyone that. You can't say, 'Oh, I can write anything,' and expect them to believe you. I had not technically done an action/adventure show in Saturday-morning animation, but if you had asked me what I would have come out here to do in the beginning, I would have said, 'Oh, action/adventure.' I really only got sidetracked into comedy and preschool. I knew action/adventure better than I knew anything else. Everything else I've had to learn, but I was ready to do action/adventure. So, I felt fairly ready to do this show.

"I definitely felt that this was an opportunity to do Spider-Man the way Spider-Man should be done," Semper elaborates. "That was exciting. It was an opportunity to bring to the screen—and I've said this before—the kind of thing that was going on in the comic book when the comic book really got going. Good drama, a realistic sense of a very unreal thing—of what a superhero was, if in fact a superhero existed—good storytelling, and the two words that would get me into a lot of trouble: *soap opera*. I remember that's what made Spider-Man my favorite comic book. I loved the characterizations, I liked the stories, and I loved the soap-opera aspect. I thought, 'Well, if I'm ever going to get a chance to do that, this was probably it.'"

Working on Spider-Man had been one of his dreams, particularly when he went to work for Marvel Productions in the early 1980s. At that point, the company was an animation outfit that was producing television shows for Hasbro, such as *G. I. Joe*, *Transformers*, and *Defenders of the Earth*, the last a series that teamed up, among others, Mandrake the Magician, Flash Gordon, and the Phantom. "It was the closest I'd come to doing anything comic book

related," he says. "But that company was a total disaster. It ultimately went out of business." Two of the perks of that job, however, were that the company was called Marvel and that Stan Lee had an office in the same building.

"The whole time I was there," he states, "I would chat with Stan, who really is a brilliant guy, and fantasize about doing Spider-Man. So I thought [*Spider-Man: The Animated Series*] was going to be an opportunity to really fulfill that dream. Through all the difficulty of working on that show—and it was the most difficult show I'd ever worked on—that was the thing that kept me alive. Every once in a while I had to look at myself in the mirror and say, 'Hey, damn, I'm doing *Spider-Man* and I'm doing it the way I've always wanted to do it. That's pretty damn cool.' In my career, I always have to take the good with the bad. Or the bad with the good. But the good was *so* good that it didn't matter how bad the bad was. And it was horrible, but it didn't matter, because I knew that what would end up on-screen would be the most true to the comic-book form of Spider-Man that I could manage to get out the door, despite all the production drawbacks."

When Semper arrived for his first day at work, he was met by impressive posters of Spider-Man that were hanging virtually everywhere, announcing that Spidey would be coming to television in the fall. Excited, he greeted Virginia Ruth, his new story coordinator, and asked to be brought up to speed. Unfortunately, to his surprise, there wasn't anything to tell. All that his predecessor had done was write a bible for the show, but instead of being a concise breakdown of the series' characters and settings, it was an exhaustive history of the character in the comic books—essentially useless as a blueprint for a new TV series. Even worse, there were no scripts written for the show.

"I began to realize that nothing had been done," he says, "and the reason nothing was done is that nobody could agree on anything. Then I started to become aware of the political undertones. What I soon found out was that *everybody* was at odds."

According to the writer, egos were running rampant, with various producers and TV executives at odds over who should be doing what, and which production entities should have final say. *Spider-Man: The Animated Series* brought an all-new meaning to the term *creative differences*. "If all I had to do every day was deal with the politics, that would have been a full-time job all by itself," says Semper. "But the problem was, I also had to get a show out the door and the show had to be good. My ability to keep getting employed in this town is based on what people see on the screen, not what goes on behind the scenes. The fact that I survived the politics of the show is meaningless, because all anyone responds to now so many years later is whether or not the film looks any good, whether the stories are any

good. That's the hard part. Somewhere in the middle of all that bullshit you have to find the time to write, to conceptualize, work with other writers and get them to do their best work, because every other writer that arrives on the scene, no matter how good they are, once they see the absurd chaos going on all around them, all they're interested in is the paycheck. So you have to inspire them to do their best work; you have to deal with their egos and emotions. I really had two lives on *Spider-Man*. One was dealing with the politics, which were ridiculous, but the other one was dealing with myself and my team of writers and trying to get the best show out the door. That was the *real* challenge."

Politically, throughout the first season things on *Spider-Man* were positively volatile. Semper admits that he was stunned by the duplicity all around him, and eventually got word that a plan was afoot for his executive producers to fire him after the first thirteen episodes. Deciding to take matters into his own hands, he chose to play political hardball and more or less performed a bit of manipulation of his own, pitting Fox against the decisions of the execs, which ultimately led (once the dust settled) to Semper keeping his position for the rest of the show's sixty-five–episode run. "Ultimately, it was Avi's decision to renew me, and, to his credit, he did. We eventually got into a good working rhythm on the show, and he started to trust me more. For a while we had a nice collaboration, and that's when the show really took off. Avi has wild ideas—mostly for individual scenes—and my job was to put them into some kind of shape. And they weren't bad ideas. Once he started giving me more freedom, I could fit his ideas into my story structure. It was the best of both worlds. But always there were people whispering in his ear that everything I was doing was 'all wrong' and that I should be suppressed in some way. So I always had to fight that."

Creatively, Semper went about designing what he hoped would be the best version of Spider-Man to date, capturing the essence of the comics as well as the character itself. "Truthfully," he says, "you can't really do Stan's comics, brilliant as they are, on television, because they don't work. They were written for a different medium. But you can get close. That's why in our Lizard episode Spider-Man is really talking all the way through. I remember a few people complaining about that, but I thought, 'Yeah, but that's Spider-Man; that's just the way it is. You've got to play the character right.' He's Hamlet. He's constantly having these monologues with himself, these interior monologues. Spider-Man is ultimately all about teenage angst and it's really about nothing else. The villainy is pretty straightforward. You kind of have a little bit of fun when you get to the Green Goblin and all that stuff, but it's really about a teenager who's wrestling with every problem that teenagers wrestle with. If you

lose that focus, you really lose Spider-Man. If you try to make Spider-Man about the powers and the web-slinging, it really doesn't differentiate him from any other superhero out there. In this over-saturated superhero world in which we live, that gets to be a problem. He starts to look a little dated. But if you keep him firmly rooted in the teenage stuff, in the coming-of-age stuff, then you stay very close to what the original spirit of the character was."

His other ambition was to deviate from previous Spider-Man shows by creating a serialized form of storytelling rather than just a series of stand-alone episodes. This was met with a lot of resistance.

"The person who was really against it at first was Avi," he says incredulously. "He wanted every episode to be self-contained. Avi was dead set against soap opera, because all he could think about was *Robotech*, and they had tried to do serial storytelling with *Robotech*. The cartoon and the toy line failed miserably, so the attitude was that, therefore, you can't do serial stuff. I was adamant. I said, 'No, that's what the fans want out of Spider-Man.' But in the beginning, I lost that battle, and so in the first season the episodes were self-contained. To me, it's boring to know that Spider-Man is going to meet a villain, some stuff will happen in the middle and he'll defeat the villain in the end.

"To go off on a tangent for a moment," continues Semper, "a lot of people don't know this, but *Batman: The Animated Series* did not set the world on fire in the ratings. Never was a big hit. The reason Warners continued making it was because they branched off and created their own network. If you remember, *Batman* began on Fox and then segued over to Warners. Because it was an established franchise, they kept making new episodes. But *Spider-Man* routinely beat the spandex off of *Batman*. You may not remember this, but when they premiered *Superman*, they put it on opposite *Spider-Man* and *Superman* failed so miserably that in order to keep it alive they had to pair it up with *Batman* as the *Superman/Batman Hour*. Then they had to take that show away from being on opposite *Spider-Man*, because *Spider-Man* was clobbering it."

In his opinion, one of the problems with the *Batman* series was that after the initial thrill of the show's look and character style, things fairly quickly fell into a bit of repetition. "By the time you got to the fifth episode," he muses, "you were all done. Why did you need to keep watching? That bothered me. I knew we were not going to get the same kind of money to spend, so it was going to look more like the *X-Men* series rather than *Batman*. But *X-Men*'s talented head writer, Eric Lewald, was getting number-one ratings with continuing story lines for the most part, so I knew we had to do that, too. And sure enough, *X-Men* and *Spider-Man* were always in a virtual tie for number one on Saturday mornings."

His short-term response to the rejection of his desire for serialized scenarios was to propose a number of two-parters in the first season. Although Arad was reluctant, he ultimately gave in—thanks, again, to a bit of manipulation on Semper's part.

"What was my first two-parter? 'The Spider-Slayers.' Why? Because Avi had a toy line coming out called Spider Slayers." He laughs. "So I went to Avi and said, 'Guess what? We can do a two-parter based on your toys,' and he said, 'Oh, I like that idea.' To a great extent, from Avi's perspective, these shows were designed to sell his toy line, so any time I wanted to push something through, if I could wrap it around one of his goofy toys, then all of a sudden it would happen.

"Pretty easy, huh?" Semper adds with a laugh. "Connect the dots. You, too, can run a show."

Figuring out how to play the game, Semper found himself more and more able to craft the kind of series he felt the Spider-Man character deserved. In the end, *Spider-Man: The Animated Series* truly was the best adaptation of the character to date, with flesh-and-blood human beings for characters. Additionally, beginning with year two, there were also season-long story arcs that allowed for genuine story development that mirrored—in tone if not in detail—many of the early comic-book scenarios, a number of which had spanned four or five issues. As such, *Spider-Man* became the example to which all other adaptations of the wall-crawler would be compared.

Interestingly, the one aspect of the comic books that Semper avoided—despite its immense popularity—was Peter Parker's romance with Gwen Stacy, as well as her death at the hands of the Green Goblin. Instead, he elected to go with Felicia Harding (who was beefed up significantly from her vague persona in the comic books), and then ultimately led Spider-Man, as was the case in the comics, to love and marriage with Mary Jane Watson.

"I didn't use Gwen on this show, because everything with Gwen would ultimately have to lead to her dying," he says. "We can't do dying on Saturday morning. The *Batman* guys always managed to get away with stuff like that, but they always managed to get away, quite literally, with murder. They did everything we weren't supposed to do—everything I was absolutely told not to do by the censors. What happened with *Batman* initially was when they did the first season, I think the censorship was a bit looser. By the time I started *Spider-Man*, Fox was having trouble placing their shows in Canada, which was banning shows like *Mighty Morphin' Power Rangers*. Fox was being really skittish about violence and they didn't want to take any chances. So all the stuff the *Batman* guys had been doing, we suddenly couldn't do. Then *Batman* moved over to the WB network, so you've got Warner Brothers making car-

toons for the WB network, and there never seemed to be any censorship on those guys whatsoever.

"Whenever I watch an episode of *Batman*, within the first three minutes I see two or three things I could never do—fists to the jaw, punches to the face, people being thrown through glass, anything having to do with fire, children in jeopardy, and so on," Semper continues. "I would always get letters from viewers saying, 'How come Spider-Man doesn't hit anybody?' I was absolutely told I could not do that. So I couldn't do what they did, yet I got better ratings. Their show went on to win Emmys and ran for years and years, because Warner Brothers wisely saw the sense in keeping the franchise going. My show, which routinely beat *Batman* in the ratings and certainly clobbered *Superman*—not only did it end with sixty-five episodes, thanks to corporate stupidity, but it really was a show that from the beginning had far more restrictions on it than any of those Warner Brothers shows did. The original *Batman* has always received kudos and *Spider-Man* has not, yet *Spider-Man*, as far as I'm concerned, was the better show from a storytelling point of view. Not that I'm biased or bitter or anything..." He laughs.

Made better, he emphasizes, from the time he was allowed to guide the series the way that he had originally envisioned it. "When I got approval from Avi to do the elaborate continuing story line for season two," he says, "it was the greatest moment, as far as I'm concerned, of his involvement with the show. He had the power to stop me cold in my tracks, but he didn't, and I'll always be grateful for that. That was when the show became the cool *Spider-Man* show that I think people are talking about when they say they like the series. Yes, I had to push really hard for that, because it was the exact opposite of what I had been told I could do. At that moment it was all about delivering the best work of your life, which I think *Spider-Man* really is."

Rumors abound that Spidey will be returning in a new animated television series following the Sam Raimi–directed feature film. Asked recently about Semper's possible involvement, Avi Arad responded that although Semper is a talented writer, *Spider-Man: The Animated Series* was the result of many different creative voices, and that they would be going for a different take on the next show.

"What they love to say," offers Semper, "is that *Spider-Man* wasn't me, *Spider-Man* was a combination of many people. But that same combination of people pre-existed before I got on the show and there was no show. And I always point out that the second series—*Spider-Man Unlimited*—was all the same people—even some of the same writers—*except* for me. The results speak for themselves."

Episode Guide

VOCAL CAST: Christopher Daniel Barnes (Peter Parker/Spider-Man), Edward Asner (J. Jonah Jameson), Linda Gray (Aunt May), Jennifer Hale (Felicia Hardy/The Black Cat), Saratoga Ballaintine (Mary Jane Watson), Patrick Labyorteaux (Flash Thompson), Michael Horton (John Jameson), Rodney Saulsberry (Joe "Robbie" Robinson), Liz Georges (Debra Whitman), Gary Imhoff (Harry Osborn), Neil Ross (Norman Osborn), Efrem Zimbalist, Jr. (Doctor Octopus), Hank Azaria (Eddie Brock/Venom), Mark Hamill (Hobgoblin), Jim Cummings (Shocker), Martin Landau (The Scorpion), Roscoe Lee Brown (Kingpin), Maxwell Caulfield (Alistaire Smythe), Edward Mulhare (Spencer Smythe), Michael Rye (Dr. Farley Stillwell), Joe Campanella (Dr. Curt Connors), Gregg Berger (Kraven the Hunter and Mysterio), Susan Beaubian (Dr. Mariah Crawford), Don Stark (The Rhino), Dawn Lewis (Terri Lee), John Beard (Newscaster), Jeff Corey (Silvermane), Nick Jameson (Morbius), Nicky Blair (Hammerhead), Rob Paulsen (Hydro-Man), Marla Jeanette Rubinoff (Liz Allen), Alyson Court (Jubilee), Alison Sealy Smith (Storm), Lenore Zann (Rogue), Norm Spenser (Cyclops), Chris Potter (Gambit), Catherine Disher (Jean Gray), Cedric Smith (Professor X), George Buza (Beast), David Warner (Landon), Laurie O'Brien (Genevieve), Joseph Ruskin (Lewald), Brian Keith (Uncle Ben), Warren Sroka (Young Peter), John Beck (Punisher), Robert Axelrod (Microchip), Jim Cummings (Man-Spider), T. D. Hall (Blade), Malcolm McDowell (Whistler), Leigh Baker Bailey (Silvermane), Giselle Achegar (Margaret Conners), Caroline Goddall (Vanessa Fisk), Dorian Harewood (Tombstone), Townsend Coleman (Young Silvermane), Eddie Albert (Old Vulture), Alan Johnson (Young Vulcan), Mark Richman (Old Peter Parker), John Vernon (Dr. Strange), George Takei (Wong), Tony Jay (Mordo), Edmund Gilbert (Dormammu), Majel Barrett (Anna Watson), Stephanie Eustace (Maria Taina Elizando), Neil Ross (Green Goblin), Joan Lee (Madam Web), Scott Cleverdon (Michael Pingree), Michael Des Barres (Jackson Wheel), William "Pop" Attmore II (Rocket Racer), Telma Hopkins (Mrs. Farrell), Edward Albert (Daredevil/Matt Murdock), Nick Jameson (Richard Fisk), Amy Hill (Susan Choi), Alfonso Ribeiro (Randy Robertson), Iona Morris (Martha Robertson), Robert Hayes (Tony Stark), Oliver Muirhead (Dr.

Jonathan Ohn), Wanda De Jesus (Dr. Silvia Lopez), Susan Beaubian (Calypso), David Hayter (Brace Huntington), John Phillip Law (John Hardesky)

SEASON ONE: 1994–95

EPISODE 1: *"Night of the Lizard"*
Written by Gerry Conway
In an effort to regrow his missing arm, Dr. Curt Connors performs an experiment that accidentally transforms him into the Lizard.

EPISODE 2: *"The Sting of the Scorpion"*
Written by Marty Isenburg and Robert Skir and John Semper
Desperate to have Spider-Man apprehended, J. Jonah Jameson hires Farley Stillwell, a genetics engineer, to create an adversary for the web-crawler. The resulting villain, the Scorpion, has plans of his own.

EPISODE 3: *"The Spider Slayers"*
Story by John Semper
Teleplay by Stan Berkowitz
At the urging of the Kingpin, Norman Osborn hires Spencer Smythe, a master of cybernetics, to create a powerful robot to destroy Spider-Man.

EPISODE 4: *"The Return of the Spider-Slayers"*
Story by John Semper
Teleplay by Mark Hoffmeier
Following his father's death, Spencer

Smythe is contacted by the Kingpin, who wants him to pick up where his father left off and create a new Spider-Slayer. Spencer, however, is more likely to seek revenge against the Kingpin himself.

EPISODE 5: *"The Menace of Mysterio"*
Written by Marv Wolfman, Stan Berkowitz, and John Semper
Mysterio, a Hollywood special effects master, assumes Spider-Man's identity to convince the public that Spidey is a villain to be feared.

EPISODE 6: *"Doctor Octopus: Armed and Dangerous"*
Story by John Semper and Brooks Wachtel
Teleplay by Brooks Wachtel and Cynthia Harrison
When heiress Felicia Hardy is kidnapped by Doc Ock, Peter Parker, who happened to be en route to a date with her, must move into action as Spider-Man.

EPISODE 7: *"The Alien Costume, Part One"*
Story by Avi Arad and Stan Lee
Teleplay by Stan Berkowitz, Len Wein, Meg McLaughlin, and John Semper
A mysterious substance within a pair of meteorites that crash on earth envelops Spider-Man, allowing him to alter his costume and his personality as well. *Something is changing him.*

EPISODE 8: *"The Alien Costume, Part Two"*
Story by Brynne Stephens and John Semper
Teleplay by Brynne Stephens
Seeking answers, Spider-Man goes to Dr. Curt Connors, who discovers that Spidey's new costume is actually a sentient being seeking a symbiotic relationship. In the end the suit is separated from Spider-Man, but finds a new host in *Daily Bugle* reporter Eddie Brock.

EPISODE 9: *"The Alien Costume, Part Three"*
Story by Mark Hoffmeier and John Semper
Teleplay by Mark Hoffmeier
While trying to deal with the threat of the Kingpin, the Rhino, and the Shocker, Spider-Man must also take on Eddie Brock, who has been transformed into Venom.

EPISODE 10: *"Kraven the Hunter"*
Story by John Semper, Jan Strand, and Mark Hoffmeier
Teleplay by Mark Hoffmeier
Kraven the Hunter wants to be reunited with his former lover, Dr. Mariah Crawford, and won't let anything get in his way—including Spider-Man.

EPISODE 11: *"The Hobgoblin, Part One"*
Story by John Semper and Stan Berkowitz
Teleplay by Larry Brody
Wanting the Kingpin out of his life, Norman Osborn hires the Hobgoblin to kill him. Unfortunately, instead the Hobgoblin kidnaps Harry Osborn, Norman's son.

EPISODE 12: *"The Hobgoblin, Part Two"*
Written by Stan Berkowitz
Spider-Man is out for blood when Aunt May is injured by the Hobgoblin in the kidnapping of Harry Osborn.

EPISODE 13: *"Day of the Chameleon"*
Written by John Semper
Spider-Man must stop the planned assassination of a pair of foreign diplomats who have come to New York to sign a peace accord.

SEASON TWO: 1995–96

EPISODE 14: *"The Insidious Six"* (Neogenic Nightmare, Part One)
Story by John Semper
Teleplay by John Semper and David Lee Miller
Mysterio, the Scorpion, Doc Ock, the Rhino, the Chameleon, and the Shocker team up to battle Spider-Man. The battle is made even tougher by changes in Spidey's blood, which are affecting his powers.

EPISODE 15: *"Battle of the Insidious Six"* (Neogenic Nightmare, Part Two)
Story by John Semper
Teleplay by Doug Booth
The Insidious Six continue trying to kill a weakened Spider-Man, while the Kingpin battles Silvermane and the Crime Lords to maintain his own base of power.

EPISODE 16: *"Hydro-Man" (Neogenic Nightmare, Part Three)*
Story by John Semper
Teleplay by Jim Krieg
Mary Jane Watson finds herself being stalked by former lover Morris Bench, who calls himself Hydro-Man and has the power to transform his body to a liquid form.

EPISODE 17: *"The Mutant Agenda" (Neogenic Nightmare, Part Four)*
Story by John Semper and J. M. DeMatteis
Teleplay by Michael Edens
As Spider-Man's blood disorder grows more intense, he turns to the X-Men's Professor X for answers.

EPISODE 18: *"Mutants' Revenge" (Neogenic Nightmare, Part Five)*
Story by John Semper and Michael Edens
Teleplay by Francis Moss and Ted Pedersen
Spider-Man and the X-Men must work together to stop a mutant creature that feeds on electricity.

EPISODE 19: *"Morbius" (Neogenic Nightmare, Part Six)*
Story by John Semper
Teleplay by Brynne Stephens and Lydia Marano
While Dr. Mariah Crawford attempts to solve Spider-Man's blood problems, a sample from her experimentations is stolen by Michael Morbius, who inadvertently uses the sample and is transformed into a vampire.

EPISODE 20: *"Enter the Punisher" (Neogenic Nightmare, Part Seven)*
Story by John Semper and Carl Potts
Teleplay by Carl Potts
As students at Empire State University are stricken by a plasma disorder, blame (of course) falls on Spider-Man. He in turn is after Morbius, and ultimately finds himself a target of the vigilante known as the Punisher.

EPISODE 21: *"Duel of the Hunters" (Neogenic Nightmare, Part Eight)*
Written by John Semper
Spider-Man's blood disorder results in his transformation into a Man-Spider, who attacks the Punisher. The vigilante barely escapes from the attack. Dr. Mariah Crawford goes to Kraven the Hunter to get his help in administering the antidote to Spidey. Things are complicated when the Punisher moves in for a rematch.

EPISODE 22: *"Blade the Vampire Hunter" (Neogenic Nightmare, Part Nine)*
Story by John Semper
Teleplay by Stephanie Mathison, Mark Hoffmeier, and John Semper
The vampire hunter named Blade arrives in New York, believing that Spider-Man is a

vampire who has to be stopped. Ultimately he learns that the real vampire is Morbius, and a restored Spider-Man desperately tries to save Michael Morbius from death.

EPISODE 23: *"The Immortal Vampire"*
(*Neogenic Nightmare, Part Ten*)
Written by John Semper and Meg McLaughlin
Morbius is planning on transforming Felicia Hardy into his vampire queen, until he's interrupted by Spider-Man and Blade, who have decided to work together.

EPISODE 24: *"Tablet of Time"* (*Neogenic Nightmare, Part Eleven*)
Written by Mark Hoffmeier, Stan Berkowitz, and John Semper
Silvermane steals a mystical "Tablet of Time" in the hopes that it will restore his youth. At the same time he kidnaps Curt Connors, who was studying the tablet. Spider-Man is determined to get Connors back, partially because he needs the doctor's cure for the neogenic disease administered every twelve hours.

EPISODE 25: *"Ravages of Time"* (*Neogenic Nightmare, Part Twelve*)
Written by Mark Hoffmeier, Stan Berkowitz, and John Semper
Spider-Man teams up with Tombstone to find Silvermane, arriving just as the Tablet of Time makes the villain younger and Curt Connors has transformed back into the Lizard.

EPISODE 26: *"Shriek of the Vulture"*
(*Neogenic Nightmare, Part Thirteen*)
Story by John Semper, Gilles Wheller, and Evelyn A. R. Gabal
Teleplay by Evelyn A. R. Gabal
When Norman Osborn attempts to take over Adrian Toomes's aeronautical company, Toomes grows furious and takes to the sky as the Vulture. His target: Harry Osborn.

EPISODE 27: *"The Final Nightmare"*
(*Neogenic Nightmare, Part Fourteen*)
Story by John Semper and Sandy Fries
Teleplay by Sandy Fries
In a strange twist from their last battle, the Vulture finds himself growing younger and stronger while Spider-Man gets older and more frail via a blood exchange between the two, thanks to the Vulture's talons. Spider-Man turns to Curt Connors for help, but their efforts are interrupted by the arrival of the Scorpion, who also wants Connors's help with his own condition. At the same time, the good doctor is desperately trying to stop an oncoming transformation into the Lizard.

SEASON THREE: 1996–97

EPISODE 28: *"Dr. Strange"* (Sins of the Father, Part One)
Story by John Semper
Teleplay by Mark Hoffmeier and John Semper
With Mary Jane Watson missing, Spider-Man turns to Dr. Strange (the Master of the Mystic Arts) for help.

EPISODE 29: *"Make a Wish"* (Sins of the Father, Part Two)
Story by John Semper
Teleplay by Mark Hoffmeier, Elliot S. Maggin, and Meg McLaughlin
Disgusted with being branded a criminal—particularly by J. Jonah Jameson—Peter Parker hangs up his tights. His attitude changes when he encounters a girl whose greatest wish is to meet the web-crawler. Donning his red-and-blue costume, he decides to give her the thrill of her life—until Doc Ock shows up.

EPISODE 30: *"Attack of the Octobot"* (Sins of the Father, Part Three)
Story by John Semper
Teleplay by Meg McLaughlin and John Semper
As a result of their last battle, Spidey has lost his memory and is "befriended" by Doc Ock. Old webhead's only hope: the young Taina (from "Make a Wish").

EPISODE 31: *"Enter the Green Goblin"* (Sins of the Father, Part Four)
No sooner has Norman Osborn disappeared in an explosion at his chemical factory than the Green Goblin arrives on the scene.

EPISODE 32: *"The Rocket Racer"* (Sins of the Father, Part Five)
Story by John Semper
Teleplay by Doug Booth and Mark Hoffmeier
Peter tries to develop his relationship with Felicia, but once again he's got competition for her time, most notably in the form of a group of jetpack-wearing thieves, the enigmatic Rocket Racer, and the fact that Felicia seems infatuated with Spider-Man.

EPISODE 33: *"Framed"* (Sins of the Father, Part Six)
Story by John Semper and Mark Hoffmeier
Teleplay by Brooks Wachtel and Cynthia Harrison
Peter Parker thinks his days of struggle are over when a wealthy businessman takes an interest in his career, but it's only a short matter of time before he finds himself framed for a federal crime. It's revealed that his benefactor is, in reality, the Kingpin, and it's up to Daredevil to help Peter/Spidey out of this mess.

EPISODE 34: *"The Man Without Fear" (Sins of the Father, Part Seven)*
Story by John Semper and Mark Hoffmeier
Teleplay by Sean Catherine Derek
Spider-Man and Daredevil team up to take on the power of the Kingpin.

EPISODE 35: *"The Ultimate Slayer" (Sins of the Father, Part Eight)*
Story by John Semper
Teleplay by Doug Booth and Mark Hoffmeier
The Kingpin arranges for Alistair Smythe to be transformed into a cyborg with the intention of having him kill Spider-Man, but things don't go exactly as the villain planned.

EPISODE 36: *"Tombstone" (Sins of the Father, Part Nine)*
Story by John Semper
Teleplay by Larry Brody, Marty Isenberg, and John Semper
A very human story: Spider-Man steps in to save Robbie Robertson's son, Randy, from being part of a gang of criminals led by Tombstone.

EPISODE 37: *"The Return of Venom" (Sins of the Father, Part Ten)*
Story by John Semper
Teleplay by Stan Berkowitz, Len Wein, and John Semper
Eddie Brock tries to convince himself that Venom was an identity that he just imagined, but the truth makes itself known quickly enough.

EPISODE 38: *"Carnage" (Sins of the Father, Part Eleven)*
Story by John Semper
Teleplay by Stan Berkowitz, James Krieg, and John Semper
Baron Mordo arranges for murderer Cletus Kassidy to become an alien symbiote like Eddie Brock, and thus Carnage is born. The real question is whether or not Venom will side with Carnage or Spider-Man.

EPISODE 39: *"The Spot" (Sins of the Father, Part Twelve)*
Written by James Krieg
When Jonathan Ohn creates a portable interdimensional gateway, all of New York is threatened with destruction.

EPISODE 40: *"Goblin Wars" (Sins of the Father, Part Thirteen)*
Story by Robert N. Skir
Teleplay by Mark Hoffmeier and Marty Isenberg
Dr. Ohn's interdimensional technology is stolen by none other than the Green Goblin.

EPISODE 41: *"The Turning Point" (Sins of the Fathers, Part Fourteen)*

Story by John Semper
Teleplay by Marty Isenberg, Robert N. Skir,
    James Krieg, and John Semper
The Green Goblin's plans involve the interdimensional device and using the kidnapped Mary Jane Watson to draw Spider-Man to the top of the Brooklyn Bridge.

SEASON FOUR: 1997–98

EPISODE 42: *"Guilty" (Partners in Danger, Part One)*
Story by John Semper
Teleplay by Larry Brody and Meg McLaughlin
It seems as though the *Daily Bugle*'s Robbie Robertson is the head of a crime ring, and it's up to Spider-Man and—of all people— J. Jonah Jameson to uncover the reality of the situation.

EPISODE 43: *"The Cat" (Partners in Danger, Part Two)*
Story by John Semper
Teleplay by Sean Catherine Derek
Doctor Octopus gives Felicia the shock of her life when she learns that her mother is being blackmailed by the madman.

EPISODE 44: *"The Black Cat" (Partners in Danger, Part Three)*
Story by John Semper
Teleplay by Marty Isenberg, Robert N. Skir, and Sean Catherine Derek
When Felicia's father is forced to hand over his formula for creating a supersoldier to the Kingpin, Felicia finds herself first in line to be experimented on. Spider-Man, of course, has something to say about this.

EPISODE 45: *"The Return of Kraven" (Partners in Danger, Part Four)*
Written by Meg McLaughlin
Spider-Man reluctantly teams up with the Black Cat to take on Kraven the Hunter, who they believe to be behind a number of strange occurrences.

EPISODE 46: *"Partners" (Partners in Danger, Part Five)*
Story by John Semper
Teleplay by Cynthia Harrison and Brooks Wachtel
The returning Alistair Smythe kidnaps the Black Cat and forces Spider-Man to do as he says or else Felicia, too, will die. Among the challenges facing Spidey is going up against the Vulture and the Scorpion.

EPISODE 47: *"Awakenings" (Partners in Danger, Part Six)*
Story by John Semper
Teleplay by Sean Catherine Derek
Morbius the vampire reenters the picture when the Kingpin grows determined to understand the secrets of his affliction and power.

EPISODE 48: *"The Vampire Queen" (Partners in Danger, Part Seven)*
Story by John Semper
Teleplay by Meg McLaughlin and John Semper
Blade battles Nosferatu and the Queen of the Vampires, before abruptly finding himself involved in the Spider-Man and Morbius situation.

EPISODE 49: *"The Return of the Green Goblin" (Partners in Danger, Part Eight)*
Written by Mark Hoffmeier
As though Spider-Man's life wasn't complicated enough, the Green Goblin reenters the picture to create havoc.

EPISODE 50: *"The Haunting of Mary Jane" (Partners in Danger, Part Nine)*
Story by John Semper and Virginia Roth
Teleplay by Meg McLaughlin and John Semper
Mary Jane goes back to work on the film that Mysterio's actions had caused to be temporarily shut down, but she is haunted by images of her father. Mysterio, it would seem, couldn't be behind these visions as he's behind bars.

EPISODE 51: *"The Lizard King" (Partners in Danger, Part Ten)*
Story by John Semper
Teleplay by Gordon Kent
After Mary Jane accepts Peter's proposal of marriage, he attempts to let Dr. Connors

know what's going on, only to discover that Connors has been kidnapped by three reptilian creatures.

EPISODE 52: *"The Prowler" (Partners in Danger, Part Eleven)*
Story by John Semper
Teleplay by Terence Taylor
When the Kingpin has a convict freed from prison, that man becomes the Prowler, and his first goal is to take on the criminals who framed him in the first place.

EPISODE 53: *"The Wedding"*
Story by John Semper
Teleplay by Meg McLaughlin and John Semper
Peter Parker and Mary Jane Watson get married. Unfortunately, their reception is crashed by the Green Goblin.

EPISODE 54: *"Six Forgotten Warriors, Chapter One"*
Written by John Semper
Peter Parker is determined to uncover the truth about Keene Marlowe, a mysterious stranger who has connections with Aunt May, Uncle Ben, Peter's parents, and S.H.I.E.L.D.

EPISODE 55: *"Six Forgotten Warriors, Chapter Two: Unclaimed Legacy"*
Written by John Semper
A doomsday device located in Moscow triggers a deadly situation as Peter Parker

and Robbie Robinson attempt to uncover the truth behind this device. Things are made tougher when Peter is forced to change to Spider-Man and battle the Insidious Six.

EPISODE 56: *"Six Forgotten Warriors, Chapter Three: Secrets of the Six"*
Written by John Semper
Peter Parker and Robbie Robertson learn of the Six Forgotten Warriors. Spider-Man must find them before the Kingpin does.

EPISODE 57: *"Six Forgotten Warriors, Chapter Four: The Six Fight Again"*
Written by John Semper
The aged Six Forgotten Warriors team up with Spider-Man against the Insidious Six and the Kingpin, who is planning on putting the mysterious doomsday device into operation.

EPISODE 58: *"Six Forgotten Warriors, Chapter Five: The Price of Heroism"*
Written by John Semper
The plot thickens as the Red Skull unleashes the doomsday device. Spider-Man, the Warriors, and Captain America work to set things right, but they may be too late.

EPISODE 59: *"The Return of Hydro-Man, Part One"*
Story by John Semper
Teleplay by Eileen Fuentes and James Krieg
When Peter and Mary Jane attempt finally

to take their honeymoon, things go awry when she is kidnapped by Hydro-Man.

EPISODE 60: *"The Return of Hydro-Man, Part Two"*
Story by John Semper
Teleplay by Meg McLaughlin and John Semper
Peter gets Mary Jane back, but both are shocked to discover that she seems to have abilities that are very close to Hydro-Man's.

EPISODE 61: *"Secret Wars, Chapter One: Arrival"*
Written by John Semper and Karen Wilovich
In an effort to understand the nature of good and evil, a being calling itself the Beyonder sets up a "game" of sorts: it allows Doctor Doom, Doc Ock, Smythe, the Red Skull, and the Lizard to take over and corrupt a world. To combat this force, Spider-Man puts together a team that consists of himself, Iron Man, Storm, Captain America, and the Fantastic Four.

EPISODE 62: *"Secret Wars, Chapter Two: The Gauntlet of the Red Skull"*
Written by Virginia Roth
The Spider-Man–led team attempts to invade the Red Skull's headquarters, a situation that allows Spider-Man to learn a little something about himself and his ability to lead.

EPISODE 63: *"Secret Wars, Chapter Three: Doom"*
Written by John Semper, Mark Hoffmeier, and Ernie Altbacker
When the Spider-Team invades Doctor Doom's territory, they're shocked to discover a land of peace and tranquility. What the hell is *really* going on?

EPISODE 64: *"Spider Wars, Chapter One: Really, Really Hate Clones"*
Story by John Semper
Teleplay by James Krieg, Mark Hoffmeier, and John Semper
Returning to earth, Spider-Man is horrified to find that little is left of New York City,

thanks to the Green Goblin and the Hobgoblin. What he ultimately learns is that this is an alternate earth where a being known as Spider-Carnage pretty much rules—and plans on destroying other dimensions as well. Spider-Man teams up with five other Spider-Men from different dimensions to set things right.

EPISODE 65: *"Spider Wars, Chapter Two: Farewell Spider-Man"*
Written by John Semper
The battle comes to an end as the six Spider-Men go up against Spider-Carnage. The end results wrap up *Spider-Man: The Animated Series.*

Spider-Man Unlimited

One of the truths about *Spider-Man: The Animated Series* was that the show was a ratings hit, no matter how often it ran or in whatever time slot it did so. This success notwithstanding, it was obvious, given the political reality of that series, that producer/story editor John Semper would not be invited aboard the next animated incarnation of the web-slinger, *Spider-Man Unlimited*.

Too bad, because they really could have used him.

Inspired by a number of Marvel Comics from the 1970s, *Spider-Man Unlimited* spent its thirteen-episode run on Counter-Earth, a world parallel to our own with similar but slightly altered characters. In episode one, Spidey, in an effort to save astronaut John Jameson from the dual threat of Venom and Carnage, stows aboard a space shuttle and finds himself on this bizarre world, where he must struggle for survival.

In one important way, Counter-Earth is similar to home for Spidey, as there is always someone there willing to make his life a living hell. In this case, it's the High Evolutionary, a brilliant scientist from our own world who has escaped to this parallel realm to create a society he can rule. Aiding him in this quest are the Knights of Wundagore, a number of intelligent beast-men who do their master's bidding; and robot warriors known as the Machine Men. Added to the mix are Carnage and Venom, who have devised a plan to have all the people of Counter-Earth join with symbiotes before they then turn their attention to the High Evolutionary himself.

For his part, Peter Parker tries to eke out a living on this world as a photographer for the *Daily Byte*. Although Peter is the same character we've known, this take on Spider-Man is slightly different in that he's adorned in an altered costume that has (thanks to Mr. Fantastic's high-tech laboratory) a variety of enhancements that make him stronger and better-equipped than he ever was on earth.

Spidey has an eclectic group of costars on the show, beginning with John Jameson, who is determined to stay on Counter-Earth until the High Evolutionary has been overthrown; Machine Man X-51, one of the High Evolutionary's robots who has gained sentience and hopes to spread his enlightened vision to the rest of his kind; the Vulture, a beast-mutant who fights alongside Spider-Man, despite the fact that he doesn't like or really trust him; Karen O'Malley, Jameson's right hand and a fellow resistance fighter; and the Goblin, an upside-down version of the Green Goblin who actually fights on the side of good.

Veteran writer Larry Brody, who was brought in halfway through the show's production as executive creative consultant, reflects, "No one liked the alternate universe. Even Avi Arad didn't like it. I was told by Fox execs that it came about because the deal Marvel made for the Spider-Man feature film prevented them from doing 'that' Spider-Man on TV until the film was released. Wanting a Spider-Man television presence, they set out to find a loophole. Originally they were going to do *Spider-Man: Year One*, but there were deal problems with that one, too, so then someone—no one will say who it was—came up with the twin planet thing.

"I took the assignment," he adds, "because I love Spidey and wanted to save him. Also because I was told that it was guaranteed to be on the air for three years, which meant I would have a solid amount of work to do, which also meant some job security. The plan was to have Spidey on Counter-Earth for two seasons and then bring him back home at a time that would coincide with the release of the Spider-Man movie. He would return to Mary Jane, his wife, and we could continue the 'real' continuity. I thought it would be great to be able to continue the life of my favorite comic characters."

The first three episodes of *Spider-Man Unlimited* aired in October of 1999, but unlike its predecessor it was met with dismal ratings and audience apathy. At the time, the Pokemon phenomenon was raging at full force and pretty much obliterated all the competition. As a result, Spidey was taken off the air, destined to return over a year later (in December of 2000). It was not a situation that thrilled Brody. "There's nothing less satisfying than working your butt off for six months and having your work never shown to its intended audience," he mused to *Comics Continuum*. "One of the reasons I left prime time to concentrate on animation was that I was a 'pilot' writer, which meant that I wrote and wrote—for very good money—but nothing was ever shot. Very frustrating."

Frustration was the name of the game for everyone, particularly the audience. While *Spider-Man Unlimited* maintained the concept of a season-long arc established by its predecessor, the attention to details—in terms of both the animation and the characterization—seemed to be lacking a certain edge. Admittedly, things improved when Brody took over the story-editing position midway through the season, but it simply wasn't enough.

"My purpose on *Spider-Man Unlimited*," explains Brody, "was to save it from the 'suits' who were misusing the character. I didn't create the concept, but I was given this strange alternate universe that wasn't really an alternate universe premise, overseen by network executives who knew so little about film and the 'language' of film that they couldn't understand anything unless it was spelled out in literal dialogue. Overseeing them were Avi Arad of Marvel and, at that time, Toy Biz, and the 'spirit' of Haim Saban, both of whom cared only about selling toys. They would have been quite happy to gut the franchise if they could sell red, purple, orange, and silver Spider-Men.

"In animation," he elaborates, "you get only as much freedom as you can carve out for yourself, not by bullying people but by working with them and making them want to work with you. So much money is at stake that there are more fingers in the pot than in prime time, and the fact that you have almost indefinite time to rewrite (because of how long animation production takes) means that there are many more drafts and changes than in prime time. I liked my coworkers, even if I felt that for the most part they were inexperienced and naive, and did my best to guide them to some new knowledge and artistry. They aren't going to like hearing me say that, but one of the problems with TV animation is that it's done for the most part by unqualified people who are inordinately proud of, quite honestly, very little. Although generating major-league bucks, it is run by people with minor-league credentials. I think it's a real shame that animation is put together so shabbily, with such greedy overthink, but it's

a situation I don't know how to change. Unless those running the companies learn to respect their audience and the writers who try so hard to entertain that audience, animation will just get worse and worse, good characters and intentions dribbling away."

Adding insult to injury was the fact that the show ended on a cliffhanger that will never be resolved.

Notes Brody, "We did wrap things up. We had written half of the next season and had outlined all of it. By the second or third episode of the second season, the High Evolutionary would have been toppled, humans would be given full citizen status alongside the Beastials, and instead of having to lead a revolution, Spidey was going to go back to what he does best: fighting crime alone. In the course of fighting crime, he was going to find another rocket and use it to go back to Earth and Mary Jane."

What the future holds for Spider-Man on television is anyone's guess. A new series—possibly computer-generated—seems to be in the cards. That point seems like a no-brainer. For over three decades Spider-Man has filled the small screen in one form or another, and there's no reason to think that that situation will change anytime soon. For Spidey, it seems to be more a question of when rather than if.

Episode Guide

VOICE CAST: Gino Romano (Peter Parker/Spider-Man), John Payne (John Jameson), Kimberly Hawthorne (Karen), Christopher Gaze (Bromley), Akiko Morison (Dr. Naoko Yamada-Jones), Rhys Huber (Shayne Yamada-Jones), Michael Donovan (Carnage), Brian Drummond (Venom), Jennifer Hale (Lady Vermin, Mary Jane), David Sobolov (Lord Tyger), Tasha Simms (Lady Ursula), Ron Halder (Sir Ram), Mark Gibbon (Nick Fury), James Crescenzo (Green Goblin), Gary Chalk (Mr. Meugniot), Scott McNeil (the Vulture)

EPISODES 1–3: *October 1999;* EPISODES 4–13: *December 2000–March 2001*

EPISODE 1: *"Worlds Apart, Part One"*
Written by Michael Reaves and Will Meugniot
Seeing Venom and Carnage stow away on John Jameson's space shuttle to Counter-Earth, Peter Parker designs (with the Fantastic Four's Reed Richards's help) a Nano-Tech costume with a number of new features, and hijacks a shuttle to go after them. Landing on Counter-Earth, an Earthlike world ruled by the High Evolutionary, he's captured by the Knights of

Wundagore, who prepare to acquire genetic samples from him.

EPISODE 2: *"Worlds Apart, Part Two"*
Story by Will Meugniot and Michael Reaves
Teleplay by Michael Reaves
Spider-Man escapes from the Knights with the help of the Human Revolutionaries, freedom fighters led by John Jameson. He learns that Counter-Earth is ruled by Beastials, human-animal hybrids created by the High Evolutionary, who use Machine Men to enforce their laws. When Carnage and Venom, pursuing their own mysterious agenda, attack the revolutionaries' headquarters, Spidey helps drive them off. Jameson invites Spidey to join his cause, but Spider-Man only wants to convince him to return to earth.

EPISODE 3: *"Where Evil Nests"*
Story by Will Meugniot
Teleplay by Brynne Chandler Reaves and Steve Perry
Settling on Counter-Earth, Peter Parker gets to know his new landlady, Naoko Yamada-Jones, and her son, Shayne. When Shayne is captured by the Bio-Mass, an amoeba-like creature under the control of Venom and Carnage, Spidey and a mysterious vigilante called the Goblin must res-

cue him. Afterward, Peter gets a job as a news photographer at the *Daily Byte*.

EPISODE 4: *"Deadly Choices"*
Story by Will Meugniot and Michael Reaves
Teleplay by Steve Perry
Git Hoskins, a Human Revolutionary who has unusual powers due to being experimented on by the High Evolutionary, steals a canister of deadly mutagen from Sir Ram's laboratory. Spidey and the Knights must reluctantly join forces to find Git, because the canister has a fail-safe that will detonate a nuclear charge to prevent the mutagen from infecting Counter-Earth.

EPISODE 5: *"Steel Cold Heart"*
Story by Will Meugniot and Roger Slifer
Teleplay by Roger Slifer
Spider-Man and Shayne befriend X-51, a Machine Man who has become sentient and no longer wants to serve the High Evolutionary. X-51 is hunted by the Knights of Wundagore and the Human Revolutionaries, who want to exchange him for one of their own held prisoners. Spidey learns that the exchange is a double-cross and prevents it, and X-51 joins the revolutionary forces.

EPISODE 6: *"Enter the Hunter"*
Story by Will Meugniot, Roger Slifer, and
  Michael Reaves
Teleplay by Diane Duane and Peter
  Morwood

Sir Ram hires the Hunter, a human mercenary, to hunt down Spider-Man. As bait, the Hunter kidnaps Karen O'Malley, and during the course of this he learns Spider-Man's secret identity. Spidey must face the Hunter in his high-tech lair, rescue Karen, and somehow convince the villain that he's not really Peter Parker.

EPISODE 7: *"Cry Vulture"*
Written by Larry Brody and Robert Gregory-
  Browne
A friend of Naoko's is kidnapped and Spider-Man sets out to save him. While Spidey learns that the victim is going to be used as a human lab rat, getting to him becomes a race against time—which is complicated by the appearance of two new Beastial foes: Firedrake and Counter-Earth's own version of the Vulture.

EPISODE 8: *"Ill Met by Moonlight"*
Written by Robert Gregory-Browne and
  Larry Brody
The rebels want to put a lethal power plant out of business, and Spider-Man agrees to help. Little does he know that not only will he have to face off against Counter-Earth's Beastial Electro, but also against John Jameson's alter ego, Manwolf.

EPISODE 9: *"Sustenance"*
Written by Robert Gregory-Browne and
  Larry Brody

Aided by the Goblin, Spider-Man searches for the spaceship that can take him back to Earth. Together, they find the ship and a horrifying secret—the dark fate of the High Evolutionary's genetic failures, the Rejects.

EPISODE 10: *"Family Matters"*
Written by Mark Hoffmeier and Larry Brody
The deepest consequences of the Beastials' subjugation of the human race are faced by Bromley, one of the most dedicated Counter-Earth rebels, when, in an attempt to free his brother from the High Evolutionary, he agrees to betray Spider-Man.

EPISODE 11: *"One Is the Loneliest Number"*
Written by Robert Gregory-Browne and Larry Brody
Spider-Man faces one of the greatest challenges of his life when he discovers that Eddie Brock and his symbiote have been separated. Instead of celebrating the end of Venom, Spidey must face off against Carnage and re-create his toughest foe, or Brock will die.

EPISODE 12: *"Sins of the Father"*
Written by Robert Gregory-Browne and Larry Brody
When Karen O'Malley is captured by the High Evolutionary, Spider-Man and the rebels come to her rescue, storming Wundagore Castle and going head to head with the Knights of Wundagore. But all is not as it seems, because the High Evolutionary's interest in Karen is more than an attempt to defeat the rebel cause. It's personal.

EPISODE 13: *"Destiny Unleashed, Part One"*
Written by Robert Gregory-Browne and Larry Brody
The High Evolutionary's patience is at an end. He wants Spider-Man and the rebels and he wants them now, so he institutes a reign of terror designed to make them give themselves up. But the sacrifice made by Spidey and the others proves even more dangerous than anticipated when Venom and Carnage strike and the destruction of Counter-Earth seems assured.

PART THREE

Swinging to the Big Screen

A SINGLE GLISTENING STRAND OF A SPIDER'S WEB BISECTS THE
BLACK FRAME. AS CLASSICAL MUSIC CARESSES OUR
EARS, WE SEE THE STRAND CRISSCROSSING OTHERS IN A PER-
FECT ORB WEB. A SPIDER—BLACK WITH AN INTRICATE PAT-
TERN—DROPS INTO FRAME. IT GRACEFULLY GATHERS AND
WEAVES THE STRANDS TOGETHER. . . .

These words begin the screenplay for *Spider-Man*, the long-awaited adaptation of one of comics' most popular characters. It is not, however, the script filmed by Sam Raimi with Tobey Maguire in the dual role of Peter Parker and Spider-Man. In fact, the actor was all of ten years old when screenwriters Ted Newsom and John Brancato first presented this particular script to former Marvel head honcho, Stan Lee.

The point being made is that the gestation period for the Spider-Man movie was no less than seventeen years, from the time these words were written to the time Spidey finally reached theaters. As such, it represents one of the longest roads ever traveled by a film project from conception through completion.

Back in the early 1980s, Stan Lee was growing increasingly anxious that Marvel's numerous properties were not being exploited on film, whether it be on television or on the big screen. DC had already scored with the live-action *Batman* and *Wonder Woman* television series, as well as the extremely lucrative Superman film franchise, and Lee saw no reason why Marvel shouldn't enjoy equal success. Yes, the company had scored briefly with the live-action *Spider-Man* show back in the 1970s and the long-running *Incredible Hulk*, but it seemed that there was a great deal of untapped

Spider-Man director Sam Raimi

potential. In the end, Marvel needed something special, and Lee felt that he had found it in Newsom and Brancato.

The duo were writers who were determined to break into Hollywood and they felt they had found a possible inroad through a developing friendship with Lee. Intrigued by their writing style, imagination, and sheer enthusiasm, Lee hired them to pen a screenplay adaptation of the old Marvel World War II title, *Sgt. Fury and His Howling Commandos*. The plan was that Lee, armed with the screenplay and comics, would make the studio rounds to see if he could drum up some interest in the property.

"We did the Sgt. Fury script, which Stan loved," says Newsom, a film producer and guiding force behind a number of documentaries on the horror genre. "Then he asked us what we'd like to do next, and we immediately said, 'Spider-Man.' He said we couldn't do it because Cannon Films had the rights to the project."

Anyone who has followed the industry over the past fifteen years or so remembers Cannon well. The company—in its most famous incarnation—can be traced back to 1979. Israeli cousins Menahem Golan and Yoram Globus, who had achieved great success in their homeland, were able to take control of Cannon when it was a minor independent specializing in exploitation films. Under the guidance of Golan/Globus, a new means of doing business was established. Cannon would come up with titles they planned on producing, attach as many big names as they could in terms of actors, writers, and directors, and sell the projects to different international territories, thus guaranteeing a profit before a foot of film had actually been shot. It's a formula that worked for such low-budget entries as *Death Wish 2, The Last American Virgin*, and *Enter the Ninja*. It led to such higher-budget and more successful entries as *Death Wish 3, Delta Force*, and the Chuck Norris actioners, *Missing in Action* and *Invasion USA*, which turned out to be the company's biggest hits, and also managed to establish director Joe Zito (more on him a bit further on).

If you were able to find a copy of *Variety* or *The Hollywood Reporter* from the period, you would probably be stunned by the sheer quantity of ads Cannon took out to announce their projects in development. Millions of dollars were spent and essentially wasted, as a vast majority of these films never saw the light of a theater projector.

And those that actually were filmed often ended up as colossal box-office failures.

"There were a number of cheese-ball cheapo production companies that, during the eighties, decided that they would turn themselves into studios," Brancato reflects. "Instead of making B-list pictures, they tried to make the serious-money A-list pictures. Cannon was one of them, and one after the other they failed. New Line, New World, Vestron—they were all the same. But Cannon was a pretty magnificent flame-out. They didn't have the best tastes and got involved in financing a lot of lame projects. They built themselves a nice, fancy office, and I remember going to the opening of the building and there were Spider-Man promo posters everywhere. Within six months, though, everything had fallen apart. It was the meteoric rise and fall of Cannon."

Noted journalist Patrick Runkle says on the on-line inksyndicate.com, "Just when Cannon's star seemed to be rising higher, there were rumblings that it was overextended and on the rocks. The company had overstepped its bounds and wasted its money by producing some of the least successful would-be big-budget blockbusters of the latter half of the eighties. Tobe Hooper's comically overblown *Lifeforce*, a 1985 science-fiction flick based on the pulp novel *Space Vampires*, was a thirty-million-dollar investment that barely cracked ten million in returns when it was released in

America. It was a sign of things to come from Cannon's big productions."

One big-budget flop followed another, beginning with Hooper's remake of *Invaders from Mars*, and *Master of the Universe*, based on the He-Man toy line, and *Superman IV: The Quest for Peace*, whose $35 million budget was cut in half on the eve of production, resulting in the worst entry in the series and the end of Christopher Reeve's turn as the Man of Steel. Fiscally exhausted, it was only a matter of time before Cannon's collapse would be complete.

Spider-Man: From Script to Screen

In 1985, when Hollywood was still their oyster, Golan and Globus felt that the superhero genre hadn't yet reached its full potential (or, put more pessimistically, hadn't been fully exploited). Golan negotiated with Marvel Comics to option the feature film rights to the Spider-Man character. In the end, Cannon paid Marvel $225,000 plus a percentage of gross revenue for a five-year option.

Satisfied with the deal, Golan, who never truly understood comics in general or Spider-Man in particular, hired *Outer Limits* creator Leslie Stevens to write a film treatment. The result was a story in which Peter Parker works as a photographer for the Zyrex Corporation. The owner of the company, identified only as Dr. Zyrex, performs an experiment on the unsuspecting

Parker by bathing him in radioactive waves. The result is *not* the acquisition of spider-like powers, but, instead, a transformation into an eight-legged human-tarantula hybrid. For the rest of the story, Parker has to battle one mutant after another.

Needless to say, this story was rejected by Stan Lee, who had the power to veto things that he didn't feel represented a faithful adaptation, unlike today, when studios don't even have the courtesy to consult with him regarding characters he created. That's when Newsom and Brancato stepped in.

"Once Cannon hired us," says Brancato, whose writing credits include the forthcoming *Terminator 3*, "Stan suggested we write the script from his outline—which was about two pages long and more or less dealt with Spider-Man's origin."

From the outset, the duo pitched a story that differed from the comics in that it intertwined the origins of Spider-Man and Doctor Octopus. In their scenario, Doc Ock's experiments result in his being physically altered and joined with his mechanical waldos, and in Peter being bitten by an irradiated spider and transformed into Spider-Man. The rest of the origin plays out pretty much the way it did in the comics, though an attempt was made to keep a sense of realism to the characters in terms of their motivations and reactions to things. Admittedly, though, things get a little fanciful at the end, when Doc Ock's experiments involving antigravity result in the science building at Empire State University floating high above the ground while hero and villain battle it out. Nonetheless, it was an effective approach to the material.

Brancato points out: "The problem with any superhero comic, obviously, is to try and find the right tone. Spider-Man, unlike Superman, always had a tongue-in-cheek, self-conscious approach to itself. It was difficult to capture that and make it play as a satisfying action film. In a lot of ways, Spider-Man was a parody of Superman and all the other books of the time. Peter Parker, being a self-conscious, socially unsuccessful, somewhat nerdy character, is very different from a square-jawed hero. Clark Kent has some similar attributes, but Spider-Man had a much more self-conscious humor about the whole situation. The villains were pretty self-conscious and goofy. If you read those stories, they have a very different tone from the DC Comics at the time. Marvel really did put itself up as being for the slightly brainier audience out there. From the very beginning, the Spider-Man comic is laughing at itself. A lot of it is asides to the audience and everything done with a wink, which is the style Stan mastered.

"It's one of the reasons Spider-Man was so lovable," he continues. "But it was also a tough tone to capture. That was always the challenge of it. *Superman: The Movie* was so mythic and grandiose in the way it was presented, and Spider-Man could never be that.

It was always the younger brother to that story line. It didn't take itself as seriously."

But, as Newsom adds, the writers themselves knew that they had to approach the material in a serious way in terms of the audience and the characters themselves.

"We took the approach that we couldn't presuppose anyone knew anything about these characters," Newsom explains. "So what you had to do was a creation story, and if you were going to have a super-villain, you had to create him, too. It can't just come out of nowhere. So Stan had a treatment from which we worked our story. We made alterations and changes. Cannon approved that treatment and we started scripting from there. The one thing that John and I didn't agree with Stan on was his take on villains and superheroes in general. I say this with due deference, because I owe a great deal of whatever we got going to Stan. But in his story, Doctor Octopus has this horrible accident and he has these waldos placed invasively into his body. As a result, he goes crazy and decides to become the greatest master criminal in the world.

"Well," he continues after a brief pause, "people *don't* do that. That's not the way *real* people react. If you're in an accident and you lose a leg, you don't decide to become the greatest pirate the seven seas have ever known. That is not a rational, logical, or even understandable emotional leap from where you were. Despite Bela Lugosi carving Boris Karloff's face up in *The*

Raven, it is not part and parcel of being repulsive that makes you do ugly things. There are real human motivations in life that drive people. So with Doctor Octopus, he wasn't a master criminal, he was insane. Now it might very well drive you crazy if your whole body became an H. R. Giger image. You might very well go crazy, but you would still be the same person inside and you would still have the same goals, which is one thing we kept pushing. He just kept doing exactly what he was doing, but he just happened to have four mechanical arms at that point."

Lee didn't like that particular approach, finding it too confusing. He remained steadfast in his feeling that Doc Ock should have his accident and come out of it with a lust for world conquest.

"Nothing's wrong with that if you're doing a comic book," muses Newsom. "One of the blessed things about Marvel, and Stan's work in particular, is that there was an element of sophistication about it that hadn't been present in comic books before that. You actually dealt with human themes and motivations and back stories, which you really didn't have in the DC stuff or Charlton Comics. There was a depth to Marvel that had not existed before. So we tried to stay with that. Look, is James Mason the villain of *North by Northwest*? He's the antagonist, but if you sat down and asked him, he would not say he's doing bad things. His goals are absolutely pure as far as

he is concerned. Most anybody, if you ask them, unless they're sociopaths, will tell you that their goals are pure as far as they're concerned. Their goals are the best that they can see. You have to have somebody like that as a villain if it's supposed to be anything else but white hat/black hat. We tried to keep the character human, despite the fact that he's an odd mutation."

Their version of Doc Ock is pretty ruthless in certain instances, violently killing people with his waldos when they get in his way. By the same token, there is a genuine sense of kindness emanating from him when it comes to his feelings about Peter's Aunt May, who the script establishes as having once been his lover.

"All of the Marvel villains, especially in Spider-Man, were sort of shaded and you sympathized with them in the same way that the heroes were less perfect," says Brancato. "It gave warts to the whole world of superheroes, which was so much of the appeal of it. Spider-Man from the beginning had elements of this sort of Batman-like origin. He is self-serving, and his uncle gets killed by the same villain he let go because he didn't give a shit. There is definitely a darker strain all the way through on Spider-Man. We tried to get that across, and the idea of Doc Ock being kind of a scary monster."

One conscious change the writers tried to make was to alter the character of Aunt May, changing her from someone who, according to Newsom, is a "pain in the ass that looks like she's about a hundred and fifty years old," to a woman more in line with actress Katharine Hepburn. "We made her very hip," he says. "Think Katherine Hepburn and you suddenly had a much more fun dynamic, because Peter Parker is not the hippest guy in the world. Peter Parker's a schlub. That's the joyous part of him as a character—he's Clark Kent to the *n*th degree, who is thrust into greatness. He doesn't go after it, it's thrust upon him. Everybody in the world is hipper than Peter Parker, so we thought, 'Fine, so's Aunt May.' Aunt May knows what the current rock hits are; Peter Parker doesn't have a clue. That, to us, was a lot more fun than doing this little old lady who's always dying."

One of the biggest questions both Stan Lee and, eventually, Menahem Golan had was exactly how they were going to pull off the effects required for the film. Back in 1985, there wasn't even a notion of computer graphics being utilized on film, unlike today, where virtually anything you can imagine can be brought to life. This issue was raised on a couple of levels, beginning with a sequence known as the "Cyclotron Implosion," in which Doc Ock's experiments on anti-gravity utilizing a cyclotron have horrible consequences and, in the end, result in the creation of both Ock's transformed appearance and Peter Parker's metamorphosis. Newsom

and Brancato described the sequence as follows:

The cyclotron rumbles, the basement shakes with the intensifying antigravity field. . . . The thick glass of the control room turns to fluid, sucked inwards to the collapsing antigravity field. The chamber's steel walls buckle like rubber, electrical wires fly and sizzle, pipes explode and bend. The shock wave of the imploding field ripples through the building. Objects melt and combine, Dali-like and surreal; the pulsing light slashes through the walls; we hear a cacophony of alarms and animal noises. Everything warps in a bizarre and terrifying nightmare. Doctor Octavius's hideous scream echoes and dies. In the aftermath, we see: a chair melted and mixed into a silly-putty wall . . . a dog molecularly melded into its wire cage, twitching and whimpering pathetically . . . and, finally, Doctor Octopus. The four steel waldos have become part of his torso.

On September 10, 1985, the writers offered their opinions on this aspect of the script, as well as the approach to Doc Ock and Spider-Man. Basically, the question was how in hell they would be able to accomplish such effects on a total budget of $15 to $20 million.

Under the heading "Cyclotron Implosion," they wrote: "Doc Ock's colossal accident is the first chance for the effects and art direction people to have a good time. We've established the rather mundane, seedy 'reality' of the university lab, and suddenly everything goes berserk. Much can be done through fast cutting and juxtaposition of image, but the real effects should be exciting, things we've never really seen before. Thick shafts of 'liquid light' knife through solid objects—these are optical effects, mostly, composites of live-action footage and light images done in the water tank. Effects people are used to this sort of thing; it's one of Spielberg's favorites. Distorted lenses and solarization of the negative can add to the bizarre, luminescent effect.

"During and after the accident, we see surreal images building up before the ultimate shock of Ock," they added. "These should be real gross-outs, bio-models akin to those used in John Carpenter's *The Thing* or H. R. Giger's imagery in *Alien*. The main ingredient in making these powerful, disturbing props is imagination, not a whole lot of money. The lab set after the accident shouldn't look like an explosion. Walls aren't blown apart, they're sucked inward, twisted and warped around. It's like the distortion of a hall of mirrors made real. These sets will have to be built, but the unsettling effect will be well worth the price. Besides, most of our final action sequences take place in this environment."

Shifting their attention to Doc Ock,

they noted that developing the character presented what would be the most intricate challenge of the film. At the same time, they felt that via a combination of effects techniques, the look of the character could be brought together "beautifully."

"The first time we see Ock's arms is crucial," they said. "A mechanical effect—i.e., sticking the metal arms to his body—would make the audience shout 'Fake!' and we'd lose them. Instead, we can take a cue from Cronenberg's *Videodrome* and construct a latex torso for our Ock actor. This should be as horrifying to the audience as it is to Ock himself. In this one shot, we'll see that the mechanical tentacles have grotesquely penetrated his body, they're not just glued-on prosthetics. This is the only place we need to see this, but it's essential the audience accepts the arms. Luckily, it's relatively cheap to do a cast of a man's torso. Again, it's not a question of expense, but imaginative use of existing techniques."

Doc Ock in action, they pointed out, could be achieved to a large degree by close-ups combined with quickly paced editing. Additionally, "practical" versions of the arms could work in some scenes where it would be possible to manipulate them off-camera. Helping them would be the fact that those mechanical arms shoot "outward like striking cobras," which is a shock effect that would offset potential disbelief on the audience's part.

"To use full-size mechanical devices

exclusively means too many problems," suggested Newsom and Brancato. "However, they're expensive and go wrong with annoying regularity. Marionetting them from above would help, but it means the arms can never cross each other because of the wire. Also, if the arms are fully extended to ten feet or so, the actor will lose his balance. Our specific recommendation is dimensional animation. It's not a technique appropriate for everything, but it can't be beat for giving life to mechanical objects. Think of the robot skeleton in the last scenes of *Terminator* or the demon dogs in *Ghostbusters*. When we see Ock in full fury, a process shot of a live actor with prosthetics, layered with fully extended miniature stop-motion arms, should thrill and scare. Dimensional animation can be extremely cost-effective—as long as it's done without union interference. It is essentially a one-man operation, but Hollywood unions insist on a full complement of stagehands. Jim Danforth, one of the best animators in town, found himself with a useless crew of twenty guys on a projected Disney film. As a result, a scene that should've cost $15,000 wound up at nearly $100,000. There are ways to get around this rule: farm out the effects, shoot outside L.A. city limits and so forth.

"Careful planning and mixing of these techniques," they suggested, "will make Ock incredibly frightening, plausible, and not prohibitively expensive."

Moving on to Spider-Man himself, their feeling was that although capturing the character in action would require virtually every special effect trick in the book, there were ways to achieve this without being prohibitively expensive.

"Obviously, several different stuntmen can be used for their specialties, from martial arts to gymnastics; since our hero wears a mask, doubling isn't difficult. For impossible shots that even the most brain-damaged stuntman won't touch, such as swinging several hundred feet between sky-scrapers, we can use a mechanical dummy. These robots aren't terrifically versatile, but during a swing, Spider-Man doesn't move much anyway—perhaps little more than a hand-wave to a crowd below. Old Republic serials like *Captain Marvel* and *Commando Cody* used this, the Lydecker technique, to great effect . . . and the shots still work today.

"Blue-screen shots are obvious for Spidey swinging on webs through town. Combine these with the mechanicals mentioned above, and add vertiginous point-of-view shots of approaching sidewalks and buildings, and Spider-Man's swinging will be a visceral, dizzying, and exhilarating experience. The effects on the Spider-Man TV series were occasionally well done. Some of the wall-crawling scenes work: a stuntman scaling a building assisted by an unseen wire from above. They also used vertical walls that were in reality horizontal. Refining these techniques for the big screen should be simple. For clinging to interior walls and ceilings, we'd love to see a rotating set (in addition to split-screen, hidden supports, and so on). Think of Fred Astaire's floor-to-ceiling dance in *Royal Wedding*. Kubrick also used this technique in *2001*, and it's a real treat.

"The famed web-shooters could be simple streams of line, shot from a hidden high-pressure airgun. At close range, liquid latex would work, since the stuff leaves a goopy wad. For distances, when the webbing becomes ropes for swinging and enraveling, we can use reverse-motion (as in the TV show), but 'undercranked' for high speed."

Finally, they addressed the climactic battle between Spidey and Doc Ock within the previously mentioned floating science building.

Explained Newsom and Brancato: "The battle with Doc Ock in the rising science center uses every technique mentioned above, and then some. Like the climaxes of *Raiders of the Lost Ark* and *Ghostbusters*, we pull out all the SFX stops for a visual spectacular. However, these movies, successful as they were, made a dramatic error—they left their heroes out of the climactic action. Indiana Jones was tied to a stake; the Ghostbusters hid and watched. Our climax uses outrageous special effects as the backdrop for an involving physical contest between hero and villain. The floating building will be a large-scale miniature with blue-screen aerials of New York. Clouds can be used in many of the shots, hiding our 'seams.' A partial set of the building exterior with battling actors on a blue-screen stage, combined with an aerial view, combined with the miniature, combined with optical electrical arcs—this is the slam-bang finale image, our money shot. Luckily, we won't need to see it more than a few times. The life-and-death struggle of our characters is strong enough (we hope) to overshadow even these flamboyant effects.

"*Spider-Man* doesn't have to cost a fortune," they concluded. "It's not a miser's dream, certainly, but with preplanning, storyboarding, and clever intercutting, the special effects bills can be kept down. *Star Trek II* and *Terminator* had only medium-scale budgets, and their special effects are tremendous. Still, what really sold these pictures was character and execution. Like in the comics, *Spider-Man* is, at heart, a character piece. The effects sequences should be fabulous, but they shouldn't dominate the picture."

Their arguments were persuasive, resulting in Lee and Golan agreeing to go forward. With the ball in Cannon's court, Golan lined up Tobe Hooper to serve as director, though he wouldn't stay in that position for long.

By 1985, New York native Joe Zito had proven himself to be an innovative director, taking relatively low-budget films and providing them with a sense of scope despite the limited resources available. His success with Paramount's *Friday the 13th: The Final Chapter* (1984) caught the attention of Golan, who brought him on board to direct the Chuck Norris action film *Missing in Action* (1984), first in a wave of "return to Vietnam" adventures along the lines of *Uncommon Valor* and *Rambo: First Blood Part II*. Quickly becoming Cannon's most profitable film ever, Zito next helmed 1985's *Invasion USA*, another Norris adventure in which the cinematic hero battles terrorists who bring their war to American soil (which, naturally, has taken on a chilling resonance since the events of September 11, 2001). Enjoying near-equal success to *MIA*, that film secured Zito with his choice of Cannon projects, and he immediately focused his sights on one in particular.

"By the time *Spider-Man* came along, I had the number one and two film in Cannon's history," says Zito. "What happened was that I was in the elevator with Menahem Golan. At the time, they used to take lots of full-page ads in the trades and they had one which was a full-page ad for *Spider-Man* and it had no director's name attached to it. So I was in the elevator with Menahem Golan and I said to him, 'I want *Spider-Man*.' He turns to me slowly—it's like the *Phantom of the Opera* with the slow turn—and he said to me, 'You want *Spider-Man*? Okay, I'll let you know in twenty-four hours.' I had a multiple-film deal at that point, so they had to give me two films a year or they'd have to pay me anyway. *Spider-Man* was the one I wanted to do. What I did *not* know, and I'm sure he doesn't believe it, but I swear to you I didn't know this, is that Tobe Hooper was supposed to do the film. There was an agreement for him to do it. I didn't know this because his name wasn't in the ad. So what happened during those twenty-four hours is that they went to the set of *Invaders from Mars,* talked to Tobe Hooper and Tobe ended up giving up *Spider-Man* and they came back and said that I had the project."

The thing that had attracted Zito to *Spider-Man* was the fact that he felt the character had a "magical" quality, and he had more or less already been directing comic-book movies.

"In *Missing in Action*, the guy goes into Vietnam and kills three hundred Vietnamese and gets out without even a scratch," he laughs. "This is not *Apocalypse Now*, this is a comic-book version of it. I was interviewed once, I think by *Newsweek*, and they said, 'Now that *Platoon* is out, do you feel that *Missing in Action* is very frivolous?' I said, 'It's not to be compared to *Platoon*. I think *Platoon* is wonderful and is doing what it was targeted to do. We were targeting something completely different. It wasn't like we were both striving for the reality of Vietnam and Oliver Stone did it better.' I was striving for a comic book that was a guiltless, old time cowboys-and-Indians adventure, without cowboys or

Indians, in which the good guy prevails. That's what it was supposed to be.

"In any event," continues Zito, "I had been doing comic-book-type movies and I liked those strange, dark worlds. There was no Batman movie yet, remember, and I had this vision of having this dark world with Spider-Man being the burst of color at the center of it. We had wonderful designs for the film. It was going to be a very stylish movie, and my conversations with Cannon were that I had really made my films with them with very little input—situations where they pretty much just funded the projects—and I didn't want to be interfered with. I told them that *Spider-Man* in particular had to be done completely differently from the way things had been done before. We would be bringing in a British crew—a very high-end British crew—and I was supposed to shoot in England, but by the time we got our production far enough along, Sidney Furie was going to do *Superman IV* on the stages in England, so we moved to Rome."

Zito's enthusiasm for the project is obvious to this day. He points out that the excitement of the project was that he would be dealing with a character who is conflicted and has to deal with real dilemmas. "He had to save the world," offers the director, "but on the other hand, he couldn't get laid. He was struggling through school. It was fun and real and it was a way to take something that was such solid comic material and have

it touch the world. It wasn't like Superman, who had no moral dilemma. He was completely conflicted. I loved it, and I was *not* a Spider-Man buff as a kid. I was in a good place at Cannon at that point. I felt that if I asked the company for something, they'd let me have it."

The "something" included his own writer. Although Zito initially began working with Newsom and Brancato, it was obvious that the three didn't quite see eye to eye on things. Says Brancato of the director, "He didn't really seem like a powerful creative force in the process." Rumors are that the writers, for whatever reason, pretty much ignored Zito's efforts to inject his vision into the script and, as a result, were replaced by Barney Cohen. The fit was a good one, considering that Cohen had written Zito's *Friday the 13th Part IV: The Final Chapter*, and would go on to create *Forever Knight* and adapt *Sabrina the Teenage Witch*.

On the *Friday the 13th* script, the writer offers: "I had not seen any of the slasher movies, so Joe told me to go see the first two films at a double feature in New York. I was on the 86th Street bus going back home after the movies, and I realized I had blinked or turned my head away on every one of the hits. I had to get off the bus, go back and keep my eyes open and see the double feature again to truly understand the genre. I think there's two ways to work as writer. One is to know something so fully that it's just in you and you don't have to worry about anything except expression. The other way is to know nothing about something, so the joy of learning it is communicated to the people that you're learning it for. I became a real fan of horror after I'd learned how to do it. The same thing with Spider-Man. I had to learn Spider-Man from the comics.

"Now I had never read a Spider-Man comic," Cohen elaborates. "When I was asked by Joe Zito to rewrite the script, they flew me out to Los Angeles from New York, where I stayed for three months. During that period, I read dozens of Spider-Man comic books to familiarize myself with the character. My only exposure had been the comic strip in the New York *Daily News*. I thought, 'What a great character,' then we had a meeting with Menahem Golan and I realized that he *hadn't* familiarized himself enough with the character to understand him the way Stan Lee did. One of the problems with the Newsom and Brancato script, which I made worse in Golan's eyes, was the character's duality. What I mean by duality is that he would rescue somebody, and then garbage would fall on his head. Then he couldn't get a date and things like that. Menahem went nuts when he saw my first draft, because he thought I was doing exactly the opposite of that. He really saw Spider-Man as a young Superman in a different outfit. I don't know if Menahem would know Superman as a socialist realist hero, which he was, but that's how he saw

him: as this proud, handsome piece of goods. He just did not get the duality and it was very difficult to explain to him why Spidey is self-deprecating, why garbage falls on his head, why he swings on a web and lands on the wrong thing. He just didn't get it. That wouldn't happen to Superman. Finally, Zito, who did get it, convinced him and we ended up with a pretty good script."

Dated April 1, 1986, Cohen's script, to a large degree, follows the structure of the Newsom/Brancato draft, although there are several additions. Most notable among them was that Doc Ock suddenly develops an underling—Weiner—who performs burglaries for the good doctor in an effort to drum up some extra cash. During one such burglary, Weiner kills Peter's Uncle Ben, thus tightening even more the origins of and connections between Doc Ock and Spider-Man.

Twenty days after the script's date, Golan himself handed in his own pass on the material, resulting in a script credited to him, Cohen, Newsom, and Brancato. This version of the story was fairly similar to the April 1 draft, though Golan added some odd topical references (i.e., the Hillside Strangler) and dialogue. "Here's a for instance," offers Newsom. "There's a sequence where Peter Parker is first realizing that something is wrong. He's gotten bitten by the spider and he's surging with radioactive Spidey power. He walks onto the street, a truck barrels at him and he leaps, finding himself four stories up. Then he climbs to the top of the building and tries to figure out what the hell's going on. Now that's comic-book stuff, that is precisely what happens in the Spider-Man origin, which is why we used it. It's perfect the way it is. But Menahem added other things that were way out of character for Peter Parker—i.e., Spider-Man—to do, because Menahem didn't grow up with the thing. He didn't understand who this character was. This guy was more Charles Bronson than Peter Parker. You have specific things that Peter Parker would say, do, or think, likewise Spider-Man because you're talking about the same guy. He wouldn't just beat up on a guy because he looked sideways at a girl. That's not what Spider-Man would do. But Menahem didn't see that because he didn't grow up on this shit. What John and I tried to do is keep the essence of Peter Parker there and keep what we thought was fun about the character."

Cohen, for his part, observes that "three interesting things" happened while he was working for Cannon. "When I first came out," he says, "Cannon was located at 6464 Sunset Boulevard. About three or four weeks later they moved to a new building that they had taken over. The first day there, because this was an Israeli company, we had a bomb scare. So they had to empty the building in the middle of everything. Everybody was evacuated. The other thing was that the building was pretty much done

except that the elevators didn't work. What was totally amazing to me was that it was only a six-story building, but people were using the stairs all the time and within two weeks everyone started looking great. The third thing was that this was a point when Menahem, a great risk taker who was always rolling the dice, was trying to make Cannon a mini-major, like New Line became. He was funding a lot of movies and he had this very complex and probably sharp business plan where he rolled one thing into another. This was when he'd hired Sylvester Stallone to do *Over the Top*, and he'd brought in people like Dustin Hoffman, Julie Andrews, and several other people. Stars and funders would come by this particular office we were working out of, because this was the twenty-million-dollar movie. This was a major motion picture. We were like a stop on the tour, we were like credibility. The interesting thing is that most of these people would come by because they were interested in Spider-Man and they all knew the character better than I did. To be honest, though, the whole experience was just a lot of fun. But then, Menahem told Joe that he had to lower the budget."

Zito explains that at that point, approximately $1.5 million had been put into the project's development, including the script and storyboarding the entire story. "Then," he says, "Cannon started getting into financial difficulty and they started limiting the amount of money. As an edict from the bank they had to limit their budgets to five million per picture. We didn't have to spend five. Originally the studio thought it would cost thirty million. I think we actually budgeted it in the upper teens, but thought it should cost more. Then I got a phone call asking if I could do it for fifteen million. We had a five-million-dollar effects budget back then. We were talking to Richard Edlund about doing special effects. *Then* I got another call when they were going through even more difficulties with banks and that kind of thing. They asked me to come back to Los Angeles from Rome. I went to Golan's home. There I met with Golan, Globus, and the head of production. Globus said, 'I have ten million for your Spider-Man.' I said, 'Ten million? Look, we've got a five-million-dollar effects budget. You're kidding yourself. You can't make this movie for ten million. If that's all you can spend, you ought to not make this film.' Ten million is a lot of money and you could make a real good film for that amount of money. Maybe two really good films. But not *Spider-Man*, with the level of effects you would need to make it competitive as an A-level film that you're going to base the value of a company on. So I advised them not to do it and that's how we didn't do it. But they would always say that they should have made *Spider-Man*, because it was going to be their *Batman*—it was the film that was going to change the value of

the company. Unfortunately, it came at a time when they could not afford to make it. Had we gotten the thing off the ground six months earlier, we would have made the film and it would have changed Cannon. The film we had in mind was a film that would have worked."

Unfortunately, by 1987, not much was working for Cannon. Not only were there the box-office failures to be dealt with, but the studio had apparently overstated the value of its stock and was being investigated by the Securities and Exchange Commission. All indications were that Cannon would go bankrupt, until it was taken over by Pathe Communications, Giancarlo Parretti's holding company, whose presence would most definitely be felt over the next few years, most notably in its acquisition of MGM.

In 1988, and with Parretti's money behind him, Golan turned his attention back to Spider-Man, deciding to go a less-expensive route. "The idea was that they would do a cheap version for a couple of million dollars," explains Joe Zito, who more or less stepped away from the project at that point. "Albert Pyun had been directing these low-budget films with Cannon that looked really stylish. They thought, 'Well, we own the property anyway,' because they had the option on the rights and they thought to knock it off as a low-budget picture."

Golan turned to actor/writer Don

Michael Paul to tackle the next draft of the screenplay, and his was the most drastically different from the Newsom/Brancato draft to date. While the origins of Spider-Man and the villain are connected, Doc Ock is nowhere to be found. In his place is the Night Ghoul, a hybrid between a human and a vampire bat that was created via genetic manipulation. While the Night Ghoul seems like a mindless creature, it's ultimately revealed to be an altered scientist who has set about avenging the deaths of a group of other scientists who were brutally murdered. While the characterization has a lot in common with many a Marvel villain—whose external appearance belies a more sympathetic soul—the script itself was fairly violent and bloody. And it was still too expensive.

Next up to the plate was Ethan Wiley, whose assignment was to write a *Spider-Man* script that could be produced for no more than $5 million. According to Wiley, at the time there was some concern that the rights to Spider-Man would be expiring shortly, so Cannon desperately needed to get the film into production as quickly as possible.

"There were a couple of things—baggage, you might say—that came with the project," he says. "It was never explained to me what the actual rights were that they owned. What I was told was that they owned the Spider-Man character, but there was some ambiguity as to whether they owned the other characters from the comic. That didn't make sense to me, because I used Uncle Ben, Aunt May, and certain characters like that. But I was instructed *not* to use any of the villains, like Doctor Octopus. So for my script, I then invented my own Spider-Man villain, which was fun. I tried to create a character that was true to the character, attitude, and approach of the comics. So I came up with a man who was a disabled doctor, a paraplegic, who was experimenting with genetic research. He was making incredible, groundbreaking advances in that field, but ultimately had a very personal motivation, because he was paralyzed from the waist down and wanted to walk again. So, in the climax of my script, he injects himself with this dangerous serum and takes on the properties of a scorpion. So he was kind of a scorpion man instead of an octopus man.

"Again," he continues, "I was trying to use elements where they would feel like they were true to the comic. I had the classic elements of Peter Parker living at home with his aunt and uncle, and getting bitten by a spider that's been genetically mutated, instead of [using] radioactivity. It was the late eighties and I tried to come up with something that rang a little more true for the times. The era of *The Man with the X-ray Eyes* seemed a little dated to me, so I wanted to do something a little bit different than just, 'Radioactivity created this situation.' The other interesting thing, and maybe this is why I was hired to do it, is that I was told to write this as a low-budget movie. They knew that they would have to make the film quickly and that there wasn't a lot of money."

Wiley was just coming off of the one-two punch of *House* and *House 2*, a pair of low-budget, effective, effects-driven horror movies which were produced on far lower budgets than even this lower-tier version of the web-slinger. Added to this was Wiley's background in special effects, acquired while working for Industrial Light and Magic and Chris Walas, Inc., on such films as *Return of the Jedi* and *Gremlins*.

"I was coming to the scriptwriting process not just as a writer but someone with production experience, effects experience and actual directing experience," he muses, "and was someone who could shape a movie that could be done at a budget like that. And, of course, write something that would be realistic to that approach. So my general structure—and concept—was actually to have Peter Parker become Spider-Man almost at the end of the movie. My thinking was that I wouldn't have the money to have him flying all over the city, doing lots of what would have been at that time blue-screen shots. This was before the age of digital filmmaking. And also the practicality of giant set pieces and shooting in the middle of cities. So I avoided a lot of that and really focused on the evolution of Peter Parker into Spider-Man. I

kind of explored that aspect of the story in more detail perhaps than earlier or later drafts did."

The real question, of course, is how such an approach would affect an audience who had obviously spent their bucks to see Spider-Man. "I think the appeal would have been watching the transformation take place," he says, "watching him metamorphose into this character. Early on, we started playing with the fact that he was developing powers and could walk on walls. At first it was just exploring things they only touched upon in the comics, such as his trying to figure out how to make money with these new powers. I had a scene—maybe similar to other drafts—where he tries to get an agent and gets onto the *David Letterman Show* and is humiliated by Letterman. It turns out to be a terrible experience in much the same way that other people, like Farah Fawcett and Madonna, have been humiliated and made fun of. It leaves a bitter taste in his mouth about show biz. So he kind of struggles with ways to turn it into his gain.

"It was also his coming to terms with his moral responsibility to society," Wiley adds. "One of the things that I always loved about the Spider-Man character—and I'm no diehard comic book freak by any stretch of the imagination—is that he was the first teen-aged superhero. I thought that was an interesting thing, so I really looked at it as a metaphor for him being a teenager growing into a man and taking on the responsibilities of what it means to be an adult; getting involved in society, responsibilities for family. As I recall, I had that classic scene, taken from the comics, where he's thwarting a crime and he's forgotten that he has Aunt May's heart medicine that he's supposed to get back to her. By the time he gets back home, she's being hauled off on an ambulance. He's almost killed her and he realizes, 'Here I was stopping this street crime, for someone I don't even know, and I forgot that I had to get the medicine back to her.' So, to me, that would crystallize the conflict in Spider-Man. Those were the things that I emphasized in the storytelling, as well as his coming up with the idea of becoming a superhero. How does he start designing the costume? How does he get it together and where do his own personal tragedies finally propel him to become a vigilante, essentially? The script ended with his finally realizing that this is his destiny, to become Spider-Man."

As far as he's concerned, one of the most enjoyable aspects of low-budget filmmaking is being forced to work within limited parameters. "I actually thought it made a pretty compelling story," he says. "Now the idea was that if it did well and was successful, then you were really set up to do a series of Spider-Man movies. You kind of use the first movie to set up the premise of the following sequels. In story number two you've got money because the first one was successful; now you jump right into the adventure and you don't have to tell his origin. At least that was my clever idea, but not clever enough, I guess."

Wiley remembers two meetings with Stan Lee: one before he began writing and one after he handed in his script. Unfortunately, Lee, he says, was not pleased with the final screenplay.

"He objected to the use of strong language and adult themes or situations," he explains. "His vision was something closer to the birth of the comic book, as I recall, and he wanted it to be a much more innocent, children's kind of story where the biggest conflict is with the bully down the street who has been picking on Peter Parker, and where Peter's greatest motivation is to get the girl. Very simple kind of teenage love story. I felt that the times called for something more sophisticated than that, something edgier. My script had a lot of comedy in it, because I tend to write with a kind of humorous angle toward things, and even some slapstick, but it also had a dark, urban vision for Peter Parker. I really had him living in a contemporary ghetto, which is very different than the earlier drafts, as I recall. That's something that has been held over to the final movie—it's set up that he lives in a Queens neighborhood and it's a little edgier. Maybe not as much as my draft, because I had a very dark plot revolving around the doctor who was doing this experimentation with genetics—

had been ostracized by the medical community because of practices they considered to be unethical. Peter Parker, who works for this doctor and learns late in this story that he's not the upstanding medical professional he claims to be, discovers that he has been duped into assisting this doctor in his very ethically dubious experiments. And the way the doctor is financing them is that he's found a by-product of his experiments that has created a super cocaine-type of drug that is very dangerous. He sells this to the mob to finance his own experiments. He feels that since he's been ostracized from the medical community and financial sources, this is his only way to finance his experiments. This drug is destroying the teenagers that Peter Parker associates with, and Peter learns later in the story that he is inadvertently responsible for this drug epidemic. Like I said, pretty dark and edgy. At the same time I thought it was kind of true to the best elements of the Spider-Man comics while bringing a real modern, contemporary angst to the character."

This drug was called T-Devil (in homage to the Tasmanian Devil), and it was pretty much a heightened type of crack-cocaine. People would take the drug, get superhuman powers as a result, get an ultimate high, and, ultimately, their hearts would explode. Again, Lee was *not* amused.

"He was actually angry and unhappy with this plotline," the writer explains. "He thought it was very morbid and cynical. He said, 'Why would people take a drug knowing it would kill them?' I could only smile and say, 'Stan, isn't that what *all* drugs do?' My point was an exaggeration of reality; that people take cigarettes, take alcohol, take heroin, take crack-cocaine and nobody tells them it's going to make them healthier. We all know these things are going to kill us. So it was taking this to this kind of bizarre extreme, and was also saying that teenagers with no purpose in their lives would rather be a superhero for twenty-four hours, even with the risks that went along with it. But when Peter Parker realizes that he had a direct hand in manufacturing this drug that's killing his high school friends, he realizes that, although it wasn't through any fault of his own, maybe he didn't look deep enough; that he ignored the early warning signs that something wasn't right, that he kept his faith in authority and the father figure and has been betrayed by that. At the end he comes back to the warehouse to confront the doctor with his evidence, and the doctor is now fully transformed into this kind of scorpion man. This leads to the Spider-Man and Scorpion Man duking it out with equal kinds of powers—a *mano a mano* epic battle in the contained warehouse, which was more of a low-budget theory. We could build a set, tear it apart, and—most importantly, they're not flying all over the city. He gets there by swinging over a building or two, but that was the big finale. In the end, when he's defeated the doctor, that's when he realizes he must use his powers to help protect society and that he can't continue to ignore his responsibility. Even when you're not directly responsible, you can be indirectly responsible because of your passivity.

"So I disagreed with Stan Lee," Wiley notes, "but I had a responsibility to come up with a script that would speak to a contemporary audience. In some ways, in his arguments about the project, he was ignoring the later evolution of the comic itself and harking back to maybe his own personal vision in the earlier days of the comic, which is completely valid but two different points of view. But even though he didn't like the script very much, it was still a thrill to meet him."

In 1989, the situation with Cannon was not improving, and Menahem Golan was seen as an impediment. Parretti began making moves that would have the filmmaker fired from his own company. In assessing the situation, Wiley opines: "It's always tough for independents. And it's always a struggle. A couple of the success stories in independents—Miramax, New Line, for example—were really defined by one really major hit movie that exploded onto the national consciousness and the national box office. New Line had struggled for like twenty years as an art house kind of company and Miramax had struggled along with lots of Oscars but not a lot of money, and then *Nightmare on Elm Street* and *Scream*

turned into huge hits. A lot of these independent film companies needed that big, defining cash cow, and I think that that had eluded Cannon. I think there was a possibility you could get in there with a little fun movie, but with Menahem Golan at the helm I don't know if he had the strongest sense of what would make a commercial hit in America at the time."

In any case, Golan's "time" with Cannon was coming to an end. The future was not bright for the company, and Golan was seen by Parretti as the sacrificial lamb. "When Golan was forced out of the company," remembers Joe Zito, "he was offered a 'golden parachute,' which was supposed to translate to a great deal of money. But the deal never could close, so in negotiation he took properties with him, and *Spider-Man* was one of them."

Golan formed 21st Century Films with the hopes of bringing back the "golden age" of Cannon. His first step was to renegotiate the *Spider-Man* deal—originally set to expire in August of 1990—with Marvel, which he managed to do. He immediately put writer Frank LaLoggia—the writer, director, composer, and star of the thriller *Lady in White*—on the project.

Next up in the writing bullpen was Neil Ruttenberg, who had previously written the film *Deathstalker II* and would go on to write *Mad Dog Coll, Viper*, and *Prehysteria 3* before giving up Hollywood for a career in teaching. Ruttenberg admits that his experience on *Spider-Man* wasn't exactly fulfilling. He desperately wanted to get back to the character's roots, but no one at 21st Century seemed particularly interested in doing so.

"I wanted to go back to the comic book," he relates. "I had a good relationship with Stan Lee, though he was more of an idea guy. It wasn't really hands on for him. He liked to sit around and talk a lot. We had a pretty good working relationship, and I had a pretty good relationship with Menahem Golan, because I respected him. Even though a lot of his films weren't very good, I think he knew a lot about film. I think the flaw in his whole organization was the people he had working for him. Menahem knew a lot about movies and had good taste in the projects he chose, he just was unable to translate that to his own films. He had a story editor who would continually derail the process and I had no more contact with Menahem after that because this guy put himself between me and Menahem.

"After I finished the draft," Ruttenberg adds, "Menahem was very happy, but the whole project seemed to be derailed again. Menahem's company always seemed to be struggling. He wasn't real respected in the community, having made some really terrible movies—though they probably wouldn't be considered terrible by today's standards. He just didn't have the reputation that he actually deserved. Again, his organization

and his cheapness just kind of did him in. After that, I kind of moved on."

In terms of the film itself, Ruttenberg wanted to deal with Peter Parker's adolescent angst, which he feels is what underlined his entire story. Additionally, he wanted to use Doc Ock as the villain.

"The better the villain, the better the movie," he says matter-of-factly. "Doc Ock, to me, was the only Spider-Man villain that was worth a damn. Spider-Man's greatest flaw was that most of the villains were never any good, but Ock was crazy and had appendages. The whole idea of Doc Ock was that you could really go to town with the prosthetics, which is what gives you your bigger bang for the buck. At that time prosthetic devices were not really well advanced, but they were still pretty good.

"Roger Corman was the king of exploitation, and that's who I trained with," he says, "but even Roger understood that there had to be some intellectual content, even though that failed to translate years afterward. He would hire directors who didn't understand what exploitation really was. Again, it was exploitation with breasts and crude jokes, but it didn't work. I would say my script didn't work for the reason that the chemistry with the executives was all wrong. Menahem would tend to grab on to an idea, love it, then divorce himself from it and let his staff deal with it and move on to the next big deal. He was running toward the end of his career, but he was still trying to play the kingmaker."

Ruttenberg's feeling is that comic-book characters in general are difficult to translate successfully to film. "At the same time," he says, "the whole idea of an adolescent slipping into someone else's skin, to be cool and develop his persona was interesting. That's what adolescence was all about. That's what I was looking for, and I never got that. It was really hard. He understood the intellectual content, Menahem, but his crew didn't and they didn't care. He could have made *Spider-Man* and it would have probably been pretty good. I haven't read all the successive scripts, but it would have been decent. I've only read a few drafts of the final movie, but what should have been a really simple story seems to have become something overly complicated."

Interestingly, he wrote for a slightly higher-than-expected budget, somewhere in the $10 to $15 million range. "I was looking at it as a big-budget movie for that time," he says. "I wanted a lot of aerial acrobat kind of thing, that was my vision of it. But I'm sure as their money coffers dwindled, they started making them lower and lower. I never tailored my script to anything. Rereading it now, I know it's not as good as I could make it today, but I know in my mind what I wanted to get, and I know what I was stopped from giving it. There was a huge age difference between me and the executive. He was in his sixties, and he

was of a different generation, too. He wasn't like somebody from the sixties who grew up with it and understood teenage angst. He was much older than that. He was coming at it purely from the exploitive, 'How can we do tits and ass?' school of thought, which didn't appeal to me at all."

The word "exploitation" was seemingly destined to drop away from the *Spider-Man* project as it moved on to its next phase.

Enter James Cameron

Golan's next step was to try and raise the money to finally shoot the film, which he accomplished by selling the worldwide television rights to the proposed film to Viacom, with Columbia Tri-Star stepping in to handle the home video release. Then there was yet another independent studio, Carolco, the company behind such hits as *Basic Instinct, Rambo: First Blood Part II*, and *Total Recall*. Meeting with Golan at the 1990 Cannes Film Festival, Carolco's Mario Kassar and Peter Hoffman convinced him that they would be able to finance a $50 million version of Spidey, for which 21st Century would receive $5 million, while Golan himself would receive $1 million. He signed a deal with Carolco, adding that his years of pushing the project would require that he be listed as the film's producer in the credits. While this didn't seem like a sticking point at the time—despite the baggage that Golan's name inevitably brings with it—it was a contractual decision that would end up biting everyone in the ass. That became apparent with Carolco's choice of writer/director in late 1991.

By that point, James Cameron had become one of Hollywood's most powerful filmmakers—years before *Titanic* became the highest grossing motion picture of all time. Cameron's credits up until then included *Piranha II: The Spawning, The Terminator, Aliens, The Abyss, True Lies*, and *Terminator 2: Judgment Day*, and Carolco, for whom he had made *T2*, felt that he was the right man for the job of bringing Spidey to life. Cameron was paid a cool $3 million for coming on board, which was bad news for Golan—it seems that Cameron's standard contract gives him approval of every credit, and he was adamant that Golan's name *not* appear on the film. Again, it had completely to do with what a Menahem Golan film had come to mean. Believing that this was his last shot at legitimacy, by April of 1993, Golan had filed suit against Carolco, which, heading toward bankruptcy, sold its rights to *Spider-Man* to MGM.

At that moment, all hell broke loose, with anyone who had ever signed a contract pertaining to the *Spider-Man* movie hitting the courtroom.

In early 1994, Carolco sued Viacom and Tri-Star in an effort to do away with the Cannon-agreed-upon deals pertaining to television and home video rights. Tri-Star and Viacom, naturally, launched a counter-suit against not only Carolco, but 21st Century Films and Marvel as well. Due to the fact that MGM was owned by the Pathe Group, it was their corporate belief that the rights to *Spider-Man* belonged to them, especially since they had begun with Cannon (plus the deal with Carolco), sued Menahem Golan, Yoram Globus, 21st Century Films, Parretti, Tri-Star, Viacom, and Marvel. Things almost got laughable when, within the next twelve months, 21st Century Films, Marvel, and Carolco all filed for bankruptcy.

Between all of these lawsuits, Cameron, who at that point was still attached to the project, wrote a 57-page "scriptment," which was a combination script and story treatment that was designed to hit all of the high points of his proposed scenario. In Spidey according to Cameron, Peter Parker's transformation into the web-crawler is fairly different from the comic. Peter and his classmates are on a field trip in order to study flies that have been genetically altered. One of them escapes from its container and finds itself trapped in a spider's web. The owner of that particular web chows down on the fly and then ends up biting and changing Peter—a fairly convoluted way to get to the same results. The villains this time out are Strand, who acquires the power of near invulnerability and electricity (à la Electro), and his henchman, the Sandman, who has the ability to morph his body into sand that is soft like that found on a beach or hard as a rock. Considering what Cameron was able to accomplish with the Terminator of *T2*, one can only imagine the "cool factor" in this version of the Sandman.

A primary difference between this Spider-Man and the one we're used to is that his webshooters are actually organic, the webbing being emitted from his wrists instead of from a device created by Peter Parker. Additionally, there's a darker thread running through this scenario than in most of the other scripts, and Peter has a tendency to break into *serious* profanity when he's pissed off.

None of this really mattered, of course. What Cameron had written was not perceived to be nearly as important as the fact that he had written anything at all, and that the plan called for him to direct—*if* the project's legal headaches could be dealt with.

One person anxious for the project to be brought to life, and growing more tired of waiting by the day, was Dan Poole, an independent filmmaker from Baltimore, Maryland, who actually filmed a fifty-minute live-action Spider-Man adventure called *The Green Goblin's Last Stand*, based on the death of Gwen Stacy comic-book story line. It was created, he says, in the hopes of attracting Cameron's attention.

"It was really the idea that James Cameron was going to be my audience," he says, "and that I had to impress him. I said, 'I've got to shoot the best thing I can possibly shoot.' *The Green Goblin's Last Stand* was made as a resume. It was specifically designed to get me a position on the *Spider-Man* movie—*any* position at all. That was the *only* goal. I only made it for him to watch. Anything that's going on now is different, but when I started out making it, it was born of watching Stan Lee on *Good Morning America* speaking about James Cameron helming the new *Spider-Man* movie. In that instant it became very clear what I had to do—I had to swing around a building, I had to get blown across a warehouse, I had to just do the most severe stuff that I could possibly do in that costume. Anything I had to do to have Cameron watch that film and say, 'Damn!'

"My hopes were kind of dashed when they would never watch it and kept sending it back, no matter what agent I got," he continues. "I tried different ways to sneak it in; an agent with a letter of indemnity, because it was unsolicited—they didn't ask for it so they didn't want to see it. They were so gun shy about lawsuits and didn't want anything to do with it. So they completely stonewalled me. I finally convinced his personal assistant to watch it and sent her the comic books that it was based on to prove that it wasn't even my story line. I said, 'I own nothing rights-wise about this project, just please watch it.' About six months went by and I heard they were gearing up to do *Titanic*, and the tape came back to me without a letter or anything. I thought, 'God, how absolutely ignorant.' So that was the beginning of me realizing I had to look out for myself, write my own script and do it myself."

Perhaps one of the most faithful adaptations of Spider-Man done to date, *The Green Goblin's Last Stand* is certainly worth checking out (www.alphadogproductions.com). What those who log on will find is an impressive—albeit low budget—Spider-Man adventure, which has paved the way for writer, director, actor, and stuntman Poole to begin work on an original superhero adventure, *Natural Forces*.

Things on the *Spider-Man* front grew fairly quiet over the next couple of years as the lawyers continued to flex their muscles. But, finally, it all came to an end, on March 1, 1999. On that day, Sony issued the following press release:

> Sony Pictures Entertainment (SPE) and Marvel Enterprises have signed an agreement that sets the stage for launching the long anticipated Spider-Man filmed entertainment franchise. The agreement will enable SPE and Marvel to produce motion pictures and television series based on the Spider-Man character. Additionally, Marvel and SPE have established a joint venture to exploit picture-related and series-related merchandise. The announcement of the agreement was made by SPE Chairman and CEO John Calley and Marvel Enterprises President and CEO Eric Ellenbogen and Chief Creative Officer, Avi Arad.

> "This is a great day for the studio," said Mr. Calley. "I am delighted that we will be able to bring this long sought after comic book hero to the world of Sony film and television entertainment."

> "Spider-Man is the crown jewel of Marvel's vast character library," noted Mr. Eric Ellenbogen. "Our pact with Sony is a giant step forward in leveraging Marvel content to the fullest across all media. I can't imagine a more momentous new beginning for our company."

> Marvel's Arad added, "In Sony we have a partner who completely understands the unlimited potential of Spider-Man. I couldn't be more pleased with the enthusiasm and direction of Sony's creative team."

> In making the announcement, Mssrs. Calley and Ellenbogen also noted that the pending lawsuits between the two companies over Spider-Man have ended and all claims have been settled between both parties, In addition, the disputes between Marvel, SPE, and MGM on this matter have been resolved.

How was it all resolved? The entertainment industry trade publication *Variety* summed up the situation as follows: "Litigation began in 1993 between 21st Century, Carolco, Sony and Viacom. MGM entered the fray in 1994, having purchased the rights from 21st Century and Carolco, both now bankrupt. Last year, Marvel, emerging from its own bankruptcy, came roaring back into the rights dispute, claiming that it had the exclusive right to make a Spider-Man film and that all the rights that had been granted had long since expired. With the case headed for a trial set to start Tuesday in L.A. Superior Court, a round of frenzied activity began. Last month, Judge Aurelio Munoz granted Marvel's motions for summary judgment against MGM," noting that MGM's rights had expired in 1996. All rights, ruled the court (including the Cameron scriptment), were back in Marvel's hands. Immediately thereafter, the deal with Sony was struck.

The only downside to all of this was the fact that during all of the litigation, James Cameron had filmed, released, and been crowned king of the world for *Titanic*, and he had gone a long way in making it clear that he was no longer interested in working on any project that he did not originate. Obviously, Spider-Man was not his, so he was no longer interested. As Lightstorm Entertainment president Rae Sanchini noted, "We have not been involved in the Sony-Marvel negotiations and are not currently attached to the project."

On April 5, 1999, Sony announced that David Koepp would be adapting Cameron's scriptment into a full screenplay. With writing credits that include *Death Becomes Her, The Shadow, Jurassic Park, Mission: Impossible, Lost World: Jurassic Park*, and *Stir of Echoes*, he seemed like the perfect choice.

Koepp's first draft, dated November 5, 1999, followed Cameron's scriptment extremely closely, with Electro (given that name by J. Jonah Jameson) unleashing a plan to disrupt the New York Stock Exchange. Things would go through more radical shifts beginning with Koepp's second script, dated April 14, 2000. The Spider-Man origin went back to tradition, avoiding the whole "fly eaten by a spider that bites Peter Parker" scenario. Also lost was Electro and the Sandman, who were replaced by the Green Goblin (a.k.a. Norman Osborn) and the film project's perennial standby, Doc Ock.

The combination of the Goblin and Doc Ock was not greeted with a great deal of enthusiasm by most fans. To some, this felt a little too close for comfort to what Warner Brothers had done with the Batman film franchise.

In Tim Burton's original (1989's *Batman*), an effort was made to tie Batman and the Joker's origins together, and from a dramatic point of view (whether or not you felt the film as a whole worked), that held together fairly well. For *Batman Returns*, the Dark Knight went up against the Penguin and Catwoman. *Batman Forever* introduced Robin to the big screen, and had the Dynamic Duo take on Two-Face and the

Riddler. *Batman and Robin* added Batgirl to the mix, and the rogues' gallery featured Mr. Freeze, Poison Ivy, and Bane. How in God's name was anyone supposed to keep up with what was going on, and how could the filmmakers have ever hoped to provide a story that would service all of those characters? The answer was obvious: they couldn't.

When Newsom and Brancato had written the first draft of *Spider-Man* in 1985, their intention was to have Spider-Man battle Doctor Octopus, and to tie their origins together. *That* was a dramatically sound idea, even if it didn't mirror comic-book continuity. But to shoehorn the good Doctor and the Goblin together felt like a major mistake. Much of the rest of Koepp's second draft followed the first, right down to the adventure at the stock exchange.

As the film moved into production, rewrites were continuously being done, some by Koepp, others by Alvin Sargent

and Scott Rosenberg. Throughout this development, the decision was made that Spidey should take on only one baddie for his first adventure. Despite the fact that Doc Ock had been waiting in the wings for some fifteen years, he was dumped in favor of the Green Goblin. One of the primary differences between this Goblin and his comic-book progenitor is the fact that his outfit is far more mechanically based than it ever was before. His clothing is more like armor (à la the Batsuits from the Batman films), equipped with a variety of weapons and devices.

In all, and despite all the fits and starts the project had been through over the course of a decade and a half, the final shooting script held the promise of an epic Spider-Man adventure; an adventure that would prove faithful to the comics without being a slave to them. It may have taken forty years, but Spider-Man was finally ready for his close-up.

Spider-Man: The Movie
Day by Day

Back when Warner Bros. was getting ready to release *Superman: The Movie* or even—ten years later—Tim Burton's *Batman*, fans of those characters anxiously waited for the next issues of *Starlog* and *Cinefantastique* magazines to be published for any sort of nugget of production information, or interview with someone involved with the production.

Things would occasionally come out in the mainstream press, but any kind of in-depth coverage was reserved for those types of genre publications, and it was nerve-wracking, waiting for word on what was happening. By 2002, things changed, thanks largely to the Internet. On a film like *Spider-Man*, for instance, you can log on each day and learn something new. Hell, Spider-Man Hype (www.spidermanhype. com), for example, not only serves as *the* source for official and unofficial information on all things Spidey, but is often quoted in the mainstream press. S-M-H (as the site is often referred to) is far from the only source of information. Fans can check out www.aint-it-cool-news.com, www. darkhorizons.com, www.comicscontinuum. com, www.comics2film.com, among others. All provide a wide range of information, from script reviews to casting sessions to top-secret details from the special effects department.

"I've never seen anything like the Internet," *Spider-Man* director Sam Raimi admitted to Spider-Man Hype. "It's like if you were a plumber and you had forty thousand other plumbers looking over your shoulder to see how you were putting it all together and they all have a really strong opinion and it's printed for everyone to see. It's not like they keep their opinion to themselves. It makes it difficult to replace the pipe. I think directing the picture is even a harder job than plumbing. It's filled with a thousand creative decisions and none are right or wrong."

Once the announcement was made that Sony would be going forward with *Spider-Man*, the Internet came to life with postings about the film. Some would turn out to be remarkably accurate, others off base, and the vast majority outright lies. The following is a look at the making of *Spider-Man* from the Internet's point of view.

May 24, 1999

Rumors began that Ron Howard would wrap up production of The Grinch *and segue over to* Spider-Man. *The names of other directors would follow, among them Stephen Sommers*

(The Mummy, The Mummy Returns), *Ivan Reitman* (Six Days, Seven Nights), *and Tim Burton* (Sleepy Hollow, Planet of the Apes).

July 1999

While promoting Mel Gibson's The Patriot, actor Heath Ledger was asked about rumors he might be starring as Spidey. "There have been some discussions," said the actor, who would go on to star in A Knight's Tale, "but it's too early to know what will happen with that one."

November 1999

Screenwriter David Koepp was interviewed in the pages of Hollywood Scriptwriter, where he was asked to compare the blockbusters he writes to the lower-budget films for which he serves as both writer and director. "I enjoy big adventure movies and there are a lot of obvious temptations to do them," he said. "I'm doing Spider-Man now as a writer. I'm still in the script stage. There's no producer and no director, and I'm already dealing with four executives at the studio, including the chairman of the company, the head of the comic book company, and a vice president. Six executives already. When the final voices are in, there will be a dozen people with input into the script. That's just guaranteed to iron out any idiosyncrasies or personal touches you can put in. So it's got its ups and downs."

December 9, 1999

Variety *reported that the two directors in the running to helm* Spider-Man *were Chris*

Columbus (Harry Potter) and David Fincher (Seven)—*wrong on both counts. On January 5, 2000, Sony's Amy Pascal added Jan De Bont* (Twister, Deep Blue Sea) *to the mix. The following day, Sam Raimi* (The Evil Dead *trilogy,* The Gift) *was mentioned as a possibility. This, of course, would turn out to be the truth.*

January 14, 2000

The Internet posters got around to the subject of casting, suggesting that the lead role of Peter Parker/Spider-Man could go to Rushmore's *Jason Schwartzman,* American Beauty's *Wes Bentley, or* Buffy the Vampire Slayer's *Nicholas Brendon.* Entertainment Weekly *would eventually add the names of Leonardo DiCaprio, Freddie Prinze, Jr., and Jude Law.*

March 1, 2000

The Aint-It-Cool-News website posted a report that Sam Raimi would want John Dykstra to handle Spidey's special effects challenges. This rumor turned out to be fact.

April 11, 2000

The Aint-It-Cool-News website reported that shooting of Spider-Man *was supposed to commence on December 4 for a summer 2001 release. At the time it seemed like an impossible schedule to keep, due to the sheer quantity of special effects shots needed for the film.*

April 17, 2000

While shooting The Gift in Savannah, Georgia, director Sam Raimi was visited by actors

Chris Klein and Liam Neeson (who had previously worked with the director on Darkman). This immediately gave birth to rumors that Klein was being considered for the role of Spidey and Neeson for the Green Goblin.

April 22, 2000

A website called the Daily Radar reported a rumor that Spider-Man would be played by actor Ryan Merriman, best known for playing the young Jarod on the earlier NBC series, The Pretender.

May 3, 2000

Sony Pictures and Marvel Comics held a conference with 400 potential lincensees and some journalists for Spider-Man on the UCLA Campus. Revealed there was the fact that the movie would feature both the Green Goblin and Doctor Octopus. Among those attending the conference were director Sam Raimi and executive producer Avi Arad, who offered a number of comments to the press:

RAIMI: Ever since I was a little kid, I loved Spider-Man. My older brother, who was the smartest guy I knew, was reading him and for some reason was enamored of these comics. I finally put down my Superman and Batman comics and took a look at one of them. Then, I understood why. The writers, Stan Lee primarily, got into the character of Peter Parker. He's a real human being. He's not from the planet Krypton. He's not some mutant. He's one of us who wins the spider lottery. He becomes this superpowered person, but he still has the everyday troubles that we all experience when he's not in the outfit. That makes him interesting and accessible. What I hope to put into the movie is what I found so attractive about the comic books. He is not pretending to be somebody, like Superman pretends to be Clark Kent. Superman is really cool and unstoppable and he winks at us with the glasses and says, "I'm just pretending to be a nerd." But Peter really is. He never loses sight of who he is and that's what's great about him. He's still us in that costume. It makes a big difference as you follow the action of the picture. But like any high school kid, Peter goes through a lot of teenage angst and he's got a lot of learning to do. And I think in some sense it'll be a very simple coming-of-age story. A story of a teenager who has teenage goals, but when he becomes Spider-Man and has the power to achieve these goals, he forsakes them to accept a greater responsibility—the responsibility of great power.

ARAD: Spider-Man has gone through a lot of changes and so has Peter Parker in the last thirty-eight years, but we're going to stay very close to Stan Lee's original version. Obviously there are some changes, because you only have a couple of hours to tell a pretty big saga. But the same guy—Uncle Ben—dies. Mary Jane is still very important. Aunt May is very important. We make her even more important than in the books. Peter is Peter. There's no reason to change him. The fans are going to love it.

There will be no controversy. Everyone is going to get what he or she wants out of it.

RAIMI: *I don't think there's ever been a time in history up until now—this year and next year—that you really could've made this Spider-Man picture. Where you can really create these digital cities and we can soar with a Spider-Man above Manhattan. What I want to do is show it like you'd show a great Olympic skating routine. He's not a muscle-bound brute. He is a live and beautiful dancer who soars above the skyline, and it'll be the work of an acrobat, the work of a gymnast, the work of all the finest performers in the art of physical what-have-you. But they are going to be long takes, like in a Fred Astaire picture, of Spider-Man climbing and leaping off a building and doing a number on a flagpole like an Olympic gymnast. Then it will become the work of a dancer in the sky. I hope it will become a thing of beauty that twenty years from now, people will still enjoy watching and we really get to fly with him.*

May 4, 2000

Again, Marvel Enterprises noted that the villains from the James Cameron/David Koepp efforts (Strand [Electro] and Sandman) would be replaced by the Green Goblin and Doc Ock. In the end, Doc Ock would be dropped.

June 14, 2000

In an interview with the Boston Herald, *actor Freddy Prinze, Jr., detailed his future aspira-*tions. Noted the paper: "Prinze intends to play one of his comic book superheroes some day in a movie—but not just in any movie. He was pursued by 20th Century Fox to come aboard X-Men, *but passed. He's hoping instead to play one of his real superheroes such as Peter Parker, the Spider-Man created by the legendary Stan Lee."* On that same day, Prinze participated in an AOL chat in which the subject of Spider-Man *came up. "I have spoken with director Sam Raimi,"* he explained, *"but no decision has been made yet. However one will be made soon. I think if they want to go kind of young and make him little and scrawny, if that's the case, you probably won't see me slinging webs."*

Aint-It-Cool-News had a story on Spidey's costume, noting: *"The costume will be something you've never seen before, although they didn't show the exact one, they showed five or six prototypes that did away with the old-school web pattern and basically came up with a new web pattern for lack of a better word, but it looks very modern and sleek and pretty cool, much like the transition from old school Batman to the Dark Knight."*

June 16, 2000

The trades reported that Scott Rosenberg, whose credits include Con Air *and* High Fidelity, *had been hired to rewrite the David Koepp screenplay.*

June 27, 2000

According to an on-line interview, Heath Ledger was indeed offered the leading role of

Peter Parker/Spider-Man, but felt it necessary to turn it down. "I'm not really a big fan of putting on tights or anything like that," he said. "I talked to Sam Raimi and it's a great script and will be a great movie, but I don't want to bear the responsibilities of being an action hero. You sort of become that and it's not just doing one movie, it's the option of the next two also. And the next thing of turning up in supermarkets for Spider-Man functions. I don't want to live as Spider-Man or be remembered for one role in my life."

June 28, 2000

The London Evening Standard *reported that Ewan McGregor (Obi-Wan Kenobi in the* Star Wars *prequels) was up for the role of Spider-Man. This would turn out to be false.*

July 7, 2000

Laura Ziskin, producer of such films as Pretty Woman *and* As Good as It Gets, *was officially tapped to serve as producer of* Spider-Man.

July 15, 2000

Felicity's *Scott Speedman was the latest actor mentioned for the role of Peter Parker/Spider-Man.*

July 28, 2000

Vince Vaughn—the actor who genre fans probably best know from Lost World: Jurassic Park, *the ill-conceived reshooting of* Psycho *(remake would be too generous a term), and the Jennifer Lopez horror thriller* The Cell, *was being considered for the role of Peter Parker's "nemesis," Flash Thompson.*

A wacky rumor was the possibility of Jeff Goldblum as Doc Ock. Physically, the actor looks absolutely nothing *like the character.*

According to Variety, *actor Tobey Maguire tested for the lead role of Peter Parker/Spider-Man.*

July 29, 2000

Tobey Maguire was confirmed by Sony to be cast as Spidey. Offered Sony's Amy Pascal: "I am delighted with this choice. Tobey's acting ability and incredible screen presence and Sam's creative vision are a powerful combination to bring Spider-Man *to the screen." Added Raimi: "As an actor, Tobey is a director's dream. He has all the qualities we were looking for in our Peter Parker."*

August 2000

More casting rumors: Nicolas Cage, John Malkovich, and Kevin Costner as the Green Goblin, Vincent D'Onofrio and Laurence Fishburne as Doc Ock, Liev Schreiber as Dr. Curt Connors (a.k.a. The Lizard), and Julia Stiles as Mary Jane Watson. All wrong!

August 3, 2000

Despite the fact that there had been readings by numerous actors for the role of Spider-Man, director Sam Raimi supposedly wanted Tobey Maguire from the beginning. As Cinescape *reported, "Raimi wanted Maguire from the get-go, though the studio wanted him at least*

Tobey Maguire

to meet with other guys, more traditional leading man guys. . . . To convince the doubting execs of his potential as an action-hero type, Maguire is said to have put himself through a workout regimen prior to the screen test."

August 8, 2000

Vincent D'Onofrio, rumored to be in the running for the role of Doc Ock, told TV Guide Online, "I wouldn't do it. There are certain things you cannot do."

August 16, 2000

Soundtrack Magazine *reported that Danny Elfman had been signed to score* Spider-Man. *The composer's previous credits include* Batman, Batman Returns, Mission: Impossible, Sleepy Hollow, Men in Black, A Simple Plan, Darkman, Army of Darkness, *and Tim Burton's remake of* Planet of the Apes.

August 20, 2000

The on-line site 4Filmmakers noted that Spider-Man *would begin actual production within the next few days.*

August 24, 2000

Aint-It-Cool-News reported that Scott Rosenberg's rewrite of the David Koepp screenplay had dropped Doc Ock from the story.

September 2000

It was officially announced that the release date of Spider-Man *had been changed from November 2001 to May 2002, and no one seemed happier about this fact than Marvel's Avi Arad. "We decided that we are much better off with a movie in the summer, especially after [the success of]* X-Men," *he told the Comics Continuum website. "We'll be starting in the summer, like* Gladiator. *I like summer movies. What it does for us, it's the first movie of the summer, it starts the whole business. It also makes it a summer movie in Europe."*

*Several days later, Raimi discussed the movie with SFX magazine: "*Batman *and*

Superman *are great movies, but they're more fantastic-world movies with these superheroes and outrageously funny villains in them. Spider-Man, I want to make more real-world. Peter Parker is cool, and something fantastic happens to him."* On October 6, Raimi discussed the fact that Maguire was pumping himself up physically for the lead role, telling the Internet Movie Database, "We're kicking his ass in the training room. He's working out every day with a stunt coordinator and with his yoga instructor. He's on special diets. He is undergoing a tremendous physical metamorphosis. He's got a great desire to see Spider-Man up on the screen."

September 1, 2000

Comedian Chris Rock told Jam! Showbiz that he desperately wanted to play Spider-Man. "I begged to be Spider-Man," he said. "I wanted an audition. But I couldn't get in, man. I couldn't get in . . . Tobey Maguire, he'll be fine. Small actually works on screen sometimes. He'll put on a suit and there will be muscles. But I would have been a great Peter Parker, man. But I can never be Peter Parker because I'm a black man."

September 3, 2000

The Coming Attractions website reported that Spider-Man would feature cameo appearances by Dr. Curt Connors and Dr. Otto Octavius as a means of laying the groundwork for future films. Nice idea, but ultimately not one that would turn out to be true.

September 7, 2000

Filmmakers reported that Kate Hudson had been added to the cast of the film, most likely in the role of Mary Jane Watson.

September 14, 2000

In an interview with Comics Continuum, Marvel's Avi Arad commented on the loss of Doc Ock from the script. "I would have liked him, but it just became very difficult to have two major villains in this movie," he said. "There was so much to tell in the origin—there's Peter, there's Spider-Man, Norman and Harry, the Goblin and Aunt May and Mary Jane Watson. It wouldn't have done justice to him. So I like the fact that they decided not to do a throwaway with such an important character as Doc Ock."

September 19, 2000

The Dark Horizons website had a report on Spider-Man's possible special effects, with a post stating: "I was talking to Ken Hahn, who was a big special effects guy on Hollow Man, and he told me that they are currently creating an entirely CG Manhattan for the movie. They are even thinking of making Spider-Man in costume CG. With the technology they created for Hollow Man, he said it would be a breeze."

October 5, 2000

The Internet Movie Database reported that Tobey Maguire had already begun a rigorous series of training sessions for the film. Noted director Sam Raimi: "Tobey's already been working with a wire man, he's got really good physical motion and I think he's studying right now how to move in an insectoid style, so he's working on it."

October 6, 2000

The Hollywood Reporter *announced that James Franco was in negotiations to costar in* Spider-Man *as Peter Parker's friend Harry Osborn, who happens to be the son of Norman Osborn, who in turn is the Green Goblin.*

On the same day, Sam Raimi was interviewed by Cinescape, *when he revealed how he got the directing gig:* "I was surprised that I was awarded the job," *he admitted.* "The first thought that came to my mind when they told me was, 'Are you sure?' But I had the presence of mind not to say that on the telephone to them. . . . I [had gone in and] pitched them on what I always loved so much about this great character and how much I loved the comic books and how I saw it taking the next step into becoming a motion picture."

October 8, 2000

More casting rumors: Alicia Witt as Mary Jane Watson and the previously mentioned James Franco as Peter Parker's buddy, Harry Osborn. Witt wouldn't be cast, Franco would. From there it was John Malkovich addressing rumors he would be playing the Green Goblin, explaining, "It's not really my genre particularly, and there were scheduling difficulties and what they offered wasn't in any way an inducement for me to do it. I mean, if I'd have loved it, obviously I would have done it, but those sort of films aren't art films, they're business propositions."

October 11, 2000

Kate Hudson reportedly passed on the role of Peter Parker's girlfriend, Mary Jane Watson.

October 22, 2000

The New York Daily News *reported that wrestler Macho Man Randy Savage would be appearing in the film. The role would ultimately be the wrestler that Peter Parker goes up against for some quick cash while he's still trying to decide what to do with his newly acquired powers.*

October 26, 2000

Spider-Man Hype *featured a report that* Dawson's Creek's *Katie Holmes might be portraying Gwen Stacy in the film, while Gary Cole was being considered for J. Jonah Jameson. In the end, neither would be true, and Gwen Stacy wouldn't even be part of the script.*

October 29, 2000

Dark Horizons *noted that the climactic battle between Spider-Man and the Green Goblin would be fought in New York's Times Square.*

November 8, 2000

David Fincher, probably best known as the director of Alien 3 and Seven, revealed to Cinescape why he didn't get the Spider-Man assignment. "I'm not very reverential of comic books," he said, "but I love the operatic nature of them, that they deal with things in a very mythic way. I wanted to do a much more operatic version of it and everybody went, 'Gulp, we want the creation story.' . . . The thing that I always loved about Spider-Man was the Gwen Stacy story. That was the one I was interested in."

November 10, 2000

Cast in the role of the Daily Bugle's J. Jonah Jameson was Oz and Law & Order actor J. K. Simmons. Rosemary Harris was cast in the role of Aunt May.

November 14, 2000

In an interview with E! News Daily, Tobey Maguire said of being cast: "I don't know what to expect, really. I'm just looking forward to doing something very different than anything I've ever done."

November 17, 2000

It's official: Willem Dafoe, whose credits include Platoon, Clear and Present Danger, and Shadow of the Vampire, is cast as the Green Goblin.

November 20, 2000

Academy Award winner Cliff Robertson (who took home the gold for 1968's Charly) was cast as Peter Parker's Uncle Ben. Admittedly a small role, Ben is also pivotal in that his death is the impetus for Peter's becoming a crimefighter.

November 24, 2000

In an interview with the Mothership website, Sam Raimi discussed his approach to casting the film: "Audiences have great expectations that we all have an obligation to meet on a film and that's brand new for me. They already have in their minds who Peter Parker is and who Aunt May is and you can get it wrong. So not only have I got to meet their expectations, I have to go beyond that and say I've got to choose who is also the soul of the character."

November 28, 2000

While announcing that James Franco had been cast as Harry Osborn, Sony also summarized the plot of Spider-Man: "The film centers on student Peter Parker who, after being bitten by a mutant spider, gains superhuman strength and the spiderlike ability to cling to any surface. He vows to dedicate his life to fighting crime. Harry Osborn, Peter's friend, is haunted by the relentless desire to live up to his father Norman's expectations. Unbeknownst to both Harry and Peter, Norman is the Green Goblin, Spider-Man's archenemy."

A few days later, while making the official announcement that Willem Dafoe was playing Norman Osborn/The Green Goblin,

Willem Dafoe

the studio elaborated. "The Green Goblin assumed his ghoulish persona after an experimental formula blew up in his face. The formula increased his intelligence and strength, but also drove him insane."

December 12, 2000

Kirsten Dunst—whose credits include Interview with the Vampire, Small Soldiers, Bring It On, and Crazy Beautiful—was officially confirmed as Mary Jane Watson. To play the role, Kirsten would have to dye her hair red.

December 14, 2000

Producer Laura Ziskin's husband, Alvin Sargent, was put on the film to perform a dialogue rewrite on Scott Rosenberg's script.

December 17, 2000

EON magazine interviewed Willem Dafoe on the subject of playing the Green Goblin. "I like very much the fact that it's a double character," he said. "It's a character with a dark alter ego. It attracted me. I mean, we all can relate to that."

December 18, 2000

Sam Raimi noted that the script was still being rewritten, despite the fact that shooting was scheduled to begin within a month. "I'm not happy with it yet," he said at a press conference for his film The Gift. "But I think it's a very good script now. What we need to do is make it more than great, though. That's the problem."

January 4, 2001

Sony Pictures held a press conference for Spider-Man in which Sam Raimi, Tobey Maguire, Kirsten Dunst, Willem Dafoe,

James Franco, John Dykstra, and Avi Arad took questions from those gathered.
The transcript follows.

Q: *There has been some debate about the organic webshooters and I was wondering if those were still in the movie and what your thoughts were about them?*

RAIMI: I'm familiar with the debate, but I haven't followed every bit of it. I know that in the Spider-Man comic books, to clarify that issue, Spider-Man is beset with these powers. The webshooters and web fluid that he builds, he puts it in the webshooters and that's how he shoots the webs. But, what we're trying to do in this Spider-Man picture is not just stick to the level of the comic books. We're trying to capture the spirit of the picture. Now, we've always seen the great strength of Spider-Man and the fact that he's a real person, he's one of us. He's a kid from Brooklyn who doesn't have a lot of money. He doesn't get the girls, he's got acne, he's an average-looking kid. He's one of us, unlike Superman who's from the planet Krypton, or other fantastic heroes. He's really a kid who we can identify with. And this kid is vested with these great powers, or perhaps cursed with these powers. But the important thing is that he's one of us. In the comic book, which I'm a giant fan of, he is a genius and we're going to keep that. He's a very smart kid, but when he can develop a material that even 3M corpora-

Kirsten Dunst

tion can't seem to develop, it stops and distances him from a normal human being and an average kid in high school. So we thought the best thing to do was, since he's bit by the spider and takes on the powers of the spider—crawling walls, the ability to leap some spiders have, the great proportional strength of a spider he's developed on the inside—we thought it was a logical progression to let it also spin its own web, and that way keep him a complete human being that we could identify with. But once he's

James Franco, Willem Dafoe, Tobey Maguire, Sam Raimi, and Kirsten Dunst at the Spider-Man *press conference*

bitten by a spider and takes on all the powers, why not take on all five and not just four out of five? In addition, it was another device to create alienation, because Peter Parker has always been an outcast, and Spider-Man a misunderstood hero. And I think that's a lot of the appeal of Spider-Man, that teenage kids understand who think that they're not understood just like Spider-Man. So having yourself change physically distances you from your friends and peers and I think the advantage outweighs the disadvantages.

Q: *For Tobey, what sort of training did you have to go through to get in shape and how comfortable will you be playing Spider-Man?*

MAGUIRE: I've done all kinds of training for flexibility and acrobatic grace, also just to push up some iron. I've enjoyed it thoroughly. I'm a little nervous, getting the premovie jitters. It's been a long time in the coming. I think I've been cast since July, and the anticipation of the work, which is now Monday. It's all on me now, but I'm excited and I can't wait to get in the middle of it. As far as people's expectations, I'm not too concerned. I put all that responsibility onto Sam. I'll just show up and do my job.

Q: Superman *came out with the catch phrase, "You will believe a man can fly." Let me ask about the burden of belief in this film.*

RAIMI: They did a great job on *Superman*. I loved that picture—it was really emotional and uplifting, and you did believe a man could fly. We're faced with the great challenge of making Spider-Man believable, the kids really want to soar with Spidey sixty stories up, dance with him in the aerial acrobatics that he performs. Those illusions are going to be accomplished a lot of different ways and I don't want to reveal too much because I don't want to spoil it for the kids. I don't want to have them picking apart the effects as tricks, but instead have them swept up into the thing. Tobey will be performing a lot of the pieces himself, with backgrounds put in. And then John Dykstra will be helping him with some CGI.

DYKSTRA: The challenge for the filmmakers is to use the technology in an effective fashion, and being part of this team I feel as if I can't go wrong. We're going to enhance and help along the spirit and the soul of Spider-Man where the physical realities fall short. *Superman* was great at the time, but I think the audience has become much more sophisticated and much more adept at determining what's real and what isn't, and that's our challenge. I believe you will be hard-pressed to tell the places where we've helped reality. But we will press the limits and we're going to do things that haven't been done, but I'm loath to tell you because then you'll look for them.

Q: *For Willem Dafoe, what is your motivation for characters like in* Shadow of the Vampire *and the Green Goblin?*

DAFOE: I think my role as Norman Osborn first and the Green Goblin grows from an aspect of Norman Osborn. Norman Osborn is an interesting character, because he's got a dark side and a light, positive side. He believes in science and is interested in developing the physical and mental capabilities of the human being through science. Before I even read the script, Sam talked me through the film and I loved the way he talked about it in such incredible, psychological terms. I also liked how we talked about the relationship between Norman and his son, and Norman and Peter in particular. It's very rich. The other aspect that attracted me to it was the physicality of it. I come from the theater and still work in the theater, and sometimes what I miss in films is the real, tangible, physical investment of things. And in this I have lots of things to play with. I'm really looking forward to it.

Q: *What can we expect for the look of Spider-Man?*

RAIMI: Regarding the outfit, we've decided to get back to the classical red and blue look of Spider-Man. To add some dimensionality to it, to take a slightly more subtle approach to the coloration of the outfit, to increase the flexibility for Tobey Maguire where he can show maximum flexibility to show his athletic prowess. That's what I think the audience really likes about Spider-Man, not the Arnold Schwarzenegger look, rather the fact that he's this graceful dancer.

Q: *Could some of the producers speak as to why it took so long to get a Spider-Man movie rolling?*

ARAD: Marvel will be having a very big party today, because we've been waiting for this for a long time. There is kind of a bloody history here. There's bankruptcy in the past and lawsuits, and then we finally had to get the movie to where it should be made in the first place. It's been a long road and all this has been written about. The good news is it's all here, the rights are clean, it's in the right place, it's in the right hands. Sam was an obvious choice, because what we look for in our universe and our pictures is passion. People have to come in here feeling that this is something they've always wanted to do. Sam can tell you the stories about his pajamas, and climbing behind his bed, and he still climbs the walls every so often. Everybody in this movie is in it for the passion and for being part of the history.

Q: *Have you looked at any other superhero films to see what worked or didn't?*

RAIMI: That was my plan. I thought to myself early in pre-production, "I'm going to watch every superhero picture ever made and try to understand why they worked and why they didn't work." But suddenly, I was overwhelmed with this outrageously gigantic job of making *Spider-Man*, and the pre-production of all these departments and their responsibilities. As far as I got was the first half of *Superman: The Movie*. I never got around to seeing the rest, although I did see *X-Men*. So I can't say that I've had time to learn from any of those movies. I do remember that I loved the first half of *Superman*, and *X-Men* was a blast.

Q: *Could you discuss Stan Lee's involvement?*

ARAD: Stan will be in the movie. We have a long-standing tradition that in our pictures we have Stan do a walk-on for posterity and, obviously, to show respect for the man who created this. Stan is not involved in making pictures. He's involved in other endeavors of writing, and this will be a tribute.

Q: *Kirsten, one of the well-known lines from the Spider-Man comic is when Peter Parker and Mary Jane meet for the first time. She says, "Face it, Tiger, you just hit the jackpot." I'm sure comic-book fans out there would want to know, are you going to be saying that line?*

DUNST: I guess it's in there now. No, that's not the first line I say to him, but I do have a "Tiger" in there.

Q: *Is this going to be stylistically like Darkman, which many consider to be as much like a Marvel comic as any film has ever been?*

RAIMI: It's going to have its own style. The guys and girls who read Spider-Man comic books are so into the outrageous movement that Spider-Man generates as he swings to these tremendous arcs, ninety miles per hour through the city of New York. It demands a much more visceral camera style than we presented with *Darkman*. [Darkman] didn't demand the same type of exciting movements that Spider-Man demands. I think it will be a lot more interesting camera movement, a lot more visceral in its feeling, but not so much that the audience says, "Oh, that's a cool shot." I don't want to pull them out of the movie. I've got some great actors here. I'm going to try to make it exciting without making myself known.

Q: *In your earlier films, you established these great visual styles, but in your last three movies*

The cast at the press conference

you've concentrated on more dramatic, performance-oriented stories. What have you learned from those films, and how do you plan on combining the two?

RAIMI: I'm learning that I don't know anything about actors. In every picture that I make I learn a lot from the actors. I got into motion pictures because I liked what cameras were and how they captured reality and how they replayed it. The fact that you could shuffle that reality in editing was outrageous to me. I got into it to study what were the effects of camera movement, lighting, and sound. Those horror movies that I made, they were about the exploration of what film was. Presenting the world of the supernatural was a great medium for that, because you had to present something that doesn't exist in our world. It was a great grounds for experimentation. But at some point in my life I began to think, "I should make the type of movies I like to see," because the films that I saw were not horror films, yet I was making horror films and I thought that was dishonest in some way. So I started to look for better material, and that attracted a finer caliber actor. I'm still learning to work with actors and what they bring to the film. The more I do that, the more astonished I am about the wonders that they create. Great stories are about human beings and their interaction. There's nothing wrong with a great visual. This picture is a great chance to combine both and make

it visually interesting and exciting, but still work with great actors and a really fine script. It's a film director's dream to work on a movie like *Spider-Man*.

Q: *James, can you tell us about your character, and is it difficult for someone who is mainly experienced in TV to go into such a high-profile movie?*

FRANCO: I play Harry Osborn, son of Norman Osborn. I guess what we're developing is the dynamic that I'm searching for love from him that he will not give, and I can't satisfy his demands. It's pertinent in this day and age, with so many problems between parents and children. In our film, all our parents are either absent or abusive. I'm very excited to be working on a film of this caliber with such talented people.

Q: *How ready is the script? We've heard about all the rewrites.*

RAIMI: The script is not in trouble. It's one of the best scripts I've had an opportunity to work on, actually. Like many pictures in Hollywood, it had a lot of writers. I say this because it's true. *Spider-Man* has a long history of many writers. Although it was created by Stan Lee, and he steered the ship for many years, different writers have come aboard, sometimes on a monthly basis even, to write the various episodes. Spider-Man has really gone beyond being one person's creation to being owned by the world now. It's such a powerful character, and it means so much to everyone. It's okay to me that a number of different writers have worked on it. I think it's fitting to this particular project, seeing as how the comic book has had different writers for thirty years. It started with a James Cameron treatment that was really a fine piece of work, then David Koepp came along and did the lion's share of the work, turning it into a screenplay and working on it for many years. Scott Rosenberg did some work for us, and so did Alvin Sargent. Everybody's contributed a great deal. I'd say David Koepp is the main writer, and nobody is really ever off the picture, we need all of those talents. It's not unlikely that I'll be calling some of those writers again to help on a problem scene, or for some advice on particular pieces of business I need help on.

Q: *With the success of recent films like* The Matrix *and* Crouching Tiger, Hidden Dragon, *where everyone is doing kung fu, will Spider-Man be doing any kung fu?*

MAGUIRE: No, I don't think Spider-Man is a martial artist. He has his own style of fighting. First of all, he's so strong that he if hit regular people like that, he could seriously injure them, and he's too responsible a man to do that. I personally can do any style of fighting that they ask, and I did a demonstration for Sam, begging him to please let

me show off my skills. But, no, we have to stick to the comic book.

Q: *Kirsten, are you worried about getting typecast when you do genre films?*

DUNST: I think that I've done enough independent films like *The Virgin Suicides* that I've broken up my work between that and genre films. Every character that I portray, hopefully, has been very different. I also have another movie coming up called *At Seventeen*, which is completely different than anything anyone has ever seen. My goal is to stay a moving target so that nobody can put a finger on me. The last thing I want is for people to see me as only one thing.

Q: *Could you talk about the special effects?*

DYKSTRA: I think the basis for this movie is having its feet in reality, so that we are extending from a real world into a world that is hyper-real, and how it affects the people involved. I believe our challenge, and it's a significant one, is to make a seamless transition between things that we can do and make the effects not become obvious and not become distracting. So that's the challenge. We have to take these people and this environment and the spirit of this film to places that we can't go for real. I'll leave it to you to figure out what these things are, but hopefully the pieces that we create will be such contributors to the film that you won't notice. So, yes, we will break the limits, but you won't be able to tell when we do.

Q: *Did you study the fighting patterns of real spiders in preparation for this movie?*

RAIMI: Like any good director, of course, I studied all the different species of spider. I don't want to embarrass you with my knowledge here, in front of the press, but I don't want to give anything away [*at which point the press conference came to an end*].

January 8, 2001

Filming officially began on Spider-Man—sixteen years after the film was first put into development.

January 9, 2001

Sam Raimi revealed that talk of a sequel had begun, though he wanted to handle the films "one at a time." Still, according to the Comics Continuum, he voiced his interest in the Gwen Stacy story line.

January 12, 2001

The Coming Attractions website received information about the nature of the Spider-Man costume. According to the site, the costume had been designed over a period of six months by James Acheson, a triple Academy Award winner for The Last Emperor, Restoration, *and* Dangerous Liaisons. *Said*

Acheson: "It is based on tension—and is one piece—all the way from the boots to the top of the head. The boots have actually been built into the suit." *A sunglass design company named Oakley, which had provided the Cyclops visor for the feature version of X-Men, designed the lenses for Spidey's mask. It was also noted that there would be two different designs for the costume, one representing Peter's first efforts as he tries to use his newly acquired powers to win some money wrestling. This particular outfit is somewhat baggy and not as sleek-looking, but it eventually evolves into the costume fans know and love.*

In The New York Times, *Sony VP of Marketing Dwight Cainies discussed the fact that they planned on taking full advantage of the Internet for promoting the film. "One of the things we have realized in the past couple of years is that the Internet audience is actually the same consumers as those moviegoers we get opening weekend," he said. "When these guys become evangelists for you, their demographic profile looks just like early-weekend frequent moviegoers, and that's the best kind of evangelist to have."*

January 16, 2001

Enthused Tobey Maguire to the Comics Continuum website: "We're trying to honor the comic as much as possible, but we're trying to make our own movie. I think it's going to be a really good movie. We have all the ingredients for it. It's a pretty complicated character and there's a lot going on."

January 17, 2001

Identifying himself as a production assistant, someone reported on line that the Green Goblin's body armor would be pretty impressive. "Look for the eyes to be bulbous beyond belief," said the poster, "like golf balls and coated with Oakley's 24k iridium coating which has real gold in it. Very cool. The armor plating on the Goblin is coated with the same expensive stuff."

On that same day, director Sam Raimi began shooting the film's big wrestling scene. Peter Parker, dressed in his first Spider-Man costume, takes on the massive "Bone Saw McGraw." An extra in the sequence—identifying himself as Quantum Mechanic—posted some of his observations: "Tobey was in a makeshift costume, with warm-up pants and Nike red sneakers, with a red long-sleeved shirt with the classic black spider figure emblazoned on it. He also wears a crude makeshift red mask that only shows his uncovered eyes. Obviously since this was a point in time where he had not yet designed his famous costume, this amateur get-up was totally on the money."

Quantum Mechanic added that the stuntman who took Maguire's place after the entrance did a great job. As Buzz Saw McGraw charged him, Spider-Man did a straight upward jump. "The camera placement," he wrote, "was pure genius here. To the viewer, it is going to look like Spidey just jumped far and high right in front of you, leaving a collison with Bone Saw imminent.

Although it was filmed out of sequence, the next shot finds the web-slinger perched, spider-like, on the side of a cage as he looks down to the enraged face of BSM, who bellows, 'What are you doing up there?' Spidey retorts something to the effect of, '[Staying] away from you for three minutes,' which will, as explained earlier in filming, net Peter a cool 3,000 bucks. As BSM rattles the cage to shake down our hero, Spidey leaps off the cage and somersaults to the ground on the complete opposite side of the ring. As Bone Saw wheels and charges Spidey again, we get our first glimpse of the fabled webshooting action. . . .

"On an observational note," he continued, "everything about this scene is totally consistent with the comic and Stan Lee's vision of Spidey as a confused, 'ordinary' hero placed in extraordinary circumstances. The director took extreme pains to let the crowd know how Spidey is supposed to react to our jeers, and eventually our cheers, as he finally realizes during the course of the fight that he isn't simply the lowly Peter Parker anymore with his new powers."

January 26, 2001

When photos of Spider-Man from the film began making the rounds on the Internet, many sites claimed that there was no way that Tobey Maguire was the person in those shots. Laura Ziskin went on line to dispute those claims. "Tobey has been in that costume many times," she said, "and I was there for the photo shoot. It is absolutely Tobey Maguire in costume in those photos. . . . We knew that we had to have Tobey in the suit because that's what fans would expect."

On the same day, Raimi admitted to Cinescape that he was feeling "terrified." "I feel like I'm in a tidal wave," he explained, "and I'm currently upside down and I don't know which direction is up. It's frightening because there are so many kids who Spider-Man means so much to. I've got a grave responsibility on my shoulders because he is their hero, so I have to decide what lessons in the movie does he learn that exemplify what it means to be a hero."

January 30, 2001

Actor Michael Papajohn, according to the Birmingham News, was cast to play the role of the burglar who ultimately murders Uncle Ben and sets Peter Parker's destiny in motion.

February 16, 2001

Joining the crew were editors Bob Murawski and Arthur Coburn, both of whom had frequently collaborated with Sam Raimi in the past.

February 27, 2001

In an article that appeared in England's Daily Telegraph, Sam Raimi defended the choice of Tobey Maguire: "He's not a Clark Kent or a Bruce Wayne. He is Peter Parker, an insecure teenager who is going through puberty and is a little bit of a loser. He has acne, he is a science geek and is something of a social outcast. What

some people consider to be Tobey's weaknesses, I consider his strengths."

February 28, 2001

On the Countingdown.com site, Willem Dafoe spoke a bit about the Green Goblin: "Norman sees a lot of himself in Peter. He has great affection for him. The dark aspect, though—the Green Goblin—has a codependent relationship with Spider-Man. There's one point in the story where he wants to enlist Spider-Man as an ally—it's very intense. It's a deadly relationship."

March 6, 2001

Tragedy hit the Spider-Man set when two cranes accidentally collided, killing a construction welder.

March 11, 2001

Cast as J. Jonah Jameson, J. K. Simmons (Oz, Law & Order) shared the fact that he researched his role by reading "just about every Spider-Man comic that highlighted predictably juicy JJJ episodes, and downloaded information off the Internet."

April 1, 2001

Director Robert Rodriguez admitted to syndicated columnist Cindy Pearlman that he actually turned down the opportunity to direct Spider-Man. "You go meet with a studio over these big films," said the director of—among other films—Spy Kids, "and you realize it's not a movie. It's a big corporate project. It's a pre-sold idea. I don't like to close my eyes and know it's a home run . . . I want to be there before McDonald's has signed on to do the merchandising."

April 4, 2001

On April 3, Sony Pictures let it be known that four Spider-Man costumes had been stolen from the studio lot. The following day, they offered a $25,000 reward for their safe return. Anyone fearing that Spidey would have to swing through Manhattan in his underwear, though, needn't have worried, as there were plenty of other costumes on hand. Apparently the studio simply didn't want them out and about.

April 7, 2001

Syndicated columnist Cindy Pearlman interviewed both Tobey Maguire and Willem Dafoe about their respective roles of Spider-Man and the Green Goblin. "[Spidey's] a great character," mused Maguire, "because he's so relatable. He's conflicted about it in our script, which makes him interesting." Added Dafoe: "All you can hope to do is respect it [Spider-Man] and treat it right. If you do, the fans will take the trip with you."

April 11, 2001

Word got out that the Spider-Man production would be coming to New York for shooting between April 14 and May 4.

April 13, 2001

Composer Danny Elfman was reportedly writing a love theme for the film that would be sung by country superstar Faith Hill.

April 16, 2001

Aint-It-Cool-News posted a story that stated the Spider-Man costumes were getting pretty beaten up during production. "This relative of mine," offered one post, "was walking down a hallway near some of the studios where the green-screen filming is going to take place, and a stuntman in a Spidey suit passed him on the way to a shoot. According to my source, both of the lenses in the mask were broken and there were rips and tears all over the uniform."

April 23, 2001

London's The Sun reported that Lucy Lawless—forever known as Xena, Warrior Princess—would have a small role in Spider-Man as a punk rocker.

On the same day, Comic Book Galaxy posted an interview with Stan Lee, in which Lee discussed his filmed role in the project. "I don't want to give anything away," he said, "but I can tell you that I say something to Peter Parker. . . . There is one funny thing I'll tell you. There was a second when there was this little girl standing there next to me and an explosion goes off and I'm supposed to lift her up and run to safety with her. I started to lift her and she was too heavy. I could hardly get her up, so Sam Raimi calls me and says, 'Hey, Stan, you

Lucy Lawless

Marvel.com posted an interview with Avi Arad in which he said the following about the Spider-Man movie: "This movie shouldn't have been made until now. There wasn't the technology to make the movie what it is today. It's very complicated to make Spider-Man fly and swing and shoot webs. It's very complicated to make the Green Goblin fly through the skies and have the kinds of action scenes it dictates. Spider-Man's powers are such that it's really not well covered by normal physics."

May 18, 2001

Lucy Lawless gave an interview to the SciFi-Wire in which she described her cameo in the film as a punk rocker: "I had a stud in my nose, a short spiky wig and lots of earrings. I'm dragging on cigarettes. So I do this tiny little, blink-and-you-miss-it cameo, but it was such fun. It was all fun and no responsibility."

May 23, 2001

In an interview with Detour *magazine, Kirsten Dunst admitted, "I just saw a brief clipping of* Spider-Man *and I had tears in my eyes. It was so beautiful. It really is such a beautiful, human story. . . . I'm so happy to be in the film."*

May 24, 2001

Entertainment Tonight *reported that Kirsten Dunst and Tobey Maguire had become an "item" during production of* Spider-Man, *but*

better forget about trying to lift her up. If you keep trying to lift her, this movie will be a miniseries,' which I thought was a funny line."

May 2, 2001

While talking to the Comics Continuum website, Marvel's Avi Arad noted that a new Spider-Man animated series in development would be based on the feature. Said Arad: "The movie, obviously, is an origin story, but done in 2002. We want to get Peter to New York as soon as possible. But it stars a young Peter."

that things had already cooled off between them romantically.

May 28, 2001

In an article printed in England's The Mail, Kirsten shared more of her feelings about being a part of the film. "Spider-Man *is this huge monster movie, the biggest thing I've ever done,*" she explained. "*It will be next year's massive film. I feel a great sense of responsibility to the fans, but I am not scared. When I got the chance to star in the film, I knew it would change my life. This is the type of movie that comes along once in a lifetime.*"

May 29, 2001

Talking to Comics Continuum, special effects supervisor John Dykstra made mention of the CG Spider-Man that will be seen in certain sequences. "*We're going to make a character that is indistinguishable from the live actor,*" he said. "*It's an incredible collaboration in the sense that Tobey is going to be the persona and soul of the character, and we are going to give that soul the enhanced capabilities.*"

June 4, 2001

Marvel's Kevin Feige surprised the Comics Continuum by mentioning during an interview that principal photography of the film had concluded at some point during the previous four weeks, and that Raimi was, at that point, in the editing room.

June 5, 2001

Actor Bruce Campbell, a frequent cast member in Sam Raimi's films and who plays the ring announcer at Peter Parker's big wrestling match, enthused to Empire Online about Tobey Maguire, "*I can't think of anyone better. He's really brought the character to life, and I honestly believe you'll be blown away when you finally get to see* Spider-Man *on the big screen.*"

June 12, 2001

At the 2001 Licensing Show, the Hollywood Reporter expressed its belief that Spider-Man would be one of the main films to provide merchandising "sizzle."

July 21, 2001

Marvel announced that Stan Lee would be adapting the movie script to a comic-book version. Pretty appropriate considering that Lee created Spider-Man in the first place.

July 22, 2001

Spidey fans attending the annual San Diego Comic Con were excited to see a filmed presentation on Spider-Man, *but they were even more delighted when director Sam Raimi showed up to take a couple of questions. Following are Raimi's comments and answers to the gathered crowd.*

RAIMI: I can't believe it hasn't been made into a movie by now. I guess it had plenty of legal problems that tied it up, but finally—

no one's happier than me as a fan of Spider-Man to finally see it on the big screen. I'm thrilled to be here with you guys, who are, as Stan Lee would say, "the true believers," to talk about it a little bit and to answer any questions you might have. So, right now, where we are in the process of making the picture is, we've shot the film, we still have some additional shooting to do—probably two more weeks, I don't know when that's going to be scheduled. So, I'd say ninety percent of the movie is in the can and another ten percent of the effects shots are being created every day. We're editing the film. I've got a fine editor in Bob Murawski, who is heading a team of editors in Sony Pictues Studios in Los Angeles. We're about to show a first cut of the movie, even though it's fairly incomplete, to Sony, probably next week. Right after this convention, I'm going to race right back to the cutting room. I haven't done this before, so please guide me. I'm joking, of course. Are there any questions about Spider-Man that I can answer?

Q: *I'm curious about how much leeway Sony gives you in deciding the length of the picture.*

RAIMI: Well, basically they say "jump" and I say, "What color?" What happens is that they had input throughout the process—the script process—but really, they've pretty much been hands-off so far. The creative aspects of the picture have been determined by myself; our producer, Laura Ziskin; Avi

Arad from Marvel Comics; and the writers, obviously, who have all contributed to it. Sony has really given us a free hand in telling the Spider-Man story. The editing could be another story, but so far, they've been very supportive and allowed us free creative rein.

Q: *Have you read the scriptment by James Cameron and how has your directing been influenced by the Coen Brothers?*

RAIMI: Well, the script that I work with, a number of writers have contributed to. It originally started as a scriptment by James Cameron, which was like this eighty- to one-hundred-page half-script/half-treatment. Then David Koepp came aboard and he spent a number of years developing it into a screenplay, and then Alvin Sargent came aboard and he did the last draft or two of the script. Although Scott Rosenberg came on briefly, I don't think we ended up going in that direction that he took the script in. As far as the Coen Brothers—I'm good friends with Joel and Ethan Coen and I really love their pictures. I think because of our friendship—we've lived together for a number of years in Los Angeles—we've probably influenced each other quite a bit. Specifically, it's hard for me to point out one particular film of theirs or script, but just being with them and taking part in their sense of humor, I've probably been influenced by them.

July 23, 2001

Advertising Age *magazine reported that* Spider-Man *had already pulled in about $40 million from corporate sponsors, among them Taco Bell and the Kellogg Company.*

August 4, 2001

In an interview with Cinescape, *composer Danny Elfman discussed the challenge facing him in terms of the demands of fans. "I've already been down that road with* Batman," *he said. "Whether it's* Planet of the Apes, Batman, *or* Spider-Man, *you can't worry about what hard-core genre fans are going to perceive. . . . I'll do the best I can do with it."*

August 16, 2001

In an interview with FeatsPress, *Tobey Maguire explained what the film was about: "Identity and self-discovery and figuring out a little more about who you want to be and who you think you should be. That's what's so intriguing about the Spider-Man concept: the fact that Peter Parker openly raises his doubts so that the readers of the comic strip could share his worries and fears. . . . He's very mortal, someone who agonizes a lot about his role in life."*

August 17, 2001

SFX *magazine featured an interview with Avi Arad, in which he discussed the upcoming film. "When you see Spider-Man, it's truly amazing," he enthused. "It plays so much on the emotional level. Obviously there is the* spectacular aspect of being Spider-Man—it's what you expect in this kind of event movie. But when you watch Tobey and Kirsten, you totally believe in the story. She is Mary Jane, he is Peter Parker and Cliff Robertson is amazing as Uncle Ben."*

August 20, 2001

FX guru John Dykstra appeared at the WizardWorld convention, where he offered some information to gathered fans. "Spider-Man does things that people can do," he said. "So, to keep the reality quotient high, so that you don't come out of your seat going, 'Oh, yeah, they just did a CG guy there,' we have to try and make sure even though he's ten times stronger than a human being, that he's capable of doing these things within the mechanics of a human move." The Green Goblin, he added, did not need any CG enhancements. "The costume exists, in reality, as a costume. He's complete. He's three-dimensional. He's there. At this point he can walk around without any CGI enhancements. When it comes to flying his glider, inasmuch as that technology doesn't really exist, he's either a stuntman on a rig of some kind that supports the glider, or a CGI character. The glider itself, when you see it in flight, will half the time be a composite or it will be computer-generated."

New means of accomplishing the impossible, he added, were necessary. "If you begin a movie that takes eighteen months to two years to make using only known technology," Dykstra mused, "by the time the film is finished it will be obsolete. So, going into any film, whether it's Spider-Man or another movie, you must promise to do more than you have any hope of achieving, through a clever combination of baffling them with bull and actually being successful with some of the things you attempt. You've got a composite of existing technologies and innovation that results in the final images. There's a lot of happy accidents involved."

Of working with Raimi, he said: "The thing that's fun with Sam is that he's not afraid to try things that other people wince at. This is a movie that is being made by Sam Raimi. It's his interpretation of Spider-Man, and I don't think that the fans will be disappointed."

August 23, 2001

Due to the accidental death of welder Tim Holcombe on March 6, the Spider-Man production was fined nearly $59,000. Noted a representative of Columbia Pictures, "We deeply regret the accident and continue to cooperate fully with all investigative agencies as we have from the outset. We are doing everything we can on an ongoing basis to assure that crews on all our productions follow very strict safety procedures to minimize the risk of accident."

On the same day Freddy Prinze, Jr., appeared on the Howard Stern Show and continued to complain about the fact he hadn't been cast as Spider-Man. It should be pointed out that it's one thing to feel passion-ate about something, but quite another to be so obsessive. Move along, Freddy.

September 4, 2001

In an interview in the Brazilian newspaper Jornal do Brasil, Sam Raimi explained: "The studio wanted someone strong and handsome [as Spider-Man]. But the character has never been this way. He's always been someone different and misplaced in society. Without piles of muscles, but with a great heart. When I saw The Cider House Rules, I felt that Tobey Maguire was the right choice, due to his sensibility to express the condition of someone who suffers such a great impact in life."

September 12, 2001

In the wake of the terrorist attacks on New York City, and the resulting loss of the Twin Towers, Sony pulled both the trailer and teaser posters for Spider-Man, as both (particularly the trailer) featured the Towers prominently. Offered Sony, "Due to the devastating events that took place, and out of respect for those involved, Sony Pictures Entertainment is requesting that all Spider-Man teaser posters and trailers be taken down and returned to the studio."

September 15, 2001

One last change needed to be made in Spider-Man's world due to the terrorist attacks against America: a scene of villains attacking New York City was removed from the Spider-Man ride at Universal's Islands of Adventure in Orlando, Florida.

September 28, 2001

Actor Benjamin Bratt, late of Law & Order—*and Julia Roberts—made the following statement in* Entertainment Weekly *regarding* Spider-Man: *"Tobey Maguire, whatever. He can play Peter Parker. I don't want to wear tights and stuff, but I'd make a better Spider-Man."*

October 10, 2001

Rumor had it that the Spider-Man *production would be back in New York during Halloween week for a number of reshoots.*

October 12, 2001

Filmmaker Quentin Tarantino was asked his opinion of the movie Iron Monkey *by a reporter for the Memphis, Tennessee, newspaper, the* Commercial Appeal. *"I've waited my whole life to see a Spider-Man movie," he admitted. "Now they're getting ready to do one, with Sam Raimi. And then I said, 'Wait a minute, the whole beginning of* Iron Monkey, *that's the way I always thought a Spider-Man movie should be, with Spider-Man hopping across the rooftops. . . . Now Sam's gonna have to raise the bar."*

The need to "raise the bar" seems to be something that Raimi himself was well aware of and he obviously felt that he was up to the challenge. There were a lot of "bodies" left in the wake of *Spider-Man's* development, from studio executives to writers and directors, to studios themselves. For a project that had the odds stacked against it, whether it be the production practices of Cannon Films or the myriad of lawsuits that swung through Hollywood the way Spider-Man swings around New York City, it seems to have been a miracle that the film was made at all.

One of the people grateful that Spider-Man has been brought to life is director Joe Zito, who was intimately involved with the project for several years when it was at Cannon.

"I'm very philosophical about this," says Zito. "To me, *Spider-Man* is not the great thing that got away. Yes, I really wish I had done it. It was also a wonderful adventure preparing the movie. Working with them on it and setting the film up in London and then in Rome was a fabulous adventure. In truth, when the project came to its end because of financial reasons, it was obviously not the right time to make that movie. I would feel much worse having ruined the character and the film. I'm thrilled that the film has been made. I was very happy when Cameron was going to do it and I'm happy that Sam Raimi has done it.

"I know this sounds self-righteous," he adds, "but I swear it's true: I wanted that film to live in front of an audience. If I couldn't make it under the Cannon circumstances, I had no negative feelings about it. I never tried to make it again. Once it didn't have its moment, that moment passed. When it got resurrected, I thought that was great. To me, every project is an extraordinary adventure. Working on *Spider-Man* was one of my great film memories, whether or not it actually got made. So I don't curse Sam Raimi, I congratulate him."

And there are millions of Spidey fans around the world who do the same. Sam Raimi, and the rest of his cast and crew, lived up to the responsibility that came with great power. No fan of Spider-Man could ask for anything more.

237

APPENDIX

Spider-Man Rogues' Gallery

A

ABSORBING MAN

NAME: Carl "Crusher" Creel

POWERS: Possesses the ability to take on the properties of anything he comes into contact with. Can reassemble himself over time if broken into pieces. His strength level varies based on the property he takes on. At times, though, he can be nearly as strong as the Hulk. Crusher also has a ball and chain that has the same powers of transformation that he does.

ORIGIN: A former prison inmate, Crusher is the creation of Loki, the Norse god of mischief. His powers are magical in nature, and were derived from a potion composed of rare Asgardian herbs which were added to his drinking water. These powers were granted to him in exchange for his solemn word that he would use them against Thor.

FIRST APPEARANCE: *Journey into Mystery* #114, March 1965

FIRST SPIDER-MAN APPEARANCE: *Amazing Spider-Man* #283

THE ANSWER

NAME: David Ferrari

POWERS: The ability to develop any power necessary to resolve a given situation, meaning that his powers are incalculable.

ORIGIN: Formerly a hit man for the Kingpin in the Las Vegas division of Hydra, the Answer was used as a human guinea pig in an attempt to gain superpowers.

FIRST APPEARANCE: *Spectacular Spider-Man* #92

ARCADE

NAME: Unknown

POWERS: No known superhuman powers to speak of. He is known for killing people in extraordinary ways, and brought that to light with the creation of "Murderworld," a complex built solely for his own enjoyment and consisting entirely of high-tech death traps. He has a genius I.Q. and has great prowess in technology, architecture, design, and mechanics.

ORIGIN: All that's known is that he's the son of a millionaire who he himself murdered. Discovering a "talent" for murder, he decided to become a hit man.

FIRST APPEARANCE: *Marvel Team Up* #65

ARMADA

NAME: Unknown

POWERS: Employs a number of robots emitted from his back that are similar to a fleet of armed ships. His "pets" are equipped to pick locks and fire blasts, among other things. He has the ability to fly and emit blasts from his palms, and has use of super strength derived from his armor, which can self-charge. He is a gifted inventor and is considered the finest corporate thief in the world.

ORIGIN: There are only assumptions to be made, the biggest being that he designed his own armor.

FIRST APPEARANCE: *Sensational Spider-Man* #0

B

BASILISK

NAME: Unknown

POWERS: Superhuman strength that enables

him to lift upward of 800 pounds. Can emit bodily generated microwave energy through his eyes; can lift himself in the air by the same means and fly with the help of the Alpha Stone, which brought about his powers.

ORIGIN: Unknown

FIRST APPEARANCE: *Marvel Team-Up* #16

BEETLE

NAME: Abner Jenkins

POWERS: All derived from a battle suit designed to give him a very high degree of protection and which augments his strength many times over due to its circuitry. Gloves contain pneumatic suction-grippers and can shoot an electrostatic blast as well as stick to areas. Has Mylar wings that enable him to fly at speeds ranging from 60 to 100 miles per hour.

ORIGIN: All powers are man-made.

FIRST APPEARANCE: *Strange Tales* #123

FIRST SPIDER-MAN APPEARANCE: *Amazing Spider-Man* #21

BIG MAN

NAME: Frederick Foswell

POWERS: Criminal genius, master of disguise, and incredible marksman with a gun.

ORIGIN: None

FIRST APPEARANCE: *Amazing Spider-Man* #10

BIG WHEEL

NAME: Jackson Wheel

POWERS: With a great speed and destructive abilities, Jackson Wheel's device can also scale walls. It has mechanical arms, guns, rocket launchers, and a wide variety of other weapons.

ORIGIN: With a great scientific mind, Jackson Wheel sought aid from the Terrible Tinkerer in assisting him in the construction of a machine similar to a tank but shaped like a single wheel. Though he sought aid in the construction of his ultimate weapon, the only death that resulted was his own.

FIRST APPEARANCE: *Amazing Spider-Man* #182

BLACK FOX

NAME: Unknown

POWERS: In his sixties, the Black Fox has thrived in a career of thievery. He has succeeded in many attempts, but as an elderly man has been halted by Spider-Man. He carries a weapons pack containing smoke and flash grenades, a glass-cutting device and a burglar detection neutralizer.

ORIGIN: Unknown

FIRST APPEARANCE: *Amazing Spider-Man* #255

BLACK TARANTULA

NAME: Carlos LaMuerto

POWERS: Carrying on "family tradition," Carlos donned the identity of the Black Tarantula many years ago. He has the power of immortality and great skills in hand-to-hand combat and martial arts, as well as possessing superhuman strength, great agility, and speed. Also known as the "Immortal Warrior."

ORIGIN: Unrevealed

FIRST APPEARANCE: *Amazing Spider-Man* #432

BOOMERANG

NAME: Fred Myers

POWERS: A great baseball pitcher from Australia, Fred Myers became connected with criminal organizations where he used his incredible accuracy with a boomerang. He has many gimmick boomerangs, including the "gassarang," the "razorrang," the "screamerang," and the "bladerang." He can fly with the use of bootjets.

ORIGIN: Fred developed his powers on his own.

FIRST APPEARANCE: *Tales to Astonish* #81

FIRST SPIDER-MAN APPEARANCE: *Amazing Spider-Man* #280

BULLSEYE

NAME: Benjamin Pondexter

POWERS: Bullseye has the uncanny ability to use any object as a weapon and to throw that object with precise, superhuman aim. Objects he's used in the past include playing cards, pencils, pens, golf balls, brushes, paper airplanes, teeth (!), and many others. He also uses the more "traditional" weapons such as handguns, knives, darts, whips, plastic explosives, etc. Much of his skeleton has been reinforced with Adamtium, a metal almost unbreakable. Bullseye is also an Olympic-level athlete.

ORIGIN: A former baseball pitcher on the major-league level, Bullseye has always had a talent at aiming objects and does so with deadly results. He eventually becomes a mercenary as he slowly grows simultaneously insane and sadistic.

FIRST APPEARANCE: *Daredevil* #131

FIRST SPIDER-MAN APPEARANCE: *Spider-Man*, Vol. 2, #6

BURGLAR

NAME: Unknown

POWERS: The Burglar has no powers, but has hurt Spider-Man more than any super-villain could have. He is most noted for murdering Peter Parker's Uncle Ben and has had a life of crime before and after. He later gets out of prison, only to be captured by Spider-Man, and he eventually dies of a heart attack. He is arguably the most interesting character, since there is very little known about him.

FIRST APPEARANCE: *Amazing Fantasy* #15

C

CARDIAC

NAME: Dr. Elias Wirtham

POWERS: Super strength, speed and agility. Has possession of a beta-powered pulse staff that he uses as a weapon. Also has use of a remote-controlled Hover hawk/Stingray glider he uses for short- to medium-distance transportation while using his staff for the glider/hawk to cling onto.

ORIGIN: Elias surgically replaced his own heart with that of a compact beta-particle reactor that gives him great energy. He depends on this beta-particle energy, which allows his heart to work properly. He also had his skin laced with a Vibranium pseudo-nerve network. He focuses this energy into his muscles to obtain his powers.

FIRST APPEARANCE: *Amazing Spider-Man* #344

CLETUS

NAME: Cletus Kasady

POWERS: Super strength and powers similar to

Venom, but much worse. He has a
psychotic killer's personality and can create
sharp daggerlike objects with his body
thanks to the symbiote spawn within him.
Can crawl up walls in a similar fashion to
Spider-Man and Venom and has the
ability to nullify Spider-Man's spider-
sense.

ORIGIN: When he is sent to serve a life sentence
for murder, Cletus's cellmate turns out to
be Eddie Brock (Venom). While helping
Brock get out of prison, Venom's symbiote
body spawns off a part of itself and bonds
with Cletus, creating a killing machine.

FIRST APPEARANCE: *Amazing Spider-Man* #344

CARRION

NAME: I—not applicable (clone of Michael
Warren); II—Malcolm McBridged III

POWERS: Can lift up to 10 tons and
telepathically read minds. He can reduce
the density of his body to become
intangible, can levitate and propel himself
into the air, and has teleporting abilities.
Malcolm originally had only the ability to
turn living matter to ash. Carrion also uses
red dust that can render his victims
unconscious or can burn through flesh,
metal, and other substances.

ORIGIN: Carrion I and II are the results of a
genetic replicator virus left by Professor
Miles Warren (Jackal) and his mutated
DNA.

FIRST APPEARANCE: *Spectacular Spider-Man* #25

CHAMELEON

NAME: Dmitri Smerdyakov

POWERS: One of the greatest living masters of
disguise; a quick-change artist and actor

supreme. He is also a master at creating
lifelike masks and disguises. His flesh can
assume the features of any person. Has used
a hologram projector in his belt to aid him
in further disguising his abilities.

ORIGIN: Little is known other than Dmitri was
a servant boy to Kraven the Hunter when a
young man, and had a somewhat strange
relationship with him until Kraven took his
own life many years later. The Chameleon
spent years trying to gain Kraven's respect
by following him to America to commit a
series of crimes.

FIRST APPEARANCE: *Untold Tales of Spider-Man*
#9

COMMANDA

NAME: Unknown

POWERS: An extraordinary jewel thief,
Commanda has a force field generated from
her tiara that makes her invulnerable to
injury. She also has drones that she controls
to do her bidding.

ORIGIN: Unknown

FIRST APPEARANCE: *Untold Tales of Spider-Man*
#10

CONUNDRUM

NAME: Unknown

POWERS: Can emit nerve gas at will and is a
master of illusion. His face is a mystery and
presents itself as a continuous puzzle,
similar to a Rubik's Cube, with different
expressions displayed at different times.

ORIGIN: A human enigma, little is known
about him except that he has connections
to the Kingdom of Sufind.

FIRST APPEARANCE: *Spectacular Spider-Man* #257

CRIME-MASTER

NAME: I—Nick "Lucky" Lewis; II—Nick Lewis, Jr.

POWERS: Neither crime master had superhuman powers. Crime-Master I is a powerful underworld leader and an excellent hand-to-hand combatant as well as an expert marksman. Crime-Master II doesn't demonstrate the same promise of his father as far as skills go, but is nonetheless an excellent marksman and hand-to-hand combatant.

ORIGIN: Nick "Lucky" Lewis moved up the ranks in the Kingpin's organization via displays of power and terror to other organized criminals. His son, seeking revenge for Nicky's death (which he blamed Spider-Man for), assumed his father's identity years later.

FIRST APPEARANCE: Crime-Master I—*Amazing Spider-Man* #26; Crime-Master II—*Marvel Team-Up* #39

CYCLONE

NAME: Unrevealed

POWERS: Has the ability—mechanically achieved—to increase the velocity of the air around him to near tornado levels. Like the villain Whirlwind, he has menaced Iron Man and the Avengers over the years.

ORIGIN: Unknown

FIRST APPEARANCE: *Amazing Spider-Man* #143

D

DEMOGOBLIN

NAME: Unknown

POWERS: Same as the Hobgoblin, including super strength and speed. He can use various smoke, gas, and explosive pumpkin bombs, but can create them mentally out of thin air. Demo also gets around by use of his fire-and-brimstone-composed glider.

ORIGIN: Phillip Macendale, Hobgoblin II, wanted more power, so badly that he offered his soul in exchange. His trading partner was the demon N'Astirh, who was a major player during the Inferno crisis. Macendale then shared his body with a demon that has possessed him ever since. For a time they battle over control of the body, but in the end the demon is victorious.

FIRST APPEARANCE: *Spectacular Spider-Man* #147

DOCTOR DOOM

NAME: Victor Von Doom

POWERS: Having one of the greatest scientific minds ever, Doom possesses expertise in robotics, weaponry, genetics, time travel, and the mystic arts. He wears a nuclear-powered microcomputer-based suit of armor, which includes particle beams and a force field, and also enables him to fly. Can psychically transfer his consciousness into the body of another. Has use of "Doombots," or robot duplicates.

ORIGIN: While he was a child, Doom's mother, a witch, was killed, and his father died at a later time. Doom developed prowess in the area of science and became roommate to Reed Richard (Mr. Fantastic) in college. There he survived an explosion, though his face was terribly scarred. For some years he lived with Tibetan Monks who taught him many secrets. It was while with them that he acquired his suit of armor. He decides to challenge the world, blaming others for the pain and suffering he endured earlier.

FIRST APPEARANCE: *Fantastic Four #5*

FIRST SPIDER-MAN APPEARANCE: *Amazing Spider-Man #5*

DOCTOR OCTOPUS

NAME: Otto Gunther Octavius

POWERS: Four mentally controlled, telescoping titanium steel tentacles attached to a stainless steel harness that's worn on Octavius's body. Each tentacle has three single-jointed pinchers. Able to move at speeds of ninety feet per second. Otto also possesses incredible strength. He is the world's leading authority on nuclear radiation and is a bona-fide genius. He has also employed an armored body suit that enables him to breathe while underwater.

ORIGIN: A brilliant atomic researcher, Otto Octavius designed the harness to aid him in working on dangerous experiments at a safe distance. Radioactive liquids exploded in a freak laboratory accident, bombarding Octavius with radiation and bonding the harness to his skin and nervous system. He also suffered brain damage from the accident, causing him to become criminally insane.

FIRST APPEARANCE: *Amazing Spider-Man #3*

DOPPELGANGER

NAME: Unknown

POWERS: Basically an evil counterpart to Spider-Man, with powers that mimic those of the web-crawler. He has the extra agility and use of four extra arms, but he is unable to talk and is essentially mindless.

ORIGIN: Doppelganger was created, along with many other doppelgangers of heroes in the Marvel Universe (such as Wolverine and Iron Man), by the Magus, a foe of Warlock. Doppelgangers were great participants in the Infinity War and serve to represent the evil side of Earth's heroes. All but one were destroyed with the defeat of the Magus.

FIRST APPEARANCE: *Infinity War #1*

FIRST SPIDER-MAN APPEARANCE: *Spider-Man #24*

DRAGON MAN

NAME: None

POWERS: Great strength and endurance and the ability to fly at 90 miles per hour. Can breathe fire at temperatures of 8,000 degrees Fahrenheit.

ORIGIN: Created by university professor as an experiment, Dragon Man was given life through a potion provided by Diablo, a Fantastic Four villain. The potion gave life to an artificial dragon, which would turn out to be more trouble for the FF than Spidey.

FIRST APPEARANCE: *Fantastic Four #35*

FIRST SPIDER-MAN APPEARANCE: *Web of Spider-Man #61*

D'SPAYRE

NAME: Unknown

POWERS: A demon with superhuman strength, he draws psychic energy from fear and anguish suffered by humans, and in turn can instill fear using mental powers. His telepathic abilities are limited. Possibly serves a more powerful being known as the "Dweller in the Darkness."

ORIGIN: Unknown

FIRST APPEARANCE: *Marvel Team-Up #68*

E

EEL

NAME: Leopold Stryke; Edward Laveli

POWERS: His costume's generators produce electricity on a level that can kill. Can also project bolts of electricity from his hands and is difficult to hold on to as his costume is coated with a greaselike substance.

ORIGIN: Eel wears a special costume from which all his powers are derived.

FIRST APPEARANCE: *Strange Tales* #112

FIRST SPIDER-MAN APPEARANCE: *Untold Tales of Spider-Man* #11

ELECTRO

NAME: Maxwell Dillon

POWERS: Ability to bodily generate electrostatic energy at 1,000 volts per minute and store up to one million volts. He can kill a normal man at a distance of ten feet, and can override any electrical powered device and manipulate it mentally.

ORIGIN: After being struck by lightning, an unusually configured magnetic field was created. Maxwell Dillon, a wire lineman, was right in the middle of it all. A mutagenic change occurred, followed by a life of crime.

FIRST APPEARANCE: *Amazing Spider-Man* #9

F

FUSION

NAME: Hubert Fusser and Pinky Fusser

POWERS: The twins, as Fusion, are able to emit great levels of radiation, and achieve near superhuman strength by absorbing the energy of whatever they come in contact with.

ORIGIN: After gently touching a switch on a subatomic particle accelerator, Hubert activated a burst of energy that erupted towards him so quickly that he didn't even have enough time to scream. His twin brother, Pinky, came to his aid, and when they touched, their flesh somehow merged, becoming Fusion.

FIRST APPEARANCE: *Amazing Spider-Man* #208

FUSION II

NAME: First name unknown; last name Markley

POWERS: Originally thought to be an amalgam of every hero and criminal in the city and able to duplicate their powers, Fusion II turns out to have only the power of suggestion; a "poor man's Mysterio," in the words of Spider-Man.

ORIGIN: Markley found out as a child that he was gifted with the innate ability to persuade others. He honed his powers using money and influence to develop systems to enhance his abilities.

FIRST APPEARANCE: *Spider-Man*, Volume 2 #30

G

GAUNT

NAME: Mendel Stormm, a.k.a. the Robot Master

POWERS: A master robotics creator, as Gaunt he has possession of advanced weaponry such as particle grenades and a computer-guided arm-cannon. Also has super strength while in robotic form as well as the ability to emit deadly gasses.

ORIGIN: Stromm was close to death after initially having a heart attack, but with the aid of Norman Osborn, and having tested a super-strength formula similar to the Goblin's on himself, he was found still alive years later. He was then outfitted with a special life-support suit of armor that kept him mobile. He soon assumed a robotic form with the help of Seward Trainer, who was a close friend of Ben Reilly.

FIRST APPEARANCE: *Amazing Spider-Man* #37

GIBBON

NAME: Martin Blank

POWERS: Great strength, agility, and speed as well as fighting skills similar to that of a real gibbon.

ORIGIN: Seemingly a mutant at birth, the Gibbon later joined a circus, where he did well as an acrobat. His powers were later enhanced by a potion given to him by Kraven to "unleash the best within."

FIRST APPEARANCE: *Amazing Spider-Man* #110

GOG

NAME: Unknown

POWERS: This intelligent, surprisingly quick, half-reptilian, half-ape being, named after a biblical giant, who like him used his huge powerful tail as a weapon, Gog has the ability to teleport with the help of his alien wristbands.

ORIGIN: Gog was found as an infant in an alien spacecraft in the Savage Land jungle (home of Ka-Zar) by Spider-Man foe Kraven the Hunter. Kraven watched over the alien as he grew rapidly. Gog has served Kraven by looking after him.

FIRST APPEARANCE: *Amazing Spider-Man* #103

GREEN GOBLIN

NAME: Norman Osborn

POWERS: Superhuman strength and a large arsenal of weaponry including pumpkin bombs and gas bombs. Uses electro-gloves and his trusty "Goblin Glider," which caused Norman's "death" back in *Amazing Spider-Man* #122.

ORIGIN: A co-owner of a leading chemical manufacturer, Norman Osborn was obsessed with power. He had already acquired great wealth and power, but it was not enough. He came across notes pertaining to ex-partner Mendel Stormm's chemical formula, designed to increase a person's intellect and physical strength. An explosion resulted from his experiments with this formula, and the aftereffects not only gave him amazing strength but also drove him insane. As the Green Goblin, he quickly becomes Spider-Man's most deadly villain.

FIRST APPEARANCE: *Amazing Spider-Man* #14

GREEN GOBLIN II

NAME: Harry Osborn

POWERS: Same as Green Goblin

ORIGIN: Being the son of the original Green Goblin is never easy, as Harry Osborn learns. His mental stability is already at stake due to the influence of drugs, but when his father reportedly dies, he blames Spider-Man and becomes the second Green Goblin. He eventually was placed under the care of psychiatrist Dr. Bart Hamilton, who would ultimately become the third Green Goblin.

FIRST APPEARANCE: *Amazing Spider-Man* #136

GREEN GOBLIN III

NAME: Bart Hamilton

POWERS: Same as previous two Green Goblins

ORIGIN: After learning much from his patient, Harry Osborn, from hypnosis, Dr. Bart Hamilton uses his newly found powers to become the third Green Goblin. He soon invades and battles the underground world of Maggia and even GGII. He is eventually killed by his own bomb, which he planned to use against Harry and Spider-Man.

FIRST APPEARANCE: *Amazing Spider-Man* #176

GREEN GOBLIN IV

NAME: Unknown

POWERS: The same as his predecessors

ORIGIN: The fourth Goblin was revealed to be nothing more than a construct of Norman Osborn and Dr. Angst to possibly become an heir to Norman. In the end, though, the construct decomposed as the Goblin formula ate away at him before he could be stabilized.

FIRST APPEARANCE: *Spider-Man* #88

GRIFFIN

NAME: Johnny Horton

POWERS: Johnny Horton gained his powers from a mutagenic serum given to him by scientists from the Secret Empire, a subversive organization. The Griffin possesses superhuman strength and has a very high resistance to physical injury. Its wings endow him with the power of flight.

FIRST APPEARANCE: *Amazing Adventures* #15

GRIM HUNTER

NAME: Vladimir Kravinoff

POWERS: Similar to those of his father, Kraven, in that he has great strength, speed, agility, and stamina. An expert wielder of knives and spears.

ORIGIN: While in Russia, and wanting to avenge the death of his father, Kraven, Vladimir set out to claim the full legacy in the United States and kill Spider-Man. He gained his powers with help from his advisor, Gregor, and a serum recipe obtained from his father's journal.

FIRST APPEARANCE: *Spider-Man* #47

GRIZZLY

NAME: Maxwell Markham

POWERS: Use of an exoskeleton that enhances his already great strength. An excellent fighter who has use of very sharp claws attached to his Grizzly costume.

ORIGIN: A former professional wrestler, Maxwell lost his wrestling license due to J. Jonah Jameson's declaration that he was a menace. Thereafter, he went into a life of crime with help from the Jackal, who created his exoskeleton.

FIRST APPEARANCE: *Amazing Spider-Man* #139

H

HAMMERHEAD

NAME: Unrevealed

POWERS: Great hand-to-hand combatant and gunman, whose greatest fighting tactic is that of charging headfirst into his victim with his steel alloy skull. Once had use of an exoskeleton, which enhanced his strength.

ORIGIN: A regular gunman at first, Hammerhead became involved with the organized crime family called the Maggia. Found beaten and disfigured, he had his skull surgically replaced with a steel alloy by Dr. Jonas Harrow, giving him a lethal weapon that he uses like a charging bull.

FIRST APPEARANCE: *Amazing Spider-Man* #113

DR. JONAS HARROW

POWERS: Harrow has no superhuman abilities, but is in possession of a brilliant mind. He is a gifted surgeon and inventor who has created or re-created several of Spider-Man's enemies over the years. Harrow has always been a behind-the-scenes player.

ORIGIN: Dr. Jonas Harrow was discredited as a surgeon after performing a number of nontraditional experiments. He began his career/re-creation of super-villains after his successful surgery on Hammerhead.

FIRST APPEARANCE: *Amazing Spider-Man* #114

HIGH EVOLUTIONARY

NAME: Herbert Edgar Wyndham

POWERS: Devised his own suit of protective armor and has a highly developed brain. The High Evolutionary also possesses vast psionic powers that enable him to rearrange matter.

ORIGIN: Herbert was a student at Oxford University, where he built a machine that was able to accelerate the genetic evolution of living organisms. Eventually he subjected himself to his own creation, thereby increasing his own intellect many times over. Since then, he has tried to construct a detailed replica of Earth called Counter-Earth, and also has plotted to evolve all of mankind.

FIRST APPEARANCE: *Thor* #134

FIRST SPIDER-MAN APPEARANCE: *Amazing Spider-Man Annual* #22

HOBGOBLIN

NAME: Roderick Kingsley

POWERS: Same as the Green Goblin

ORIGIN: Roderick gained the powers as he stumbled upon one of the original Green Goblin's hidden lairs, which contained costumes, weapons, private journals, and more.

FIRST APPEARANCE: *Spectacular Spider-Man* #43

HOBGOBLIN II

NAME: Jason Macendale

POWERS: Same as the Green Goblin

ORIGIN: After thinking that the original Hobgoblin was dead, Jason assumed his guise and powers. In fact, it was Betty Brant Leeds's husband, Ned, who was brainwashed into playing the part of the Hobgoblin until he was murdered under orders of the original. Up until this point, Macendale was known solely as Jack O'Lantern.

FIRST APPEARANCE: *Machine Man* #19

FIRST SPIDER-MAN APPEARANCE: *Amazing Spider-Man* #289

HUMAN FLY

NAME: Rick Deacon

POWERS: As the Human Fly, Deacon has increased healing capabilities as well as super strength, the ability to fly, and great speed. He can also create an ultrasonic backlash by beating his wings.

ORIGIN: The Human Fly was created by scientist Harlan Stillwell at J. Jonah

Jameson's request. Rick Deacon was transformed into the Human Fly when his atoms became "impregnated" with the genetic coding of a common fly. Jameson funded the undertaking to create a "hero" to rid the town of Spider-Man.

FIRST APPEARANCE: *Amazing Spider-Man Annual* #10

HYDRO MAN

NAME: Morrie Bench

POWERS: Ability to transform himself into a watery substance of unknown composition. He can mentally control every drop of water he is made up of and can propel water at high speeds.

ORIGIN: After accidentally being knocked overboard from a cargo ship, Bench made contact with an experimental generator within the ocean. The results of this energy conversion, along with being subjected to volcanic gases, is that Morrie's life and body changed forever.

FIRST APPEARANCE: *Amazing Spider-Man* #212

J

JACK O'LANTERN

NAME: Jason Macendale, Jr.

POWERS: Military training in hand-to-hand combat and martial arts. Has grenades in many forms as well as wrist-blasters on each hand. "Jack" uses hovercraft for transportation.

ORIGIN: Originally recruited by the CIA, Jason began his life of crime soon after being discharged. He used the costumed identity

as well as his scientific skills and vast combat training to aid his criminal ways.

FIRST APPEARANCE: *Machine Man* #19

FIRST SPIDER-MAN APPEARANCE: *Amazing Spider-Man* #254

JACKAL

NAME: Professor Miles Warren

POWERS: The Jackal is a brilliant mind who possesses no superhuman powers. There are razor-sharp claws in his costume that he sometimes coats with poison or drugs. He also occasionally administers shocks to his victims from an electrical device from which he is safely insulated.

ORIGIN: Miles was a professor at Peter Parker's Empire State University, where he had a great infatuation for Peter's girlfriend, Gwen Stacy. Miles later blamed him for her death and took on the guise of the Jackal.

FIRST APPEARANCE: *Amazing Spider-Man* #129

JOYSTICK

NAME: Carrie Bradley

POWERS: Strength, agility, speed. Has the ability to generate blasts through the use of wrist conduits. She uses sticks to emit energy blasts at specific targets.

ORIGIN: Little is known about how Joystick received her powers, but much of it is apparently man-made (or in this case, woman-made).

FIRST APPEARANCE: *Amazing Scarlet Spider* #1

JUGGERNAUT

NAME: Cain Marko

POWERS: Juggernaut possesses superhuman strength and is highly resistant to all forms of injury. Can mentally create a force field around himself and is able to sustain himself without food, water, or oxygen for long periods of time.

ORIGIN: Cain Marko has possession of a ruby from the lost temple of Cyttorak, which transferred its mystical energies into him and endowed him with his powers. His helmet and skullcap are composed of an unknown, indestructible metal.

FIRST APPEARANCE: *Uncanny X-Men* #12

FIRST SPIDER-MAN APPEARANCE: *Amazing Spider-Man* #229

THE JURY

NAMES: Sentry (Curtis Elkins), Screech (Max Taylor), Ramshot (Samuel Caulkin), Bomblast (unknown), Firearm (unknown), Wysper (Jennifer Stewart)

POWERS: All members have armor that is based on the Guardsman's. They're fitted with power packs that give them varied individual powers. All members also have the power of flight, thanks to the use of antigravity discs attached to their feet.

ORIGIN: The concept of the group was devised by Mr. Orwell Taylor, a man of vast resources. Orwell's son, Hugh, was killed by Venom while working as a guard at the prison known as Vault. Orwell formed the Jury from a group of Vault guards to act as a vigilante organization that hunts and captures villains so that they can go on "trial." Naturally, Venom was their first target.

FIRST APPEARANCE: *Venom: Lethal Protector* #2

FIRST SPIDER-MAN APPEARANCE: *Amazing Spider-Man* #383

JUST A GUY NAMED JOE

NAME: Joe Smith

POWERS: As his "beserker" counterpart, Joe has strength that rivals Spider-Man's. He can withstand a lot of punishment while going off into fighting frenzies and has proven to be impervious to many harmful conditions. His powers are only present during his "berserker" phase.

ORIGIN: While on the set of his first acting job, Joe was accidentally exposed to a flood of spilled chemicals that reacted with live electrical wires. The resulting shock triggered the transformation in him.

FIRST APPEARANCE: *Amazing Spider-Man* #38

K

KAINE

NAME: Kaine

POWERS: Acquired the same powers as Spider-Man, and is also able to burn his handprints into any surface, thus allowing him to leave the "Mark of Kaine." Experiences precognitive flashes that let him see into the future. Equipped with deadly claws like Wolverine's.

ORIGIN: Kaine was the first clone of Peter Parker created by Professor Miles Warren, who also doubled as the Jackal, with one genetic flaw: he is slowly degenerating.

FIRST APPEARANCE: *Web of Spider-Man* #119

KANGAROO

NAME: I—Frank Oliver; II—Brian Hibbs

POWERS: Always a great fan and researcher of mammals, Frank Oliver gained enhanced powers courtesy of Dr. Jonas Harrow. With the aid of power boots, he has great jumping and punching/boxing abilities. He eventually dies of radiation poisoning.

ORIGIN: The original Kangaroo's powers were derived from a genetic mutation and were further enhanced by Dr. Harrow's implants, which were connected to his central nervous system. The second Kangaroo is more of a mystery, with little being revealed about him.

FIRST APPEARANCE: I—*Amazing Spider-Man* #81; II—*Spectacular Spider-Man #242*

KILLER SHRIKE

NAME: Simon Maddicks

POWERS: Amazing strength and peak human reflexes. Has great endurance and resistance to injury. Ability to fly due to antigravity generator located at the base of his spine. He wears twin power blasters on each wrist.

ORIGIN: Unknown

FIRST APPEARANCE: *Rampaging Hulk* #1

FIRST SPIDER-MAN APPEARANCE: *Marvel Team-Up* #90

KINGPIN

NAME: Wilson Grant Fisk

POWERS: Although the Kingpin appears to be extremely obese, he is in peak condition, with amazing strength and agility. He is skilled in the martial arts and sumo wrestling and is extraordinary in hand-to-hand combat. He is also a gifted organizer and planner, with much knowledge on the subject of political science. Carries an "obliterator cane" walking stick that contains a 300-unit laser beam. Also has a diamond stickpin that can fire sleeping gas.

ORIGIN: The Kingpin has no superhuman powers, but has made his way to the top of organized crime through sheer strength and intellect.

FIRST APPEARANCE: *Amazing Spider-Man* #50

KNIGHT & FOGG

NAMES: Malcolm Knight and Thomas Fogg

POWERS: Knight—Heavy armor and use of a long blade that protrudes from the back of his hand. Can also use this blade to cut through brick and concrete. Fogg—Impervious to harm when in the form of a slippery green fog; similar in appearance to a misty ghost.

ORIGIN: Originally contract killers for a Liverpool mobster in England, Malcolm and Thomas were hired to kill physicist Henry Lewis. When Thomas shoots Professor Lewis, a particle cannon is triggered, which unleashes itself on the two men, transforming them forever.

FIRST APPEARANCE: *Spectacular Spider-Man* #165

KRAVEN

NAME: Sergei Kravinoff

POWERS: Superhuman strength, speed of up to sixty miles per hour, high agility, and stamina. Also skilled at taming wild beasts and uses exotic-animal–fighting techniques. Has a nerve punch that can paralyze, and uses weaponry such as darts, spears, axes, nets, whips, poisons, gases, and more.

ORIGIN: The son of a Russian aristocrat, Sergei sought employment in Africa. After meeting a witch doctor, he took an herbal potion that enhanced his physical powers.

He used these newfound abilities to further aid his big hunts, eventually turning his sights on Spider-Man.

FIRST APPEARANCE: *Amazing Spider-Man #15*

KRAVEN II

NAME: Alyosha Kravinoff

POWERS: Similar to his father's.

ORIGIN: He is the son of Sergei Kravinoff, the original Kraven, and has followed in his father's footsteps.

FIRST APPEARANCE: *Spectacular Spider-Man #243*

L

LIGHTMASTER

NAME: Dr. Edward Lansky

POWERS: Lightmaster's powers come from the powered suit he wears, which allows him to manipulate photons. He can create solid-mass objects from photons and generate beams of light that he can direct as a destructive force.

ORIGIN: As a high-ranking official of Empire State University, Edward Lansky attempted to attack New York City in response to budget cuts. Spider-Man's intervention caused a large current of electricity to flow through his body, transforming him.

FIRST APPEARANCE: *Spectacular Spider-Man #3*

LIZARD

NAME: Dr. Curtis Connors

POWERS: Super strength, alligator-tough skin capable of resisting bullets, and the ability to attain speeds of up to forty-five miles per hour. Can also communicate with and control all reptiles within a one-mile radius.

ORIGIN: Originally an amputee army surgeon, Dr. Connors studied reptiles and their ability to regenerate limbs. He discovered a chemical substance and injected it into himself, hoping to grow an arm to replace the one he had lost. Instead, he found himself transformed into reptilian-humanoid form.

FIRST APPEARANCE: *Amazing Spider-Man #6*

LIVING BRAIN

NAME: Not applicable

POWERS: The Living Brain has great strength and the ability to move upon command, and its limbs can perform various motions. It has the ability to think due to its great computerized "brain." It is short-circuited after its introduction and goes "crazy," until Peter Parker readjusts the machine, bringing it back to normal. The later version has the ability to hover and fly and is considerably stronger.

ORIGIN: The Brain was an early Mobile Computer prototype built by I.C.M. in Midtown High School, which Peter Parker attended.

FIRST APPEARANCE: *Amazing Spider-Man #8*

LOOTER

NAME: Norton G. Fester

POWERS: Super strength gained from a meteor.

ORIGIN: Norton believed he could prove meteors contain microscopic life, and in his studies was struck in the face by gas from one of the meteorites he was experimenting on. The resulting increased strength leads him down a criminal path.

FIRST APPEARANCE: *Amazing Spider-Man #36*

M

MAGNETO

NAME: Magnus

POWERS: Mutant ability to control magnetism and shape and to manipulate magnetic fields. Also an expert in genetic engineering and an excellent hand-to-hand combatant. His magnetic abilities can increase his physical strength to the 100-ton class. Has minor psychic abilities.

ORIGIN: Since Magneto is a mutant, he was born with his abilities. It took him several years to learn of his powers, as he attempted to seek revenge for the death of his daughter. His wife left him shortly thereafter, and he began his life as Marvel's second-greatest villain, behind only Doctor Doom. He is, by far, the X-Men's greatest foe.

FIRST APPEARANCE: *X-Men #1*

FIRST SPIDER-MAN APPEARANCE: *Amazing Spider-Man #327*

MAN MOUNTAIN MARKO

NAME: Michael Marko

POWERS: His only power is super strength, which is comparable to that of Spider-Man's.

ORIGIN: His strength was derived from his being genetically altered by Maggia as well as having been given racehorse steroids over time.

FIRST APPEARANCE: *Amazing Spider-Man #73*

MAN-WOLF

NAME: John Jameson

POWERS: Man-Wolf has super strength, agility, and speed, with sharp claws resembling an arctic wolf. When in the other realm known as Stargod, he can speak telepathically, manipulate energies, and uses a broadsword, dagger, and bow and arrow.

ORIGIN: As an astronaut, John came across a rubylike gemstone on the moon and wore it as a pendant. Unfortunately, he didn't realize that the stone was an alien artifact that grafted itself to his throat. As a result, whenever a full moon would rise, he would be transformed into a werewolf, with all of those inherent abilities.

FIRST APPEARANCE: *Amazing Spider-Man #124*

MINDWORM

NAME: William Turner

POWERS: The ability of a psychic parasite. He is able to gain strength from the minds and souls who live within the range of his power. He can emit "mind-blasts" from his eyes that render his victims very weak.

ORIGIN: Born a freak, William Turner gradually realized he was a mutant as he approached manhood. He alienated himself from humanity and became a recluse after accidentally killing his parents by draining their strength.

FIRST APPEARANCE: *Amazing Spider-Man #138*

MIRAGE

NAME: Desmond Charme

POWERS: As a holographic technician, Desmond easily became a costumed criminal known as Mirage. He can project three-dimensional images known as holograms to disguise himself. In the end, he is yet another criminal murdered at the hands of the criminal assassin known as the Scourge.

ORIGIN: Unknown

FIRST APPEARANCE: *Amazing Spider-Man* #156

MISTER HYDE

NAME: Dr. Calvin Zabo

POWERS: Mr. Hyde can lift upward of fifty tons. As Dr. Zabo, he has a very gifted intellect, but as Mr. Hyde he's far more bestial. As Hyde, what he lacks mentally he makes up for in enhanced reflexes, stamina, speed, and durability. Zabo must ingest a chemical to transform into Mr. Hyde.

ORIGIN: Zabo's experiments resulted in a potion that, like the character in the Robert Louis Stevenson classic, unleashed a man's inner demon.

FIRST APPEARANCE: *Journey into Mystery* #99

FIRST SPIDER-MAN APPEARANCE: *Spectacular Spider-Man* #46

MOLTEN MAN

NAME: Mark Raxton

POWERS: Possesses super strength. His skin is composed of a frictionless metal alloy coating that allows him to slip away from any kind of grasp. That same skin surface makes him impervious to injury. He is able to radiate heat up to 300 degrees Fahrenheit.

ORIGIN: Unknown

FIRST APPEARANCE: *Amazing Spider-Man* #28

MORBIUS

NAME: Dr. Michael Morbius

POWERS: Pseudo-vampire. Has superhuman strength, but needs fresh blood to survive. Victims of his bite also are transformed into vampires. He is able to glide on wind currents and quickly heals from injury.

ORIGIN: A Nobel Prize–winning biochemist, Michael Morbius was dying from a rare disease that involved the dissolution of his blood cells. Attempting to find a cure, he used a vaccine that contained elements of the blood of vampire bats. That substance, combined with electric shock treatment, transformed him into a vampire.

FIRST APPEARANCE: *Amazing Spider-Man* #101

MYSTERIO

NAME: Quentin Beck

POWERS: Skilled fighter and athlete, whose major skills are as an illusionist and master hypnotist. He is also a skilled chemist, stuntman, and special-effects artist. In the past, he has had the ability to emit blasts from his costume and at one point electrified his cape.

ORIGIN: Originally a stuntman in Hollywood, Quentin Beck had an idea to simulate Spider-Man's abilities and moved to New York to do so. While there, he worked with the Terrible Tinkerer and costumed himself as an alien. He continued his life of crime from that point on.

FIRST APPEARANCE: *Amazing Spider-Man* #13

N

NIGHTMARE

NAME: Not applicable

POWERS: Nightmare draws power from the psychic energy of the dreaming masses, particularly those on Earth. He can control those who sleep and draw on their life essence. Additionally, he can trap a sleeper's soul indefinitely.

ORIGIN: Nightmare's origin is relatively unknown, as he may or may not be human in nature.

FIRST APPEARANCE: *Strange Tales* #110

FIRST SPIDER-MAN APPEARANCE: *Amazing Spider-Man* #25

O

OWL

NAME: Leland Owlsley

POWERS: The Owl has no superhuman physical abilities, but is an inventive genius who creates many weapons, including razor-sharp talons that are attached to his forearms. He also has a special cloak and exoskeleton that enables him to fly as fast as thirty miles per hour.

ORIGIN: Leland was once a financier sought by the IRS for fraud. At that point he became a major crimelord who suffered numerous defeats. Stricken by a debilitating ailment that made him unable to walk or stand without a brace or exoskeleton, his legs were eventually paralyzed.

FIRST APPEARANCE: *Daredevil* #3

FIRST SPIDER-MAN APPEARANCE: *Spectacular Spider-Man* #73

P

PROFESSOR POWER

NAME: Professor Anthony Powers

POWERS: Wears a battlesuit that endows him with superhuman strength. Has an electronic beam implanted into the suit's forearm area, and he is able to fly, thanks to electronically powered turbines.

ORIGIN: Designed his own powersuit and created an organization known as the Secret Empire.

FIRST APPEARANCE: *Marvel Team-Up* #117

PROWLER

NAME: Hobie Brown

POWERS: Hobie has no superpowers, but an arsenal of weapons including a pellet-firing cartridge attached to a bracelet he wears. Additionally, he's armed with steel-tipped claws for scaling purposes and is skilled in hand-to-hand battle. Can leap long distances, thanks to his "shock absorber" boots. He can also glide by use of his cape, which contains pneumatic filaments that expand with air, giving it a rigid structure.

ORIGIN: Hobie Brown began his costumed career after being a window washer, and he used some of his own inventions as weapons. Over the years, he has designed each weapon that he uses.

FIRST APPEARANCE: *Amazing Spider-Man* #78

PSYCHO MAN

NAME: Unknown

POWERS: Possesses superhuman intellect and employs a number of suits of body armor made of an alien material that gives him super strength. His speed and stamina also is augmented by these suits of armor, along with metahuman durability. Built into his armor are various forms of weaponry. His most well-known weapon is a portable emotion-stimulator device that can project rays that stimulate the emotional center of the brain and can trigger three emotional states: fear, doubt, and hate.

ORIGIN: Psycho Man is the chief scientist of the planet Traan, located in the microverse, which is a group of five planets in a subatomic system.

FIRST APPEARANCE: *Fantastic Four Annual* #5

FIRST SPIDER-MAN APPEARANCE: *Spectacular Spider-Man Annual* #10

PUMA

NAME: Thomas Fireheart

POWERS: The latest of American Indians bred to be a perfect human being, Thomas becomes the Puma through intense concentration. A transformation takes place that increases his strength, speed, agility, stamina, senses, and coordination. His fingernails transform into claws and his pupils dilate, the whites of his eyes becoming yellow. He is then covered in fur, which provides camouflage.

ORIGIN: Thomas was the victim of a secret Indian tribe experiment. Combining mysticism with controlled breeding in an effort to bring about one perfect warrior to act as their protector, the tribe transformed him into Puma.

FIRST APPEARANCE: *Amazing Spider-Man* #256

Q

QUICKSAND

NAME: Unknown

POWERS: Enhanced strength and the ability to convert part of her body into a sandlike substance through sheer mental will. Can bend and extend her body or portions thereof. She can also create a sandstorm that can be used against her enemies.

ORIGIN: As a former scientist, the woman known as Quicksand obtained her powers as a result of a nuclear accident that altered her atomic structure.

FIRST APPEARANCE: *Thor* #392

FIRST SPIDER-MAN APPEARANCE: *Web of Spider-Man* #107

R

RANGER

NAME: Unknown

POWERS: Little is known about the Ranger, but he does have great strength and athletic abilities. Carries a pair of "lightning rods" he uses as weapons.

ORIGIN: Unknown

FIRST APPEARANCE: *Amazing Spider-Man*, Volume 2, #1

RED SKULL

NAME: Johann Schmidt

POWERS: The Red Skull inhabits the body of a clone of Captain America that was created when he was in peak physical condition. An excellent hand-to-hand combatant, he is also a gifted marksman and brilliant strategist.

ORIGIN: Johann was originally trained to be Adolf Hitler's right-hand man during World War II after Hitler saw a hatred of mankind in Johann's eyes. The Red Skull was used to spread terror throughout the world during and after the war.

FIRST APPEARANCE: *Tales of Suspense* #65

FIRST SPIDER-MAN APPEARANCE: *Amazing Spider-Man* #325

RHINO

NAME: Alex O'Hirn

POWERS: Super strength, speed, and endurance. Very high degree of invulnerability. Also has very thick polymer mat similar to rhinoceros skin. Can resist explosions and temperatures of minus 50 to 1,000 degrees Fahrenheit. Has two horns with two-inch plate steel that he uses as weapons.

ORIGIN: A pair of scientists named Igor and Georgi designed and created the thick polymer matted costume that gives the Rhino his great powers.

FIRST APPEARANCE: *Amazing Spider-Man* #41

RINGER

NAME: Anthony Davis

POWERS: No superhuman abilities, but does control various weapons that take the form of rings—explosive rings, freezing rings, constricting rings, and various interlocking rings that he uses as ladders, lassos, or whips. His battlesuit can form ring weapons from thin air.

ORIGIN: The Ringer obtained his weapons from an unidentified source, but the longtime Spider-Man foe, the Terrible Tinkerer, had a big hand in improving them as well as giving Anthony a new battlesuit.

FIRST APPEARANCE: *Defenders* #51

FIRST SPIDER-MAN APPEARANCE: *Spectacular Spider-Man* #58

RINGMASTER

NAME: Maynard Tiboldt

POWERS: With Nazi ties from his past, Maynard utilizes the Red Skull–created "nullatron" to take hypnotic control over whomever he chooses. The nullatron is concealed in his huge ringmaster's top hat.

FIRST APPEARANCE: *Incredible Hulk* #3

FIRST SPIDER-MAN APPEARANCE: *Amazing Spider-Man* #16

ROCKET RACER

NAME: Robert Farrell

POWERS: Intellectually gifted. Devises a cybernetically controlled, rocket-powered magnetic skateboard that serves as his means of transportation, and with which he can attain speeds of sixty miles per hour. Has gloves equipped with explosives.

ORIGIN: After his mother suffered a heart attack and was hospitalized, Robert Farrell turned to crime to get enough money to pay the family bills.

FIRST APPEARANCE: *Amazing Spider-Man* #172

S

SANDMAN

NAME: Flint Marko

POWERS: Superhuman strength and the ability to convert his body into a sandlike substance by mental command. Can increase the density of his body greatly, making him largely indestructible.

ORIGIN: After escaping prison, Flint found refuge in a military nuclear testing site on a beach and was exposed to a reactor's explosion, which bombarded him with vast amounts of radiation. Awakening, he discovered that his DNA had been altered.

FIRST APPEARANCE: *Amazing Spider-Man* #4

SCARECROW

NAME: Ebenezer Laughton

POWERS: The Scarecrow has the agility of a professional contortionist and is thus able to escape from many a tight situation. He also is well trained as an acrobat and can command birds to attack and perform various acts. The Scarecrow's body produces a mutated pheromone that affects the adrenal glands of people within twenty feet of him, triggering panic attacks.

ORIGIN: The Scarecrow was originally a variety-show contortionist who realized that he could probably make more money as a criminal than a performer. He obtained superhuman strength from surgical implants given to him by doctors working for the enigmatic "Firm."

FIRST APPEARANCE: *Tales of Suspense* #51

FIRST SPIDER-MAN APPEARANCE: *Untold Tales of Spider-Man* #22

SCHEMER

NAME: Richard Fisk

POWERS: The Schemer uses various firearms in his crimes, as he's an exceptional marksman, hand-to-hand combatant, and strategist.

ORIGIN: After fully realizing the nature of his father's work, Richard Fisk was ashamed and set out to disrupt and put an end to the Kingpin's empire, indirectly leading to a conflict with Spider-Man.

FIRST APPEARANCE: *Amazing Spider-Man* #83

SCORCHER

NAME: Hudak

POWERS: The Scorcher can direct enormous fire-powered flame blasts at his enemies. Heat is generated from the armored suit he wears. Use of a jet pack enables him to fly.

ORIGIN: A former research chemist, the Scorcher has the ability to easily create the equipment he uses in his life of crime.

FIRST APPEARANCE: *Untold Tales of Spider-Man* #1

SCORPIA

NAME: Elaine Colls

POWERS: With the Scorpion suit created by Silvermane's engineers, Elaine's strength and speed is enhanced 500 percent. She also has use of a micro-thin force field and energy blasts that take various forms.

ORIGIN: Taken from the Hell's Kitchen area of New York City, Elaine Colls was employed by Silvermane and eventually turned into Scorpia.

FIRST APPEARANCE: *Power of Terror* #2

FIRST SPIDER-MAN APPEARANCE: *Spider-Man Unlimited* #9

SCORPION

NAME: MacDonald "Mac" Gargan

POWERS: Super strength, speed, agility, and stamina resulting from a battlesuit constructed of two layers of steel mesh with one layer of insulated rubber within. His primary weapon is a seven-foot-long tail—designed by the Terrible Tinkerer—which is cybernetically controlled.

ORIGIN: Mac gained the powers of the Scorpion after chemical and radiological treatments from Dr. Farley Stillwell. The treatments caused a mutagenic change within him, resulting in the creation of the Scorpion.

SCREAM

NAME: Donna

POWERS: Same as Venom. Also can shoot strands of an alien substance in the form of any weapon she imagines. Her hair is the area most used in this manner.

ORIGIN: Donna, along with four other volunteer security personnel, was reborn in the laboratories of Life Foundation after the organization learned that Carnage received his abilities from a spawn of the alien symbiote costume of Venom's. They obtained and controlled other spawn and then combined them with the volunteers.

FIRST APPEARANCE: *Venom: Lethal Protector* #4

FIRST SPIDER-MAN APPEARANCE: *Spider-Man* #52

SHOCKER

NAME: Herman Schultz

POWERS: The Shocker has two vibro-shock units that create high-pressure air blasts that are very powerful and destructive. Also has a vibration shield that deflects blows and allows him to slip from many a grasp. Has a uniform of foam-lined fabric to absorb the impact caused by his vibro-shock units.

ORIGIN: As an unsuccessful burglar, Herman Schultz, gifted in working with tools, developed, in prison, what was to become the infamous vibro-shock units that renew his criminal life.

FIRST APPEARANCE: *Amazing Spider-Man* #46

SHRIEK

NAME: Sandra Deel or Frances Louise Barrison (no one is sure)

POWERS: Has the ability to use sonic blasts and the power to manipulate others by bringing out their fears and angers until they react violently.

ORIGIN: Gained her powers from being exposed to Cloak's (of Cloak & Dagger) darkness. May or may not have had these powers before then, either by mutation or some other unexplained way.

FIRST APPEARANCE: *Spider-Man Unlimited* #1

SILVERMANE

NAME: Silvio Manfredi

POWERS: Peak human stamina, speed, and endurance, along with superhuman strength. Also possesses superhuman senses.

ORIGIN: As a former head of the crime syndicate known as the Maggia, Silvio gained the nickname due to the premature silvering of his hair at the age of forty. At age eighty, he forced Dr. Curt Connors (the Lizard) to concoct a youth serum, which cut his age in half. He eventually goes on to become Supreme Hydra at that organization, where his son aids him as the villain Blackwing.

FIRST APPEARANCE: *Amazing Spider-Man* #73

SINEATER

NAME: Stanley Carter

POWERS: Enhanced strength and endurance. Extensive hand-to-hand combat skills. Uses double-barreled shotgun to kill his victims.

ORIGIN: Well known for the murder of Captain Jean DeWolff, Stanley Carter was injected with drugs while with S.H.I.E.L.D., resulting in a transformation of his body.

FIRST APPEARANCE: *Spectacular Spider-Man* #107

SLYDE

NAME: Jalome Beacher

POWERS: Super speed and the ability to basically "slide" out of anyone's grip.

ORIGIN: A chemical engineer, Jalome created the costume that endowed him with superior speed abilities.

FIRST APPEARANCE: *Amazing Spider-Man* #272

SPENCER SMYTHE

NAME: Same as above

POWERS: A genius when it comes to creating robots, Spencer created a number of Spider-Slayers, all of which were major threats to the web-crawler.

ORIGIN: Spencer was initially hired by J. Jonah Jameson, editor of the *Daily Bugle*, to create a robot to stop Spider-Man and failed. With each failure, Smythe's obsession with Spider-Man grew and drove him to try harder.

FIRST APPEARANCE: *Amazing Spider-Man* #25

SPEED DEMON

NAME: James Sanders

POWERS: Super strength in his leg muscles, which enable him to press over 1,000 pounds. Strongest power is superhuman speed and reflexes.

ORIGIN: Originally known as the Whizzer, James Sanders changed his name and look to the Speed Demon. Beyond that, not much else is known.

FIRST APPEARANCE: *Amazing Spider-Man* #222

SPIDERCIDE

NAME: Peter Parker (clone)

POWERS: Same as Spider-Man, plus has a malleable body like Mr. Fantastic. He also can create sharp weapons from his body, and can turn into a liquid form and rematerialize as a solid.

ORIGIN: Clone of Peter Parker created by the Jackal, who made Spidercide believe that he was the true Peter Parker.

FIRST APPEARANCE: *Spectacular Spider-Man* #226

STEGRON

NAME: Dr. Vincent Stegron

POWERS: Stegron has great speed and strength as well as mental control over the dinosaurs that inhabit the Savage Land (home of Ka-Zar). Possesses an incredibly powerful tail that he uses as a weapon and is well armored.

ORIGIN: Vincent Stegron gained his powers as a result of cell regeneration utilizing dinosaur tissue from an experiment conducted by S.H.I.E.L.D. and Dr. Curt Conners.

FIRST APPEARANCE: *Marvel Team-Up* #19

STILT MAN

NAME: Wilbur Day

POWERS: Wilbur has use of an armored battlesuit that enables him to extend his hydraulic stilt-legs up to 290 feet and also gives him enhanced strength (approximately tenfold). He can use these legs as battering rams. The stilts are coated with a silicone compound that Spider-Man's webbing cannot adhere to. Wilbur also uses gas grenades/canisters and a particle-beam blaster.

ORIGIN: Wilbur Day, while working at Kaxton Industries as a scientist, stole a design for a hydraulic ram device created by his employer, Carl Kaxton, out of dissatisfaction with his position in the company. He used the design to create an armored pair of stilts and attached them to a suit of armor. He began his criminal career by looting and robbing before going against some big-name characters such as Daredevil and Spider-Man.

FIRST APPEARANCE: *Daredevil* #8

FIRST SPIDER-MAN APPEARANCE: *Amazing Spider-Man* #237

STYX & STONE

NAMES: Jacob Eichorn and Gerald Stone

POWERS: Styx—ability to kill organic matter with a single touch due to his "living cancer" disease and immunity. Stone—uses a blaster with a variety of tools, among them gas pellets, sonic beams, strobe-bursts and nova-beams. Both villains have use of a turbo-copter for transportation.

ORIGIN: Unknown

FIRST APPEARANCE: *Amazing Spider-Man* #309

SWARM

NAME: Fritz Von Meyer

POWERS: An ex-Nazi scientist, Fritz is essentially made up of mutated killer bees—approximately 220,000 of them. Can shoot "blasts" of bees as a weapon. He has mental control of these bees and every other mutant bee around the world. Swarm can fly and is impervious to bullets.

ORIGIN: Von Meyer hid in South America after World War II. He became very interested in the breeding and keeping of bees. One day he discovered a highly radioactive oversize beehive due to a meteorite bombardment. The bees that inhabited the hive demonstrated great intelligence. Von Meyer tried to manipulate the bees so that he might train them by using a psionic beam. As a result, the bees underwent an even greater mutation. The bees attacked him and consumed his body, leaving only his skeleton behind within the living swarm.

FIRST APPEARANCE: *Champions* #14

FIRST SPIDER-MAN APPEARANCE: *Spectacular Spider-Man* #36

T

TARANTULA

NAME: Anton Miguel Rodriguez

POWERS: Great athlete with incredible agility and leaping skills. Excellent in hand-to-hand combat. Wears gloves with retractable razor blades and boots with retractable points at the toes.

ORIGIN: As a revolutionary terrorist and government operative, Anton was expelled from his small organization after murdering a guard without reason during a robbery. This is the moment when Anton went to the repressive side of the government, where they created the identity of the Tarantula for him and demanded that he serve as his country's counterpart to Captain America.

FIRST APPEARANCE: *Amazing Spider-Man* #134

TARANTULA II

NAME: Luis Alvarez

POWERS: Olympic-level athlete with incredible agility and leaping skills. Other skills and equipment similar to the original Tarantula.

ORIGIN: A captain in the Delvadian Army, "El Arana" was also the leader of a rebel fighting death squad. His government saw him as the perfect candidate to succeed the first Tarantula. He was subjected to a number of painful experiments including use of a serum similar to the one that gave Captain America his original abilities.

FIRST APPEARANCE: *Web of Spider-Man* #35

TERRIBLE TINKERER

NAME: Phineas Mason

POWERS: Originally thought to be an alien in *Amazing Spider-Man* #2, the Tinkerer turns out to be a brilliant man who excels at creating violent mechanical devices. He even equips the "Spider-Mobile" with weaponry and has had his services employed by many other villains, including Big Wheel and Rocket Racer. He also creates a super-strong robotic assistant named Toy.

ORIGIN: No outside source whatsoever for his ability with mechanical devices.

FIRST APPEARANCE: *Amazing Spider-Man* #2

THE THOUSAND

NAME: Carl King

POWERS: The Thousand is literally a thousand spiders that hold Carl King's consciousness and have the ability to liquefy the innards of a human, then walk within his hollow shell. The Thousand also has superhuman strength and agility.

ORIGIN: Carl King was trying to emulate what happened to Peter Parker when he was bitten by a radioactive spider that fateful day. He had no idea on how to irradiate a spider, so he did what he thought was the next best thing: eating the dead, previously irradiated spider that bit Peter Parker. A couple of days later, Carl's body began breaking down and consuming itself.

FIRST APPEARANCE: *Tangled Web* #1

TOMBSTONE

NAME: Lonnie Thompson Lincoln

POWERS: Mostly known for his stranglehold,

Lonnie is considered an expert hitman. Sensitive to the sun due to the fact that he's an albino.

ORIGIN: Lonnie originally had no superpowers, but eventually gained super strength after being contained in an airtight chamber with gas used in a test at an Osborn Chemical Plant. There was a mutagenic reaction to the gas, which was absorbed into his bloodstream.

FIRST APPEARANCE: *Web of Spider-Man #36*

TRAPSTER

NAME: Paul Petruski

POWERS: His main weapons are a variety of "paste shooters," which can reach targets up to 150 feet away. This paste, however, becomes rock hard within seconds and its consistency lasts for upward of five hours. In all, an effective means of rendering opponents helpless.

ORIGIN: Originally known as "Paste Pot Pete," the Trapster was a research chemist who created an extremely adhesive liquid, which he realized he could use in a life of crime.

FIRST APPEARANCE: *Strange Tales #104*

FIRST SPIDER-MAN APPEARANCE: *Amazing Spider-Man #214*

TRAVELLER & HIS HOST

NAME: Dr. Judas Traveller and His Host (Medea, Chakra, Dr. Nacht, Boone)

POWERS: Traveller is originally thought to have such powerful abilities as time travel, the power to alter his appearance, and the ability to destroy with his mind. It is later revealed that he possesses only limited psionic powers and the ability to alter people's perception of reality. Being a world renowned criminal psychologist, he is also an expert on human nature and its capacity for good and evil. The Host: Medea (expert with weaponry, fast, strong, agile), Chakra (ability to take on astral form), Boone ("Tracker Man"), Dr. Nacht (expert note taker; far from the most powerful man in the Marvel Universe).

ORIGIN: The Doctor's abilities are mutant in origin.

FIRST APPEARANCE: *Web of Spider-Map #117*

TYPEFACE

NAME: Gordon Thomas

POWERS: Typeface has a variety of letter-theme weapons, including explosive letters he calls letterbombs and Scrabble-like letters he uses to create words such as "sleep" to put his enemies to sleep, etc. Also has use of a sharp *p*-shaped letter opener and other such weapons that adorn his costume.

ORIGIN: Gordon was involved in a war (believed to be Vietnam), which left a number of terrifying emotional scars. He lost a friend in the war and almost died himself. He then became a craftsman of letters and became a sign man and educator. After being laid off from his job, he craved revenge and sought it.

FIRST APPEARANCE: *Spider-Man* Volume 2, #23

U

ULTIMATE GREEN GOBLIN

NAME: Norman Osborn

POWERS: Norman as the Green Goblin has

super strength and the ability to produce weapons from his hands—mostly in the form of fireballs. He also can jump great distances due to his incredibly muscular legs.

ORIGIN: Norman injected himself with a pure form of the drug "Oz" after seeing what it did to young Peter Parker following his being bitten by a spider injected with the same drug. What he ended up, though, was a horrible and powerful creature bent on destruction.

FIRST APPEARANCE: *Ultimate Spider-Man #6*

ULTIMATE KINGPIN

NAME: Wilson Fisk

POWERS: The Kingpin of Crime has no known superhuman powers, but he is in peak human condition with incredible strength and agility. Very formidable in hand-to-hand combat, and is brilliant strategist.

ORIGIN: Wilson is at the top of organized crime in New York City and has been doing as he pleases. When in trouble, he just buys stock in whatever company is giving him trouble. Not much is known about how he attained his criminal power.

FIRST APPEARANCE: *Ultimate Spider-Man #9*

ULTRON

NAME: Not applicable

POWERS: Expert robotist, master planner, and strategist. Has superhuman cybernetic analytical capabilities and the ability to process information at incredible speed. Has a super-strength Adamtium body, which is almost unbreakable. Also has an "encephalo" beam for subliminal commands and can project concussive blasts of energy from his optical sensors and hands.

ORIGIN: As a non-humanoid robot based on the android Dragon Man, Ultron was the brainchild of Avenger Henry Pym. The robot was inadvertently provided with self-awareness and emotion and carries a great hatred for his creator. Has even remodeled himself numerous times over the years.

FIRST APPEARANCE: *Avengers #55*

FIRST SPIDER-MAN APPEARANCE: *Amazing Spider-Man Annual #25*

V

VENOM

NAME: Eddie Brock

POWERS: The same as Spider-Man, and more, since Brock is far more conditioned and stronger in human form than Peter Parker is when he is endowed with spider powers. Can also shoot strands of alien substance in the form of webbing.

ORIGIN: An alien costume that Spider-Man once wore grafted itself to the nervous system of Eddie Brock, who shared his hatred of Spider-Man with the alien costume. The costume itself absorbed the powers of Spider-Man during a brief symbiotic relationship with him.

FIRST APPEARANCE: *Amazing Spider-Man #299*

VENOM 2099

NAME: Kron Stone

POWERS: Same as the original Venom. Additionally, can turn his molecules into a watery substance as his skin is malleable in nature and can shape-shift.

ORIGIN: Kron Stone has been spoiled since childhood, as his father was a rich and powerful man. From the start he was extremely dangerous, and received his powers after Punisher 2099 tossed Kron into a sewer, where he came into contact with the alien mutation looking for a human host.

FIRST APPEARANCE: *Spider-Man 2099 #35*

VERMIN

NAME: Edward Whelan

POWERS: He has the appearance of a humanoid rat with long, clawlike fingernails, razor-sharp teeth, and a body covered in fur. He once gains the ability to revert to human form at will. Additionally, he has a very acute sense of smell and exercises mental control over rats and dogs within a radius of a couple of miles.

ORIGIN: Vermin is the product of an experimental process involving psycho-genetic engineering designed by Captain America's archenemy, Arnim Zola.

FIRST APPEARANCE: *Captain America #272*

FIRST SPIDER-MAN APPEARANCE: *Spectacular Spider-Man #131*

VULTURE

NAME: Adrian Toomes

POWERS: Super strength, vitality, and athleticism while wearing a harness that enables him to fly due to the electromagnet anti-graviton generation built into it. Can fly at speeds up to ninety-five miles per hour for up to six hours and can attain a maximum altitude of eleven thousand feet.

ORIGIN: Originally an electronics engineer, Adrian, who was also a budding inventor, created an electromagnetically powered harness, which gave the ability of flight to whomever wore it.

FIRST APPEARANCE: *Amazing Spider-Man #2*

W

WILL O' THE WISP

NAME: Jackson Arvad

POWERS: Wisp has control over his body's electromagnetic particles and can make himself intangible or rock hard, much like the Vision. He also has the ability to mesmerize others. Jackson is a genius when it comes to the field of electromagnetics. His body gives the impression that it is an ethereally glowing sphere as the molecules of his body oscillate around him.

ORIGIN: Jackson received his powers from a "magno-chamber" that he and James Melvin were experimenting on. He was forced by Jonas Harrow to use his powers in criminal ways.

FIRST APPEARANCE: *Amazing Spider-Man #167*

WRAITH

NAME: Brian DeWolff

POWERS: Psionic powers make him capable of controlling and reading the mind of another. Can create illusions in one's mind and induce pain in his victims. Also is able to telekinetically levitate items. He is yet another vigilante/villain killed by the criminal assassin known as Scourge.

FIRST APPEARANCE: *Marvel Team-Up* #48

X

XANDU

NAME: Real name unknown

POWERS: Originally a student of the mystic arts, the man known as Xandu learns to control the minds of others through hypnotic spells. Can open pathways between dimensions.

ORIGIN: Unknown

FIRST APPEARANCE: *Amazing Spider-Man Annual* #2